REINVENTING THE
MELTING POT

REINVENTING THE
MELTING POT

THE NEW IMMIGRANTS
AND WHAT IT MEANS
TO BE AMERICAN

EDITED BY

TAMAR JACOBY

BASIC
BOOKS

A Member of the Perseus Books Group
New York

Books published by Basic Books are available at special discounts for bulk purchases in the United States by corporations, institutions, and other organizations. For more information, please contact the Special Markets Department at the Perseus Books Group, 11 Cambridge Center, Cambridge, MA 02142, or call (617) 252-5298, (800) 255-1514 or e-mail special.markets@perseusbooks.com.

Designed by Reginald R. Thompson
Set in 11.75-point Garamond 3 by Perseus Books Group

Library of Congress Cataloging-in-Publication Data
Reinventing the melting pot : the new immigrants and what it means to be American / edited by Tamar Jacoby.
    p. ; cm.
Includes index.
    ISBN 0-465-03634-1 (hc) — 0-465-03635-X (pbk.)
1. Emigration and immigration—Social aspects—United States. 2. Immigrants—United States—Social conditions. 3. Assimilation (Sociology)—United States. I. Jacoby, Tamar, 1954- II. Title.
    JV6475.R45 2003
    304.8'73—dc22

                                                                    2003017575

For Aunt Bea,
who was the last living link
to my family's Ellis Island generation

CONTENTS

REINVENTING THE
MELTING POT

PART ONE

AN EMERGING CONSENSUS

1

DEFINING ASSIMILATION
FOR THE 21ST CENTURY

by Tamar Jacoby

LIKE MANY ASIAN-AMERICANS of his generation, Eddie Liu* isn't
quite sure how to place or describe himself. Born in Taiwan to professional parents who moved to the United States when he was two
years old, Eddie grew up in a California suburb, speaking mostly
English and absorbing the manners and morals he saw on television,
hardly aware of any differences between himself and his mostly Anglo
school friends. Going to college changed all that: by the mid–1990s,
identity politics had taken over his University of California campus,
and Eddie quickly learned to see himself as an Asian-American. He
took courses in Asian-American studies, joined several Chinese-
American organizations, decided he could date only Asian women
and grew more and more skeptical about the United States—the typical trajectory of a young, hyphenated American in the age of multiculturalism.

By the time I met him, he was twenty-five, and his life reflected
both of these younger selves. He lived in a comfortable Los Angeles

*That isn't his real name.

suburb, drove an expensive late-model car, dated both Asian and white women and, though he worked for an internet company that targeted Asian-Americans, knew more about American popular culture than I did. A bright and engaging young man, he grew thoughtful and a little tentative when our conversation turned to ethnic identity. Asked whether he saw himself as an excluded minority or a "person of color," he laughed good-naturedly. "Hardly," he said. And yet, when asked about the word "assimilation," he was plainly uncomfortable. "I don't know," he mused, "not if it's a one-way street. Not if you're asking me to give up who I am and fit into some 1950s 'Leave It To Beaver' America. Of course, I'm American. But I'm not sure I'm assimilated—or want to be."

Eddie's ambivalence is far from unique. Like most immigrants in the past, the overwhelming majority of today's brand-new arrivals know why they have come to the United States: to make a better life for themselves and their children by becoming American. These newcomers struggle against all odds to fit in—finding jobs, learning the system, picking up the rudiments of the language. And with the exception of a few community leaders who draw their status and livelihood from their separate ethnicity, first-generation immigrants have no trouble with the word "assimilation." "I don't see why people would not want to assimilate," a Chinese-American newcomer said to me recently with a certainty typical of those born in another country.

But the second generation, be it Asian or Latino or some other group, is often far less clear about its relationship to the new place. Like Eddie, they know what they don't want. None seek to lose themselves and their cultural heritage in a bland, homogenized America— assimilation as defined by the conformist, lily-white suburban neighborhoods of 1950s television and advertising. Multiculturalism combined with the sheer number of newcomers arriving today has laid that dream—if it ever really was anyone's dream—to rest forever. But nor do most voice the oppositional attitudes and color-coded divisiveness associated with identity politics. They are keen to make it in America, yet reject the metaphor of the melting pot—and desperately need a way to understand just who they are and how they fit it.

American demographic realities only highlight the significance of the questions they face. One in nine Americans is now foreign-born, and together blacks, Hispanics and Asians account for 30 percent of the population. The new immigrant groups are by far the fastest growing segments of the nation, with Latinos already the largest minority. A lion's share of these newcomers have settled in a few cities and states: Hispanics make up nearly one-third of the people in both California and Texas, for example, almost half in Los Angeles and two-thirds in Miami. But significant numbers of immigrants are also moving to other parts of the country, and dilemmas such as Eddie Liu's will soon have consequences for every region.

Will the melting pot work for the new immigrants arriving today? What's at issue is partly pragmatic: whether the newcomers will succeed economically the way millions of immigrants before them succeeded, learning English, taking advantage of opportunity and moving up the ladder into the middle class. But the question also has another dimension, at least as important: will they "become American," loyal to the ideals and habits and values that have historically held the nation together? And for that to happen, we may need a new definition, or new understanding of assimilation—a definition that makes sense today, in an era of globalization, the internet, identity politics, niche advertising and a TV dial that offers a choice among a hundred or more different channels.

what are these?

Even as they live out the melting pot myth, today's immigrants and their children are searching for new ways to think and talk about it, and together, they and the rest of the nation face the challenge of updating the traditional ideal. This rethinking need not be destructive. On the contrary, it could ultimately strengthen one of our most hallowed tenets. The ferment is already taking place—in immigrant neighborhoods, on university campuses, in the media, among scholars and social critics. The essays that follow reflect and crystallize that important debate. Just what kind of assimilation is taking place today? What is possible? What is desirable? And how can we reframe the melting-pot vision to make it work for a cosmopolitan, twenty-first century America?

MAKING IT INTO THE MAINSTREAM—
AS HARD IF NOT HARDER THAN EVER

The story of immigrant absorption is as old as America, but the new arrivals and the country they are settling in are very different today than in the past. Yesterday's newcomers were ethnically more similar to the nation they were joining: like the native born, virtually all were of European stock. In contrast, today, most immigrants hail from the developing world, more than half of them from Latin-America and a quarter from Asia. Today's newcomers include skilled, middle-class people, but many are poor and uneducated and woefully unprepared to join the knowledge economy. (Some 60 percent of those from India, for example, have completed four years of college, but only 6 percent of refugees from Cambodia have, and the average Mexican arrives with 7.6 years of schooling.) Together, immigrants and their children account for more than 60 million people, or a fifth of all U.S. residents. And by 2050, if today's projections are borne out, a third of all Americans will be either Asian or Latino.

The America they come to is also different: at once more prosperous and unequal economically than it was a century ago, often making it harder for newcomers to assimilate into the middle class. The gap between rich and poor is wider than ever, creating what some social scientists call an "hourglass economy." In many cities, well-paid factory jobs have been replaced by service-sector work, and for some time now, real wages at the bottom of the pay scale have been declining rather than growing. On top of this, many newcomers settle in impoverished inner cities, where crime, drugs, gangs and broken families conspire to hinder their climb up the economic ladder. Getting an education—the most critical step in assimilating into the knowledge economy—is no easy matter in the barrios of, say, south central Los Angeles. Such neighborhoods can be so dangerous that it's hard even to get to school. And more often than not, a young immigrant's parents will have less than a high-school education, making it difficult for them to do much to help their children up the social ladder.

Some immigrant enclaves are better off: many Asian-Americans in California, for example, live in leafy, upscale suburbs. But pleasant as they are, these neighborhoods can be as insular as any ghetto: their ethnic shopping malls, ethnic restaurants and groceries, in-language newspapers, one-country Rotary Clubs, community banks, ethnic movie theaters and other amenities often make it unnecessary to have much contact with the integrated mainstream. The more newcomers arrive from the old country, the larger and more all-encompassing these enclaves—both rich and poor—grow, reducing incentives to make the difficult transition to a mixed neighborhood. Meanwhile, geographic proximity and cheap air travel allow newcomers to shuttle back and forth to their home countries and, in some cases, to maintain dual citizenship and even vote in both places.

Then there are the cultural factors that conspire against assimilation: everything from the internet and niche advertising to color-coded identity politics. The attacks of September 11, 2001, have sparked new patriotism and a new confidence in what brings us together as Americans. Some forty years after the Black Power movement and the ethnic revival it sparked among people of all backgrounds, the excesses of group chauvinism seem finally to be fading a bit. But no mere swing of the cultural pendulum is going to repeal multiculturalism or erase the profound effect it has had on the way most Americans live and view the world. From the relativism that now reigns in intellectual circles to the way Congress divides up into monolithic ethnic caucuses, multiculturalism has become the civil religion of the United States. Those—and there may be some—who no longer notice its ubiquitous effects are our era's equivalent of Molière's *Bourgeois Gentilhomme:* little do they know that they've been speaking prose—or, in this case, worshipping ethnic difference—all their lives. Welcomed by some, deplored by others and mellowing as it may be today, this emphasis on origins and encouragement to cultivate what makes you different cannot help but complicate the course that a young man like Eddie travels as he makes his way into the mainstream.

The drumbeat of ethnocentric messages can be constant and unavoidable. In an inner city high school, native-born minority classmates tease you for listening and doing your homework—both widely condemned by poor blacks and Latinos as "acting white" or "selling out." If this doesn't deter you, if and when you get to college, you'll be assailed by campus ethnic activists pressing you to question why you want to join the mainstream, racist and exploitative as it is seen to be. By the time you've finished your education, according to one study, you'll be far less likely to consider yourself an American, or even a hyphenated American, than you were as a young teenager. In many cases, by then, you'll see yourself simply as an aggrieved minority or as what some are now calling "ampersand Americans"—as in "Mexican & American."

When you reach young adulthood, politicians, pop stars, media personalities and marketers of every description will bombard you with reminders of what makes you different from the Anglos around you. The stable bilingualism taking hold in several regions of the country may make it harder for you to speak English as well as you'd like. An array of Spanish-language TV networks can spare you from subjecting yourself to mainstream television and its seductive lessons in becoming American. Nor does the government let you forget your ethnicity, reminding you powerfully at every turn with racial and ethnic preferences and other legal distinctions. The Supreme Court's 2003 decision upholding affirmative action at the University of Michigan, and enshrining "diversity" as a compelling national interest, can only further encourage new Americans to see themselves as different. No wonder many young people are questioning the traditional melting pot metaphor.

We shouldn't exaggerate the threat. Today, as before in our history when the immigrant tide was rising, nativists peddle a frightening array of grim scenarios: balkanization, civil strife, economic ruin and worse. Very few of these nightmare visions are based in fact, and all are unlikely. Indeed, as this volume shows, the nation is steadily absorbing tens of millions of newcomers: people of all ages and backgrounds who are finding work, learning English, making their way through school and up into more comfortable circumstances than they knew at home or when they first arrived in America. Still, like any wholesale social shift or personal transformation of this magnitude, the integration of today's influx needs watching—and occasional tending.

What's the worst that could happen? The most dire scenario is that today's immigrants and their children will become tomorrow's underclass. A wide array of forces would have to conspire to create such an outcome. But combine overheated identity politics with a prolonged economic downturn, rising nativist prejudice and an unwelcoming political system—and isn't hard to imagine the catastrophe that would ensue. One need not look very far afield—consider any country in Europe with a significant immigrant population—to catch a glimpse of what the future could hold. Barred from settling permanently, denied equal rights, largely without access to political power, unable to close the education gap and cut off from the job opportunities that only a college degree or better can open for them, migrants languish at the bottom of the social pyramid in many of the world's most civilized nations. Imagine then that they come under the sway of angry ethnic leaders who encourage self-indulgent, self-defeating protest politics. An overzealous Americanization movement—determined to force-feed a coercive national identity without opening real economic or political opportunity—would only make matters worse. The all but certain result would be unending racial polarization—and a permanent class of less equal citizens and noncitizens who feel they are not part of society and, as a result, remain a persistent burden.

Such a scenario is unlikely—one has to be deeply pessimistic about both the newcomers and the native-born to think it plausible. But it points clearly enough to the challenge facing the nation. There is much the mainstream can and should do to encourage immigrant integration—first and foremost, making the American educational system work for today's newcomers as it worked in the past for an earlier influx. Also necessary over the long haul: plentiful economic opportunity, real access to political power and a meritocratic ethos like the one that allowed wave after wave of previous outsiders to climb the ladder of success in America. But ultimately, nothing will be more important than <u>sustaining a culture of</u> inclusion: the culture of *e pluribus unum* that has made it possible for generations of newcomers not only to join the mainstream but, despite their difference, to feel that they belong. This, when it works, is the secret of the melting pot, and the challenge we face today is keeping it alive.

A NEW INTELLECTUAL CURRENT

But what about Eddie Liu and his doubts? Is what we as a nation want to encourage really *assimilation?* The very notion is almost a dirty word today. Some who oppose it are plainly extremists: people so taken with multiculturalism that they see being absorbed into a larger America as so much cultural "genocide." Yet Eddie is no activist, and concerns like his are widely felt, particularly in his generation. To young people like him, "assimilation" <u>implies a forced conformity</u>. They feel that it would require them to give up what makes them special, and they dread being reduced to what they see as the lowest common denominator of what it means to be American. As for the melting pot, if anything, that seems even more threatening: who wants to be melted down, after all—for the sake of national unity or anything else?

Meanwhile, at the other end of the political spectrum are those who think that, desirable as it is, assimilation is no longer possible in America. Some in this camp are driven by racial concerns: they view today's immigrants as simply too different ethnically ever to fit in in the United States. Others believe that the obstacles are cultural: that America has a distinct national ethos that cannot be grasped by any but a few newcomers—the better educated, perhaps, or those from Christian Europe. Still others feel that the problem lies less in the foreign influx than in ourselves: that in the wake of multiculturalism and the upheavals of 1960s, we as a nation have lost the confidence to assert who we are and what we believe in. But whatever their reasoning, all three kinds of pessimists have gained a wider hearing in the wake of 9/11 as the nation has grown ever more anxious about what many imagine are the unassimilated in our midst. And together, these two groups—those who believe assimilation is impossible and those who fear it—have come to dominate most discussion of the issue, leaving little room for those in the middle who take a more positive view.

That is the gap this book aims to fill, creating some middle ground between those who think assimilation is necessary but impossible and those, edging toward it, who see it as an unwelcome demand.

Hemmed in on both sides, hardly heard in the din of an often emotional debate, in fact, many of the thinkers who have thought longest and hardest about immigration believe that assimilation is still possible and indeed desirable, if not inevitable, today. They don't all like or use that word—for some of the same reasons that Eddie has trouble with it. Very few imagine that it should look as it looked in the 1950s: that it requires newcomers to forget their roots or abandon their inherited loyalties. And fewer still believe that it happens automatically—that it needs no tending or attention from the nation as a whole. Still, whatever word they use, these thinkers maintain that we as a nation not only can but must continue to absorb those who arrive on our shores: absorb them economically, culturally, politically and, perhaps most important, give them a sense that they belong. This is not a full-blown school of thought—its proponents disagree on too much else. But it is the intellectual current represented in this volume: a group of thinkers brought together for the first time in the belief that standing side by side, their arguments sound even stronger than each does alone.

The essayists in the book differ on far more than they agree upon. Academics and journalists, economic researchers and fiction writers, they hail from both the right and the left—and everywhere in between. Some feel that we should trim the number of foreigners we admit each year; others believe that if anything, immigration ceilings should be higher. Some see multiculturalism as a historic shift to be welcomed; others lament it—and fear what it means for the nation's future. Though they come together around a common goal, they disagree sharply on many if not most points of policy. Is affirmative action a good idea? Should bilingual education be ramped up or phased out? Is ethnically pitched advertising something to be encouraged—a gesture of respect or a form of bigoted stereotyping? You'll find no agreement on any of that in this volume. And even on the core issue—on just how assimilation does and should work—there are as many views as there are essays here.

What do the authors agree upon? In addition to the desirability of assimilation, most concur that it is indeed proceeding apace in the United States today. Like it or not, most immigrants and their children are becoming Americans, in every conceivable sense of the word. The essayists are divided on whether the way this happens today is the same as or different from the way it happened in the past for earlier waves of newcomers. Some emphasize how the immigrants are different now, others how the nation they are integrating into has been transformed—while still others think that none of this matters and the basic absorptive alchemy remains exactly as it has always been. Still, in considering the present, all the essayists agree that ethnicity need not be obliterated on the road to becoming American. Most if not all recognize that assimilation is a two-way street: that in the long run, the mainstream will change too, generally for the better, as it absorbs and accommodates the cultural variety of its newest members. Contributors diverge on how much—and what exactly—the nation should do to encourage immigrant absorption. Yet in the end, most understand that it is not something that can or should be forced. Punitive, coercive pressure for cultural conformity will not work: today, even more than in the past, that can only backfire.

Perhaps most important, whether or not they believe that today is different, virtually all understand that we need to find ways to talk about becoming American that will be meaningful and resonant for a young man like Eddie Liu. If assimilation got a bad name in the 1950s—or 1920s—those misleading associations must be erased. If indeed the concept needs updating in the wake of multiculturalism, the sooner we as a nation do that, the better. Most critical, whether this requires a new definition or merely a refurbished one, the new understanding must accommodate the realities of the world we live in—must work in an era of globalization, identity politics, niche marketing and the hourglass economy.

Some people will call this emerging viewpoint revisionist, but a more descriptive term might be "realist." The writers in this collection are not the first or only assimilationist thinkers to consider a new set of givens. Yet perhaps under pressure from what is happening in the world, their viewpoint is asserting itself with a new force, and the twenty-two original essays that follow represent some of the best realist thinking about assimilation in America today.

All have something to say to Eddie Liu and his perplexed peers.

A first cluster of essays asks whether Eddie is right about what assimilation traditionally meant. Did it in years past require the forced conformity he fears so much? And does it still do so today, or have times changed? Each of the five contributors in this section answers those questions differently. Still, in virtually every case, the picture they paint should ease Eddie's concerns.

The next group of essays speaks to his fear that he would be making a bad bargain by assimilating—giving up much that is meaningful to him without gaining enough in return. And although the writers in this section differ about whether we as a nation are currently living up to our side of the contract, both agree that fundamentally it remains a good deal.

A third and fourth set of essays look at how assimilation is playing out on the ground today. Four essays examine situations where incorporation seems to be working fairly well: among Mexican-Americans, Asian-Americans, in New York City, in families where parents manage to help their children resist the pull of underclass culture. And tellingly, according to the authors, in all four instances, immigrants themselves play a significant role in determining how and on what terms they will enter into the mainstream and absorb its ways.

The next part of the book—two chapters each on economic and political assimilation—contains some of the sharpest disputes in the volume. But whether or not the authors feel that immigrant absorption is working as well as it might in the area they consider, none describes an America that leaves no room for ethnic particularity. On the contrary, if anything, the two pessimists in this section feel that the balance may have shifted too far toward the immigrant side of the scale, with America now unable to assert what it needs and should ask of newcomers.

A fifth cluster of essays—another opposed pair—asks what the black experience in America tells us about the challenge facing today's immigrants. The authors have very different ideas about exactly what lessons African-American history teaches. Yet neither thinks that today's newcomers need fear a reprise of black history.

The final section of the book addresses the new immigrants' most difficult question: what exactly are they assimilating into? What does America expect of them? And what indeed does it mean to be American today, in an era of multiculturalism, globalization and the challenges posed by terrorism? Here too, the authors differ markedly: each sees the national identity through his or her own unique prism. Still, all these essays should be compelling reading for Eddie.

For ultimately, what young people like him need most is a national story about America that they can identify with. The old story from the 1950s—true or not as it may have been at the time—plainly doesn't work for them. But it's not clear that the story of the 1980s and 1990s—a story built around the idea of diversity—does the job either. Much as they appreciate their own and others' ethnic backgrounds, even young people like Eddie seem increasingly to be hungering for something else, too: a larger, shared story that allows them to escape their narrow origins and provides an understanding of what holds us all together as Americans. The nation is changing profoundly—and both newcomers and the native-born need a way to make sense of what is happening. We need a beacon: not just a rationale but a shared narrative, a common vocabulary, symbols, songs and holidays that we can all buy into together. The essays in this volume cannot provide all of that, but they sketch some outlines for the story that is needed.

A word about terminology: as an editor, I've let the essayists use their own language to describe immigrant absorption. We all know that in many circles, the term "assimilation" is unfashionable and worse—it can seem off-putting and even offensive. Some contributors defer to that sensibility; others bristle at what they see as PC euphemisms—or are simply determined to use what they feel is the most descriptive word. Still, no one in the book is advocating the kind of oppressive assimilation that Eddie and others dread. Nor should the title be taken to mean than any of the essayists argue for erasing ethnic differences, whether by assimilation, intermarriage or other means. The salad—or stew or mosaic—make strike some readers as a better metaphor. But the fact remains that the melting pot is the best shorthand we have for the age-old American tradition of integrating and absorbing newcomers.

Does the anthology have a bottom line? No simple formula can capture the complexity of the essays, but if there is a common denominator, it is that integration and identity need not be contradictory. A young man like Eddie doesn't have to choose whether he is Asian or American—the very idea is an abomination. In the end, contributors agree, assimilation is about finding a sustainable balance between what makes us different and what we have in common.

Both sides of the balance matter, and both can be difficult to get right. Yes, today more than ever, Americans need to be reminded of their commonalities. Distracted by multiculturalism and the divisiveness that can come with it, in the last decade or two, many of us lost sight of that shared identity. We forgot that we needed one—or didn't like the version we knew. And though, in the wake of 9/11, people feel a renewed need for a shared story, many are no longer sure what it is—aren't even really sure what it means to be an American.

Restoring that vision will not happen quickly or easily. What we have in common is far more important than our differences, and that may be difficult for some to accept. Though parts of the national identity are optional, most of it is not. And although it must leave room for ethnic attachments, the national ethos must also rise above them—to the point that there have to be limits on the place and role of particularity. To say that what is needed is balance doesn't mean that we can have it all. There are choices to be made. Some of them

See Mercado's book - same theme

will pinch, and some conflict will be inevitable in arriving at an answer that can hold in our fractious era and beyond. There is no point in being Pollyannish: restoring a shared sense of American identity is a formidable challenge, one we have neglected for far too long.

But the ethnic side of the balance is real too, and those who fear difference—who deplore any kind of multiculturalism and see no room for particularity—are as much of a threat as those who think that it is all that matters. The truth is that difference is as American as the Stars and Stripes. Assimilation has always left room for a hyphen. And finding unity amid diversity, be it national or religious or some other kind, is a thread that runs throughout our history, arguably the most important one. True, in recent decades, the balance between clan and commonweal seemed to be tilting out of whack, with too many people dwelling too much on their differences and too much ethnicity seeping into the public square. But there are signs that the balance may now be starting to right itself. And although plenty remains to be done to find a workable equilibrium, that is not an argument for overcorrecting.

In the long run, as the essays in this volume suggest, neither side need be quite so worried: not the questioning Eddie Liu or those who are alarmed by his doubts about assimilation. In fact, Eddie *is* assimilating, and what he's assimilating to isn't as airless or oppressive as he fears. Still, both sides need to find new ways to think and talk about what is happening, and the essays in this book are a good place to start.

2

THE NEW IMMIGRANTS: A PROGRESS REPORT

by Tamar Jacoby

TODAY AS IN THE PAST, immigrant absorption has two main dimensions: objective and subjective. The first challenge facing any newcomer is to make a life in the new country: to find a job, master the language, eventually put down roots and launch one's children toward a better life. The second dimension is more nebulous: the long, slow process of coming to feel that one belongs in the new place. Although the essays in this volume contain a wealth of information about the external story, many are more concerned with the subjective side—what assimilation means and how it is understood, by newcomers and the native-born alike. And so perhaps it is useful to set the scene for the chapters that follow with a brief description of today's immigrants: a few words—and a few numbers—about the more measurable aspects of their integration into American life.

The immigrant influx of the last forty years is a demographic shift of historic proportions. The percentage of the population that was born abroad is slightly lower than it was when the last great wave of immigrants arrived, at the beginning of the twentieth century: 11 percent now compared to 15 percent then. But the absolute number of new-comers living in the United States today is the highest it has ever been: some 31 million. Roughly 1.2 million arrive on our shores every year. One in nine Americans is an immigrant. And half the laborers entering the American workforce in the 1990s were foreign-born. Add in their families and extended families and the picture grows more dramatic still. Together, immigrants and their children now account for one in five Americans. Hispanics, at nearly 14 percent of the population, are already the largest minority, outnumbering blacks. Asian-Americans are still a relatively small share of the nation—at only 4 percent. But despite their numbers, they, too, are going to play a major part in the country's future: already, they make up between 15 and 20 percent of the students at most Ivy League colleges.

Where do these new arrivals come from? Just over half the foreign-born are Hispanic and a little more than a quarter are Asian. They hail from all the corners of the globe, though more from some countries than from others. Mexicans, by far the largest category, account for roughly one in three first-generation immigrants—almost ten times more than any other nationality. The next largest groups are Filipinos and Indians, followed by Chinese, Vietnamese, Koreans, Cubans and Salvadorans—but none of these account for more than 3 or 4 percent of the total.

What do the newcomers do for a living? They tend to be clustered at both the top and the bottom of the job ladder. A large percentage work in dirty, demeaning, low-paid jobs that native-born Americans no longer want to do: busboys, chambermaids, farmhands, nurses' aides, sweatshop workers, on the assembly-line in meatpacking plants. But a large number also work at the top of the job pyramid: as scientists, engineers, nurses, high-tech entrepreneurs and the like. Two of the statistics that paint this picture most vividly are the percentage of U.S. farmhands who are foreign-born (an astonishing 80 percent) and the percentage of patents that are held by foreigners (an equally astonishing 26 percent). Social scientists call this a "barbell pattern," and it has some predictable corollaries. Not surprisingly, today's newcomers are either quite rich or quite poor, and they are either very well educated or hardly educated at all. Roughly a quarter have less than nine years of schooling, while an equal percentage have university degrees—a much larger share than the proportion of native-born Americans who have stayed in school that long.

Where in the United States do most immigrants settle? Until about ten years ago, they were concentrated in what demographers call "gateway cities": New York, Los Angeles, Miami, Houston, Chicago. But this is changing dramatically and with profound consequences for the country. States such as New York and California and New Jersey are still home to the largest numbers. But the states with the fastest growing immigrant populations are places like North Carolina, Georgia, Arkansas and Tennessee. Even Iowa more than doubled its share in the 1990s. The cities where the immigrant population expanded the most in the past decade are equally surprising: Greensboro, N.C., Charlotte, N.C., Raleigh, N.C., Atlanta and Las Vegas. Still more of a departure, while some of today's new arrivals still gravitate to urban areas, many head straight for the suburbs, and roughly half of all Asians and Latinos now live outside the center city. True, these are often older, less affluent, inner-ring suburbs: Port Chester rather than Scarsdale, say, in the New York metro area. But all around the country, from New York to California, suburban America is increasingly ethnic.

Whether or not they are assimilating is harder to quantify. Becoming an American is a complex, personal process—the kind of transition that can take a lifetime, even two. A Mexican farmhand with a sixth-grade education takes a different path into the mainstream than an Indian engineer working on an MBA, and the sometimes mind-boggling diversity of today's immigrants can make it difficult to generalize. What's more, even when one focuses on one group, it can be hard to assess just how well or how fast they are integrating. Economic success or failure, for example, is reflected in countless and sometimes contradictory statistics, and in today's polarized immigration debate, any statistical portrait is sure to be controversial. Nevertheless, a lot is known about today's immigrants, and on the whole it adds up to an encouraging story.

Most foreigners, whether they arrive legally or illegally, come to the United States to work. Most do not come in the expectation of living on welfare: most are not entitled to most kinds of benefits for at least five years. Thanks to modern technology, they generally know from other immigrants who have preceded them from their regions whether or not work is available. And in economic downturns, when there are fewer jobs to be had, fewer immigrants seem to make the trip. After all, if you're going to be unemployed, it's much better to unemployed at home than in the United States. It's usually warmer at home and less expensive to live, and you are likely to be surrounded by a network of supportive family and friends. So while technically three-quarters of American immigrant visas are given out on the basis of family ties, the lion's share of foreigners who come to the United States get a job—or two or three jobs—and work hard at it. This isn't new: Hispanic males have long boasted the highest labor-force participation in the country, and most other immigrant groups are not far behind.

Of course, however hard they work, many poor, ill-educated immigrants who start at the bottom of the ladder remain there throughout their lives. This is not particularly surprising, and it may seem to vindicate those who claim that the United States today is importing a new lower class. But that's part of the point of our immigration policy: America no longer has this kind of working class, and it turns out that we need one. And even this does not necessarily mean the newcomers will not be absorbed into the economy or do well by it. Indeed while most brand-new arrivals make considerably less than the native-born, by the time they have been in the United States for ten or fifteen years, they are usually making more. (Mexicans seem to be an exception—and a troubling one—but despite their overwhelming numbers and the way this weights any statistical measure, the overall immigrant average is still a success story.) By the time they've been in the country for fifteen to twenty years, immigrants are also less likely than the native-born to be living in poverty.

The trajectory of high-end immigrants—those who come with some money or an education—is even more impressive. Immigrant entrepreneurship is nothing short of astonishing—in the first and second generation and beyond. Asian and Latino business start-up rates were four times the average American rate in the 1990s. Most of these minority-owned firms were small, and most had no paid employees— but that was also true of the businesses owned by native-born Americans. And indeed Asian entrepreneurs were more successful than nonminority owners on virtually every measure. More of their businesses had employees; fewer fell in the smallest-of-the-small category, or what economists call "micro-businesses." And despite the newcomers' relative lack of familiarity with American markets, an equal percentage of their concerns grossed over $1 million a year.

In some cases, immigrants are not merely assimilating into a regional economy: they dominate it. In Silicon Valley in the 1990s, foreign-born scientists accounted for a third of the scientific workforce, and Chinese and Indian entrepreneurs ran a quarter of the high-tech companies. In New York, by one estimate, Korean immigrants own 70 percent of the independent groceries, 80 percent of the nail salons and 60 percent of the dry cleaners. In Los Angeles, an increasing share of the banks are Asian-owned, and newcomers—whether from the Middle East, North Africa or Korea—control most of the $22 billion fashion industry. Whatever one calls it, there can be little question, immigrants are finding their place—and generally a productive place—in the American economy.

Of course, by definition, the first generation is transitional. Those who make the trip from the old country invariably live between two worlds and, if they arrive as adults, may never fully assimilate. Far more important in the long run is how their children fare, and to some degree, in America today, it's too soon to tell how the second generation is doing: the majority still have not reached adulthood. Nevertheless, the evidence is beginning to pour in.

There are some troubling signs—and no end of pessimistic predictions. Young people who were born abroad—or whose parents were— often start at the bottom of the socioeconomic ladder. They go to some of the worst schools in the country: failing, overcrowded inner-city schools. Many of their native-born classmates scorn mainstream success, and despite their parents' best efforts, some second-generation immigrants catch this bad attitude from their school friends. Alarmed by these conditions, many social scientists who study the second generation begin their research with a dire view of the young newcomers' chances—and indeed, the field can be divided into optimists and pessimists.

But in fact, as a group, immigrant children bring home a superb record card. The most important study of the second generation, conducted over the last decade in San Diego and Miami by sociologists Alejandro Portes and Rubén Rumbaut, found that whatever country they come from, across the board, immigrant children work harder than their native-born classmates. They do an average two hours of homework a night compared with the "normal" thirty minutes. They aspire to greater achievement, get better grades and drop out far less often—between a third and half as often. So if school performance is any guide, today's second generation will certainly outstrip its parents.

The big question for the future is what kind of jobs these young people will get—whether and how fast they will be able to move up the socioeconomic ladder. Plainly, for many, there is cause for some concern. Not even the best students from inner-city schools of the kind many immigrants attend make it to college. As often as not, when they do, it's a community college. For economic and family reasons, many of them do not finish, and of course this puts them at a disadvantage in today's knowledge economy. But here too, what evidence we have suggests that the pessimists may be overstating the case. The main difference between optimists and pessimists is about what the benchmark should be: do we expect the second generation to do as well as the native-born—or simply better than their parents? In fact, most immigrant children seem at least as driven as their elders; they have the advantage of the language and familiarity with the culture. And while second-generation Latinos, for example, still earn less on average than native-born whites, they earn more than native-born blacks, and considerably more than first-generation Latinos—about 50 percent more. What's most important, more hopeful scholars say, is the newcomers' trajectory—and it points upward.

A third key component of assimilation is language. Are today's newcomers and their children learning English? Do they even want to learn it? Many of the native-born fear not. Certainly, there is a great deal more Spanish in the air today than there was twenty or thirty years ago. One sees signs in Spanish wherever one goes. Politicians are racing to learn Spanish. Even corporate America is catching the bug, spending now up into the hundreds of millions of dollars a year on advertising in Spanish and other languages, including Mandarin Chinese. So it would be easy to surmise that immigrants are not learning English, particularly not Hispanic immigrants, who often live in large enclaves of other Spanish speakers, where, it is sometimes argued, you don't need English to get by.

But in fact the conventional wisdom driving people to campaign and advertise in Spanish is quite wrong. True, the first generation often has trouble with English. This was true in 1900, and it's true today. It's hard to learn a new language as an adult. Even in homes where the children were born and raised in America, the predominant language is usually that of the parents, and according to the 2000 census, some 10 percent of the U.S. population now lives in a household where Spanish is spoken—at first blush, an alarming number. But in fact it's a misleading number, because Spanish is rarely the only language spoken in these homes. For the Census Bureau, even one Spanish speaker—and in many cases, it's an elderly grandparent—is enough to get a family classified as Spanish-speaking. And even in those households deemed to be Spanish-speaking, some 70 percent of the working-age adults speak English well or very well.

Besides, on this issue too, what really matters is the second generation: the linguistic future lies with those who come of age in the United States. And the fact is that despite the travesty that is bilingual education, virtually everyone who grows up in America today eventually learns English. This is true for every national group and at every socioeconomic level, and it happens no matter what language your parents or grandparents speak at home. According to the Census, even in the 10 percent of households that are "Spanish-speaking," 85 percent of the children speak English well or very well. According to a 2002 survey by the Pew Hispanic Center, most second-generation Latinos are either bilingual (47 percent) or English-dominant (46 percent). (By the third generation, eight in ten are English-dominant.) And the San Diego-Miami second-generation study showed even more dramatic progress. Although more than 90 percent of the young people surveyed came from homes where a language other than English was spoken, by the end of their high school years, 98 percent spoke and understood English well or very well, and nine out of ten preferred it to their mother tongues—even if they couldn't speak it better.

This evidence can be confirmed anecdotally by a visit to any immigrant neighborhood—even the poorest and most isolated Latino enclaves. In restaurants and shops and on the streets, adults are invariably speaking Spanish. But the children—even very young children, and even small siblings in families of Spanish-speaking adults—can often be heard speaking English among themselves. Even if they don't learn much at school, children pick up English from TV and other popular culture; their parents know it is the key to their futures. And virtually no one who studies immigrants has any doubt about the long run: today as in the past, the United States is going to prove a "graveyard for languages."

Still another indicator of assimilation is home-ownership—a telling sign, after all, that a newcomer is putting down roots and investing in the new country. And on this measure, too, today's immigrants seem to be doing fairly well. True, as pessimists are quick to point out, many recent arrivals are anything but settled. They go back and forth to the old country. They often leave their families at home and maintain strong ties to the Old World. Still, after a while, they generally settle down. They ask their families to join them or they marry someone they've met in America, and within twenty years, 60 percent are homeowners. By the time they've been in the United States for twenty-five years, they are more settled than native-born Americans: a significantly higher share own their own homes. Indeed, for some years now, a research firm in California has been tabulating the most common last names among new home buyers, and the list is invariably dominated by Asian and Latino names: Garcia, Lee, Martinez, Nguyen, Rodriguez and Wong.

Similarly, with citizenship. True, today, unlike in the past, it is possible for people from many countries to maintain dual citizenship—and with it, perhaps, troubling dual or conflicting loyalties. Naturalization is a slow, gradual process, and among those who arrived in the years since 1990, less than 15 percent have become citizens. Still, among those who have been in America since 1970, as many as 80 percent are naturalized. If you stay, it turns out, you eventually join—today, as in the past, you graduate from sojourner to member. And for many newcomers, naturalization is a critical tipping point. Not only is it the moment when many begin to say "we" rather than "they" and feel that their fates are intertwined with America's; it also tends to spur other steps, like buying a house and participating in the political process.

For social scientists, the ultimate measure of assimilation is the ethnic intermarriage rate—and in America today, it is nothing short of astounding. Among U.S.-born Asians and Hispanics, between a third and a half marry someone of a different ethnicity. By the third generation, according to some demographers, the rates reach over 50 percent for both groups. And in places with large numbers of newcomers, this can have dramatic consequences. In Los Angeles County, for example, among people under forty, more than one in five marriages involves a mixed-race couple—and some 15 percent of the babies born in California are now born into mixed-race families.

Meanwhile, arguably even more interesting than this evidence from social science, a similar picture of today's immigrants is taking shape in corporate America—among people whose livelihoods depend on gauging new Americans' tastes and values. A new industry has sprung up in the last decade or so that focuses exclusively on selling to ethnic customers: a burgeoning network of advertisers, consultants and in-house marketing departments—evidence in itself of the newcomers' galloping economic assimilation. The estimates of minority purchasing power change almost too fast to keep track of them, but according to one study, Latino buying muscle grew by 160 percent in

2002 alone, and if it were a separate country, Hispanic America would now boast the eleventh largest GDP in the world. As recently as two or three years ago, most advertisers assumed that assimilation was a long, slow process—that no matter how much money Latino customers had to spend, they were best reached by Spanish-language ads produced in a stodgy old-country style and aired on Spanish-language television. But all of this is changing dramatically in response to new research about the ethnic market.

One recent survey of young Hispanics in New York and Los Angeles conducted by the California firm, Cultural Access Group, paints a picture of what its authors call the "post-ethnic" generation. These young people generally speak Spanish at home, but English with their friends. They prefer English to Spanish by a ratio of five to one. They watch at least twice as much English-language TV as Spanish programming. When they use the internet, it's virtually always in English. And when asked how they identify culturally, their answers are far more likely to be about the kind of music they listen to—most often, hip hop or mainstream pop—than about their parents' ethnic origins. Cultural Access Group didn't ask for details about whom they date, but it isn't hard to guess: anyone and everyone. (Indeed, according to another recent survey, more than 60 percent of all American teens have dated someone of another race or ethnic group.) No wonder the most savvy corporate marketers are now switching strategies: abandoning the old-fashioned Spanish-language approach and producing ads in English or Spanglish, usually with a racy, international flavor, to run on mainstream media as well as Spanish-language TV and radio.

Finally, in addition to social scientists and marketers, opinion researchers too have something to say about assimilation. What do immigrants themselves report about the fateful choices they've made and the way their lives have been transformed? Do they feel they are becoming truly American? Do their opinions shift in some tangible, measurable way the longer they live in the United States? Although it is notoriously difficult to pin down attitudes of this kind, accumulating survey data adds intriguing highlights to the picture.

When asked how they feel about America, newcomers are invariably positive—often extravagantly so. A recent survey by the polling firm Public Agenda asked immigrants whether they would still come to the United States if they were making the decision again today, and an astonishing 80 percent said yes. Asked about what their new home meant to them, a similar eight in ten said that America is a "unique country" that "stands for something special in the world." As for assimilation, according to one of the largest and most comprehensive surveys of Latinos, conducted by the *Washington Post* in 1999, 84 percent believe it is "important" or "very important" for immigrants "to change so that they blend into the larger society, as in the idea of the melting pot." This doesn't necessarily mean that newcomers want to give up who they are or the legacies they brought with them to America. The same *Washington Post* survey found that 89 percent—roughly the same portion that endorsed the melting pot—also said it was important for "Latinos to maintain their distinct cultures." Given half a chance, there is no one more patriotic than a new immigrant. But many newcomers are plainly hoping to have it all: to become Americans and hold on to their old cultures, too.

Nor are immigrants and their children immune to the identity politics they encounter in America. On the contrary, a good deal of what they assimilate to in the United States today is precisely identity politics. When they arrive, they tend to think of themselves as Mexicans or Chinese or Vietnamese, and most adults hang on to those national labels. But as the San Diego-Miami second-generation study found, their children quickly come to see themselves as Latinos or Asian-Americans, and they often believe this sets them apart from the mainstream in important ways. Still, if one takes a closer look at how immigrants' deeper, personal values change over time as they remain in the United States, identity politics can look less significant—for generally, no matter what newcomers say about themselves, surveys show that their values and priorities are gradually transformed by exposure to American life.

Consider, for example, how Latinos feel about the relative importance of family and work, about whether one's private life is more important than getting ahead. This is a profound personal issue, a key indicator of who one is and how one lives. And in general, Latinos answer this question markedly differently than native-born whites: they're much more inclined to put their personal lives first. Asked whether their first priority is work or family, non-Hispanic whites split roughly 50–50, while among Latinos, the ratio is more like 70–30, with the emphasis on family. Nevertheless, when one recent survey by the Pew Hispanic Center divided its Latino sample into two groups—first- and second-generation, or those who spoke English well and those who didn't—pollsters found a dramatic bifurcation, with the native-born and the English-dominant coming much closer to white norms, if not matching them.

The same holds true of attitudes on a wide range of personal questions from views about divorce and homosexuality to the most closely held existential values. To assess change on these topics, the Pew poll divided its foreign-born sample according to the age they had immigrated and how long they had lived in the United States, then compared the subgroups' answers. The results were startling: one could almost see the newcomers becoming more American with every passing year. The survey probed deep-seated attitudes often thought to be at the heart of Hispanic culture. Are relatives more important than friends? How important is it for grown children to stay close to their families? Can you control the future enough so that it's worth your while to make plans—or is it better to accept whatever happens fatalistically? Even on these core values, English-dominant Latinos polled dramatically differently than the Spanish-dominant. Nearly 60 percent of Spanish-speakers, for instance—compared to 15 percent of non-Hispanic whites—were so fundamentally fatalistic that they saw no point in planning for the future. But among second-generation and English-dominant Hispanics, 75 percent said that they felt they were in charge of their lives. America had already changed them that much—they had assimilated that thoroughly.

In the end, of course, the jury is still out. It's far too soon to say anything definitive about the vast and varied influx of immigrants still arriving on our shores. Their fate will depend on many things—on them, but also on us and what we expect of them. And whether or not today's relatively hopeful trends continue will rest to a significant degree on how we—all of us—come to understand assimilation. That more subjective, and prescriptive, side of the story is the subject of the essays that follow.

PART TWO

THEN AND NOW

3

THE AMERICAN KALEIDOSCOPE, THEN AND NOW

by Herbert J. Gans

I T WAS AT THE START of the twentieth century, in the midst of the last great wave of immigration to America, that the English playwright Israel Zangwill produced his signature work, *The Melting Pot*. The play presented a utopian vision of America as a crucible that blended all nationalities and races into a new American people, interethnic and interracial, who would build "the Republic of Man" and "the Kingdom of God." It is an appealing vision, hopeful that the New World might bring about the total ethnic, racial and even religious blending that was impossible in Europe. Yet even in Zangwill's time, there was no single American culture into which immigrants could blend. Long before Southern and Eastern European immigrants started arriving in the 1880s, America was already remarkably diverse, as Alexis de Tocqueville had noticed as early as the 1830s.

But while immigrants to America never really "melted," losing all trace of their origins, they did and still do undergo assimilation. This is a slower and more complex process than Zangwill imagined, and it takes several forms. For all newcomers, economic assimilation has to begin almost at once: immigrants must find work and make their first move into the mainstream American economy, or one of its ethnic enclaves. This kind of assimilation is made easier by the fact that immigrants are resigned to working longer hours at lower wages than the native-born.

Cultural assimilation has to begin almost as quickly, for newcomers have to learn enough about American ways and institutions to send their children to school, cope with landlords and bureaucracies and maneuver around their new communities. American popular culture has always been a force for assimilation, perhaps because much of it was created by immigrants. However, cultural assimilation really takes place almost automatically as newcomers learn that the habits of everyday life brought from the old country often do not work here.

But social assimilation occurs much more slowly. It does not happen until immigrants, or more likely their descendants, are comfortable enough to join nonimmigrant groups, such as neighborhood organizations, civic associations, women's clubs and mainstream churches. More important, they have to be accepted by native-born Americans; otherwise, they cannot move away from their immigrant moorings.

Today, as in the past, the factors that most influence assimilation are class and race. Middle-class newcomers have a far easier time than poor ones, since they bring along their own financial, cultural and social resources, or "capital." Among the past European immigrant groups, for example, Eastern European Jews and Northern Italians, who already came with job skills demanded in the urban economy, assimilated more easily than groups who were mainly peasants or farm laborers. This differential, or segmented, assimilation has also been taking place among the "new," post–1965 immigrants, although far fewer of them were peasants.

The most important obstacle to speed and ease of assimilation, however, is race. In the nineteenth century, swarthy Jews, "black" Irish, and Italian "guineas"—a not so subtle euphemism borrowed from the African country of Guinea—were all seen as what we today call "people of color." These immigrants terrified lighter-skinned native-born Americans, who accepted the newcomers as "white" only when they—actually, their descendants—began to earn middle-class incomes. Of course, skin color does not affect an immigrant's ability to absorb American culture. But color can play a large part in hindering economic and social assimilation: today's black newcomers, from the Caribbean and elsewhere, are often treated as part of the African-American population, with all the associated disadvantages.

"Asians"—the term Americans use for immigrants from all the countries of the Far East—are in a very different situation. Because so many are middle-class professionals, and because their children often excel in school, native-born white Americans sometimes classify Asians as a "model minority." Still, being considered a model minority does not mean automatic acceptance in white America. On-the-job glass ceilings remain in place, and when Asians, like other immigrants, compete for jobs, housing and other resources in limited supply, discrimination can rear its head very quickly.

"South Asians" are a special case, and one that demonstrates the importance of social class. Indians, for example, are currently the most highly educated of the new arrivals—over half come with college degrees—and though they are often darker-skinned than African immigrants, they are frequently welcomed as if they were whites. Whether Indians would be able to marry whites at the same high rates as lighter-skinned Asians or Hispanics is still a moot issue because Indian parents strongly discourage their children from inter-marrying, but the question will surely come up before too long.

"Hispanics"—a language group that has now been redefined as a quasi-race—are solidly in the racial middle. Lighter-skinned Hispanics are treated just about like Asians. Those with darker skin and other traces of their Indian ancestors have a harder time; and black Hispanics, notably Dominicans and other West Indians, suffer from the same discrimination and segregation as other black immigrants.

Matters are complicated by the fact that immigrants quickly pick up the discriminatory practices of their new country. Regardless of where they come from, immigrants learn that, in America, lighter is always better, darker is always worse and black is worst. Little time passes before immigrants become prejudiced against African-Americans.

This, too, is a kind of assimilation, and one that Israel Zangwill's idealistic vision never anticipated.

*   *   *

It has taken the American mainstream—including scholars—a long time to understand assimilation. A century ago, it took native-born observers a good many years to understand how the new European immigrants were slowly being absorbed into their adopted country. The journalists, social workers and amateur social scientists, almost all of them WASPs, who first wrote about these newcomers generally had a very low opinion of their manners, morals, intelligence and sanitary habits. Because the new arrivals were packed into terrible slums, many with outhouses and shared wash-stands, WASP observers thought they were opposed to bathing. (One of the more widespread stereotypes of the time had new immigrants using their bathtubs as coal bins.) Unlike Zangwill, such observers were convinced that this uncivilized mass could never be Americanized. Some of them argued for an immediate end to all immigration; others joined with advocates of eugenics in proposing that the newcomers be sterilized or sent to communities that would today be described as concentration camps.

Then, during the first decade of the twentieth century, a handful of American universities graduated the first professional sociologists trained to undertake empirical research. Some of these scholars headed for the immigrant slums. The problem was that most spoke only English, and as a result they did much of their research among English-speaking young adults of the second generation. These researchers were often no less prejudiced against immigrants than earlier writers, but as a result of their generational "sampling bias" they spoke to far more Americanizing young people than first-generation immigrants maintaining their old culture. As a consequence, these scholars portrayed a second generation that was moving away from its parents' culture and escaping from immigrant poverty. The scholars were generally pleased by the Americanization they uncovered, and the term they used to describe it was *assimilation.*

Later, other researchers posited a theory of assimilation that suggested it was happening, in effect, in a "straight line." Essentially, these thinkers believed, cultural, social and other kinds of assimilation would continue uninterrupted, without slowing, over several generations. With assimilation would come speedier upward mobility, which in turn would generate still more assimilation. Immigrant institutions would erode further and further, and immigrant culture would eventually disappear, until finally the newcomers—at least the light-skinned ones—would be indistinguishable from other Americans.

Because this process was thought to be roughly the same for all immigrants, the theory could indeed be pictured on a graph as a straight line: it began with the immigrants' arrival and ended when they had become fully American. What's more, because the theory was formulated around the time Congress outlawed further immigration to America, in 1924, it was thought that the straight line would eventually end with the Americanization of all the immigrants then in the country. In fact, the straight-line argument was a more gradual version of Zangwill's melting pot metaphor—and like Zangwill, it envisioned a single kind of new American.

Only in the quarter-century after World War II did some scholars begin to recognize that the straight-line theory was too simple. In fact, assimilation moved in many and sometimes mysterious ways, and was influenced by a number of factors. Economic assimilation, for instance, was slower among ethnic groups that dominated an occupational niche, as the Poles and other Slavs that then dominated the steel and automobile industries. Different groups' ethnic cultures and ethnic institutions also declined at different speeds: more slowly, for example, if ethnic traditionalists or ethnic churches were influential enough to hold back change. And working-class communities were generally slower to give up on their ethnic institutions than middle-class groups, which were by then sending their young people directly into the new and quintessentially American postwar suburbs.

In fact, it turned out there was no single pattern. Given their different speeds of assimilation, different ethnic groups needed their own "lines" on the chart of assimilation. In most cases, these trajectories were not straight at all, but rather wavy or bumpy, and each in a somewhat different way. Even as people were assimilating, they were reworking rather than just dropping ethnic traditions, and often they created new ethnic practices and traditions to fit present needs. As women began to demand more equality, for example, the bar mitzvah celebrating the religious adulthood of thirteen-year-old Jewish boys was complemented by the newly invented bat mitzvah ceremony for girls.

Nor could anyone say for sure where, when and how the various bumpy lines would end—if indeed they did end. For one thing, journalists and researchers periodically discovered seventh- and eighth-generation descendants of nineteenth-century immigrants who still identified with their ancestors, calling themselves Swedish, German, or Scotch-Irish, even though in all other respects they were entirely American. At the same time, however, significant numbers of third- and even second-generation descendants of later European immigrants were already intermarrying. Then the intermarried couple had to choose which of their ethnic backgrounds, if any, they would try to pass on to their children. In sociologist Mary Waters's now classic phrase, people found that they had "ethnic options."

The picture was complicated further still when social scientists realized that, contrary to the classic model, the descendants of immigrants were not assimilating into a single American culture—they were not turning into WASPs. In fact, this was not a new development. The Scandinavians and many of the Germans who came to America in the early to mid-nineteenth century were white Protestants, but even they did not adopt much of the WASP culture of Puritan America. Indeed, there was great diversity among WASPs themselves. The dirt-poor Appalachian "hillbillies" were WASPs too, after all, and just as "Anglo-Saxon" as the elite who controlled the economy, politics and culture.

The more social scientists looked at assimilation, and at America, the more complex, and in some ways contradictory, the process turned out to be. Although the straight-line theory was clearly too simple, its underlying thesis remains accurate: the institutions and cultures that immigrants bring from the old country erode further with each generation. Eventually, most of them will probably disappear, except among small groups of traditionalists and scholars working to keep them alive through ethnic festivals and in museums. At the same time, bits and pieces from these cultures persist, albeit transformed from generation to generation, modernized and supplemented by new versions of old traditions. Meanwhile, as long as the American economy needs new infusions of cheap labor, and as long as people around the world see the prospect of a better life in America, immigration will continue. And each wave of new arrivals will add its culture to the country's evolving diversity. Were Zangwill to come back and see what had happened in the hundred years since he wrote, he might agree that the best metaphor for America is not a melting pot but rather a kaleidoscope. Only that image really captures the constant flux, the persistent but changing populations and cultures, that make up the overall pattern of the nation.

*   *   *

Will the immigrants who have been arriving on these shores since about 1965 assimilate in the same way as those who came from Europe a century ago? Certainly the straight-line theory will become less and less apt. Unlike the old European immigration, which was all white and all poor, the new wave of immigrants consists of people from many different social classes and skin colors; and by now researchers understand how much those differences can affect the speed and characteristics of assimilation. Still, though it will take new and different forms, it's a sure bet that assimilation will continue.

Unlike their predecessors, today's researchers are able to study first-generation immigrants, not just their English-speaking children. We are learning that assimilation begins much earlier than originally thought, and perhaps earlier than it did in the past. Immigrants who arrive with professional schooling and middle-class habits can assimilate almost as quickly as they choose—that is, if their skin is light enough. They can also move faster into the higher ranks of the economy, previously open only to the best-schooled children and grandchildren of immigrants. Glass ceilings remain, but they are much higher than they once were. Italian, Polish, Greek and other European Americans had to wait a century to gain entry to the top echelon of American business, but today's immigrants will be allowed in earlier—and this time, not just the men.

However, despite the Americanization that today's immigrants are already undergoing, some of their children reject what is happening and question the very idea of assimilation. They proudly proclaim the virtues of their ethnic or racial backgrounds and celebrate the distinctiveness of their identities. Determined to be loyal to the communities they come from, they want to avoid being transformed into what they perceive to be mass-produced, homogenized Americans. As for straight-line theory, if it ever was accurate, they are convinced it does not apply to them.

To be sure, these reactions are not shared by all members of the second generation. Most of them are busy with everyday pursuits and practical problems; few of them use words such as "assimilation" or "identity." Concern about one's ethnic or racial allegiances—what some sociologists call "identity work"—is more likely to be undertaken by young people who do not yet have parental and other responsibilities, and by political activists. Those seeking to protect what they see as their community's cultural integrity seem to be found mostly among second-generation ethnic and racial groups who are the first in their families to attend college or to work in public agencies and other large institutions. It is particularly common when they constitute numerical minorities in the midst of not-always-friendly native-born white Americans.

What this suggests is that the public expression of ethnic or racial culture and loyalty is in part a reaction to the discrimination and subordinate status often imposed on these second-generation pioneers. "Hyphenated" Americans discover that they are still considered foreigners; students have to learn from reading lists filled entirely with the writings of those they scorn as "dead white males." Even third- and fourth-generation Asian-Americans may be asked where they learned to speak accent-free English. No wonder many of them feel insulted and respond with a stronger pride in their origins.

Of course, this movement has a political side too. Students expressing their ethnic or racial identity as a way of coping with slights and rejections may found or join a campus organization or national movement extolling community pride and group identity. Like all organizations that pursue cultural objectives and advocate ideological positions, these groups also seek power and resources. Leaders press for decisionmaking positions and jobs in public agencies, and they lobby for legislation to benefit their members and supporters. Likewise, campus activists demand ethnic and racial studies departments with faculties, courses and scholarships for their constituents.

Many people, including those whose ancestors came here so long ago that they have forgotten their own immigrant roots, are put off by such activity, now commonly called "identity politics." Although we are all supposedly multiculturalists now— most Americans are sympathetic to the ideal of diversity—identity politics can still make some people nervous. It should not be surprising that both the right and the left are sometimes unhappy with the politics of difference, particularly when its advocates fail to support public policies that could benefit all Americans.

Right and left opponents have different reasons for questioning identity politics. Some on the right worry that ethnically or racially targeted policies, and ethnic militancy in general, will threaten what they see as an already fragile nation. In some parts of the country, identity politics is being fought with opposition to bilingual education or "English only" policies that ban the official use of immigrant languages, and some even want to close the door to further immigration. What these opponents do not mention, and perhaps do not even realize, is how much they worry about losing their dominant role in American society.

Meanwhile, those on the left believe that identity politics can only get in the way of attempts to revitalize antipoverty programs and revive the welfare state. An economically and politically more egalitarian society, they believe, would benefit ethnic and racial minorities more than successful public assertions of their identities. In his classic critique of identity politics, sociologist and critic Todd Gitlin rightly accused identity movements of wasting their time by marching on college English departments to demand ethnic studies courses and politically correct language while conservatives were taking over the White House.

My own opinion is that both right and left overestimate the political power of identity politics. The world's only current superpower is not as fragile as some political pessimists believe. And even if identity politicians were to march on the White House instead of on English departments—even if they were to join the liberal struggle to build a new, more egalitarian welfare state—they still would not win that struggle, sad to say.

At the same time, it is important to recognize that whites, being the dominant American racial group, do not always realize when they are themselves engaged in racial identity politics. They believe their own intentions and goals to be free of racial underpinnings. Actually, most whites don't even realize that they are also a race, and that most practitioners of identity politics are pursuing the same American Dream as everyone else. Policies that call for African-Americans and other racial minorities to support a race-blind country are often a disguised attempt to keep whites firmly in control—in effect, white identity politics. And when white America appoints Asians as a model minority, in fact the real model, implied if not stated, is a white one. Accordingly, the appeal to other racial groups to model themselves on Asians becomes white identity politics, no matter its intent.

But whatever one's political viewpoint, today's struggles over multiculturalism need to be understood in historical context. While identity politics appears to be a new idea, in fact it was already alive and well among the European immigrants of the late nineteenth and early twentieth centuries. Concerned as they were with economic survival and better living conditions, these newcomers were also caught up in identity politics, except that it was then called ethnic politics. The big urban political machines of the day lost no time in seeking the votes of the new immigrants, and in return offered them free coal, Thanksgiving turkeys and jobs. Patronage jobs in city agencies were dealt out by ethnic group. In New York City, for example, the Irish often got the police and fire departments, Eastern European Jews dominated public school teaching, and Italians took over sanitation. As the number of ethnic votes grew, the machines presented voters with so-called "balanced" slates that included candidates from each major white ethnic group. Later, Democratic candidates for big-city mayoralties, and even for the presidency, made sure to travel to Ireland, Italy, Poland and, after 1948, Israel. Meanwhile, Republicans campaigned among Anglo-Saxons, Scandinavians and other Northern Europeans, but these were not defined as ethnic groups.

One major difference is that, for European immigrants, there was no campus-based identity politics, for the simple reason that before World War II only a tiny proportion of the population attended college. Second-generation Jews were among the first "white ethnics" to arrive on the campuses of private colleges, and they were more segregated and self-segregated than today's nonwhite students. But by the time the descendants of other European immigrants made it to college, assimilation had sufficiently eroded their ethnic identities that they had no interest in Polish, or Italian, or Irish studies.

Eventually, assimilation will also undermine today's identity politics. Some of the current activists will graduate into local and perhaps even national politics, but many of their erstwhile constituents will think more about families and mortgages than about identity. Some will vote with their racial and ethnic blocs, some will not, though most are likely to support continuing immigration. And the next generation, the grandchildren of the post-1965 immigrants, will probably behave more like the grandchildren of the European immigrants, voting in accord with their personal and national interests rather than in terms of their ethnic origins. These interests will also determine their choice of political party. Depending on the economic and social conditions of the moment, some could even become vocal opponents of further immigration.

Still, whatever the pace of political assimilation, individual ethnic identity and ethnic pride will not necessarily disappear. Ethnicity is a hearty plant, and it can easily coexist with assimilation. In fact, some people may nourish pride in their ethnic origins precisely to compensate for their continuing assimilation. After all, identifying with one's heritage does not require knowing much about it. Pride and a sense of belonging can be evoked by attending an ethnic folk festival, visiting an ethnic restaurant or merely seeing a film made in the old country. "Symbolic" activities of this kind have become one of the main ways in which white ethnicity persists, and there is no reason to think it will not also persist among the later generations of today's immigrants. Eventually, however, even such symbolic ethnicity may well prove transitory, as intermarriage creates a population so multiethnic that its ethnic options run out. After all, no one can identify with four or more ethnic cultures at the same time.

The more durable challenge to assimilation is race. Racial identity, grounded on harsher realities than ethnic identity, will persist for a good deal longer, since skin color has consequences for economic and social assimilation. Race also has consequences for intermarriage rates. About half of all Asian-Americans and light-skinned Hispanics now marry whites, and at that rate, they may be defined as near whites in a few decades. When it comes to African-Americans, however, less than 10 percent marry whites. Until they are able and willing to intermarry at the same rates as lighter-skinned people, blacks will remain a separate and segregated population. Racial intermarriage requires equal partners, and a significant increase in black-white marriage must await much greater racial equality than exists today. As a result, black identity movements may survive longer and remain stronger than others.

Still, in the longer run, and if all goes well racially, all Americans may have brown skins one day—just the right color to survive global warming. Such an outcome would prove Israel Zangwill's dream of the melting pot to have been right, though not quite in the way he thought. Once assimilation results in across-the-board intermarriage, and generations of intermarriage erase differences in skin color, eye shape, and the other visible bodily features from which we construct "race," the interracial American that Zangwill dreamed of could actually come into being. But with one qualification. The melting pot was a utopian vision, and like all utopias, it was unrealistically static. For the foreseeable future, in the real America, immigration is likely to continue bringing new racial groups and new ethnic cultures to our shores all the time. Assimilation will continue, but so will the shifting patterns of the American kaleidoscope, which will remain the quintessential image of what it means to be American.

4

REDISCOVERING THE MELTING POT —STILL GOING STRONG

by Stephan Thernstrom

TODAY, THE CONVENTIONAL WISDOM HOLDS that the "melting pot" is a myth. Of course, it is true that no single metaphor can perfectly describe the experience of every one of the tens of millions of immigrants who have come to the United States over the last century. But the fact remains that, throughout our history, the vast majority of immigrants have been absorbed into the nation—and with impressive speed. Even in the late nineteenth and early twentieth centuries, when European immigrants sought to preserve separate group identities and cultures, they eventually assimilated successfully into American life. And though today's great wave of immigrants comes largely from Asia and Latin America instead of Europe, the process of assimilation captured in the melting pot metaphor is still going strong. The melting pot does not require reinvention; it needs only to be rediscovered, to be understood as its original proponents understood it.

THE HISTORY OF A CONCEPT

Although assimilation has been taking place since the beginning of American history, the melting pot was born in 1908 as the title of a play by Israel Zangwill. Zangwill's drama was a hymn to the power of assimilative forces in American life. The hero and heroine—he a Russian Jew, she a Cossack—could never have fallen in love and married in the Old World, but in America their historically antagonistic backgrounds were irrelevant. They were living in a new land, and were reborn as a result, freed of the prejudices and hostilities that divided the peoples of Europe into mutually suspicious blocs.

Zangwill, like Mary Antin, the author of the classic immigrant autobiography *The Promised Land,* social work pioneer Jane Addams, and other melting pot proponents of the Progressive Era, did not claim that immigrants had to become English, or ape the ways of Anglo-Americans. American culture at the beginning of the twentieth century was not Anglo culture, not the exclusive property of the *Mayflower* crowd and the Daughters of the American Revolution. Even before Southern and Eastern European immigrants began to arrive in unprecedented numbers at the end of the nineteenth century, America had been transformed again and again by earlier waves of immigration. Thinkers who supported the melting pot concept believed that immigrants would be changed by America, to be sure; but they also expected that America would be changed by the immigrants. All citizens were in the melting pot together. In fact, the melting pot—far from being an oppressive or conformist notion, as is often asserted today—was a liberal, cosmopolitan social ideal. It saw American culture as being in a state of constant flux, open to the contributions of successive waves of newcomers. Becoming American did not require a complete denial of one's origins.

Unfortunately, the coming of World War I inevitably stirred deep concern about the loyalties of immigrants whose mother countries were on the other side of the battle lines. For the first time, there were demands that "hyphenated" Americans conform to the standard of

"100 percent Americanism." The leaders of this drive continued to use the melting pot term, but what they meant by it could more accurately be described as "Anglo-conformity."

This perversion of the melting pot concept was in part the work of two sharp critics of the "100 percent Americanism" campaign: the philosopher Horace Kallen and the journalist Randolph Bourne. Appalled by the superpatriotic excesses of the World War I years, Kallen and Bourne went so far as to deny that the immigrants of their day were being assimilated at all, and maintained that it was a very good thing that they were not. Writing for *The Nation* in 1915, Kallen argued that what he called true "democracy" was not the melting pot but "cultural pluralism." In *The Atlantic Monthly* the next year, Bourne made a similar plea for a "transnational America" instead of a melting pot America.

In this view, the United States was not and should not become a centralized nation-state with a strong sense of unity shared by all citizens. It should instead be a great "federation of nationalities," each group retaining its separate Old World culture in perpetuity. That would guarantee maximum diversity, which Kallen and Bourne valued above all else. Ethnic identity was primordial and inescapable: "You can't change your grandfather," Kallen said. According to this view, each ethnic group should and inevitably would pursue its own distinct destiny: its members were "like-minded," and naturally preferred to associate with others of their "kind." The children of Polish immigrants, for example, would marry only other Polish-Americans and would faithfully keep the Polish language and Polish customs alive in their homes from generation to generation. Ironically, Kallen's ethnic determinism meshed well with the racist thinking of the time, which held that black people were genetically inferior to whites and should not be allowed to mix with them in schools, restaurants or other public places. Bourne even referred dismissively to children born of ethnically mixed marriages as "half-breeds."

Although these critics of the melting pot were writing in the midst of a bloody world war that had been stimulated in part by the clashing passions of historically oppressed nationalities, neither one of them addressed the obvious question: what would keep a mere "feder-ation of nationalities" from exploding into perpetual ethnic warfare? Why would immigrants in Chicago show greater mutual respect and tolerance for each other than they were doing in the Austro-Hungar-ian and Russian empires—unless they developed a powerful sense of national identity as fellow Americans and stopped thinking of them-selves as Serbs or Croats or Slovaks first? Kallen rhapsodized about the United States as a great symphony orchestra, with the different in-struments representing different ethnic groups. Ukrainians were the oboes, Czechs the flutes, Italians the violas, yet all would play the same tune. But he never asked who would pick the tune and who would conduct the performance.

Neither Kallen nor Bourne attracted a mass following in their own time. Although most Americans during the 1920s came to share the two writers' conviction that recent immigrants had not been assimilating to American ways, the general public drew a very different and perhaps more logical conclusion. If newcomers were not Americanizing, people thought, the obvious solution was to put an end to immigration. A series of laws enacted in the 1920s not only sharply reduced the total number of newcomers but also dis-criminated against Eastern and Southern Europeans because immi-grants from those areas were perceived to be most resistant to assimilation. The refugee problem created by World War II led to some liberalization of the immigration law, but not until 1965 was the entire structure abandoned and the doors again thrown open to mass immigration.

That immigration reform followed on the heels of the 1964 Civil Rights Act and reflected the increasingly tolerant public attitudes that made possible the great victories won by the civil rights movement in that era. Unfortunately, this more tolerant climate also fostered a resurgence of the romantic attachment to ethnic diversity—and the disdain for assimilation—that had been central to the thought of Kallen and Bourne. At least among the intelligentsia, the concept of the melting pot and the very idea of Americanization acquired entirely negative connotations.

An early sign of the new mood was Nathan Glazer and Daniel P. Moynihan's 1963 volume *Beyond the Melting Pot,* a phenomenal best-seller for a scholarly book. Its central thesis was that "the point about the melting pot is that it never really happened." In fact, the authors largely ignored the conventional measures of assimilation that social scientists had always used—measures that would have yielded a quite different picture. They succeeded in demonstrating only that there were still some recognizable cultural differences among five selected groups in New York City, which had the highest concentration of recent immigrants of any city in America, and was thus a completely unrepresentative case.

What's more, one of the five groups examined by Glazer and Moynihan was African-Americans, though melting pot theorists had never pretended to explain their special situation, the product of a unique history of slavery and Jim Crow. Another of the five was Puerto Ricans, who had only very recently arrived in the city in large numbers, and had the further handicap of being racially mixed. And two out of the three European groups considered—Italians and Jews—had been in the United States in large numbers for only half a century, so that a substantial proportion of Italian or Jewish adults were foreign-born.

Shortly after the publication of *Beyond the Melting Pot,* the nation confronted movements for Black Power, Brown Power, Yellow Power, Red Power, and the supposed *Rise of the Unmeltable Ethnics* (the title of a 1972 book by Michael Novak). Bayard Rustin, a prominent black intellectual, summed up the new mood when he claimed that "there never *was* a melting pot; there is not *now* a melting pot; there never will *be* a melting pot; and if there ever was it would be such a tasteless soup that we would have to go back and start all over!"

The idea of the melting pot and the belief that immigrants should be "Americanized" have remained unfashionable ever since. Nathan Glazer may have exaggerated a bit in titling his 1997 volume *We Are All Multiculturalists Now,* but not by much. Well-argued books taking a different view of the matter, such as Peter Salins's *Assimilation, American Style* and John J. Miller's *The Unmaking of Americans,* did little to dent the widespread belief that the melting pot "never really happened." A brief review of the evidence, though, will indicate that the melting pot did really happen—and that it continues to happen today.

THE MELTING OF EUROPEAN IMMIGRANT GROUPS

When the results of the 2000 census were released, the press lavished attention on the spectacular recent growth of the Hispanic population. At 35 million, Latinos tied with African-Americans as the largest ethnic group in America, and their rapid rate of growth made it clear that they would soon outnumber blacks.

No one noticed, however, that the census actually recorded the presence of another ethnic population substantially larger than either Hispanics or blacks. In response to the question "What is your ancestry or ethnic origin?" some 43 million Americans said they were German. Many others reported partial German ancestry—the number for 2000 has not yet been released—but in the 1990 census it was an additional 12 million, making a total of approximately 55 million. These days, we hear constant references to the Hispanic or Latino "community," to Hispanic "issues" and "concerns," to Hispanic "leaders." Why is there nary a word about the far more numerous German-American "community," German "issues" or the German "vote"?

The answer is obvious. There is no German-American community, no prominent leaders who can claim to represent the "German point of view," because there is really no German ethnic group in the United States any more. There was a German ethnic group once, a huge and powerful one. But it has vanished in the melting pot. When questioned by the census taker, many millions of Americans can still dredge up memories of German ancestors. But having forebears from Germany is not a significant indicator of how these people live and how they think of themselves.

To say that one is of German ancestry, for example, does not mean that one speaks German at home. The 2000 census data on this point are not yet available, but we know that in 1990 just 1.5 million Americans lived in homes in which German was spoken, and this was at a time when 58 million people claimed some German ancestry. That amounts to less than 3 percent. The tiny German-speaking population consisted chiefly of members of religious communities like the Amish and Hutterites, groups that have made exceptionally intense efforts to remain as isolated as possible from American life. How many people in Milwaukee, once the capital of German America, still speak German? Precious few.

Nor does claiming German ancestry mean that one is of unmixed, unmelted German background. The census allows respondents to name up to three different ancestries. Two-thirds of those who claimed German ancestry in 1990 also specified at least one other ethnic element in their backgrounds. Even the one-third who mentioned only German forebears included people who were unaware of, or simply chose not to report, the non-Germans in their family trees. This is striking testimony to the powerful effects of intermarriage on the American melting pot.

That being of German ancestry seems to be of such minor, purely symbolic, significance to most who report it explains an otherwise mystifying fact. In 1969, when the Current Population Survey first asked a question about ancestry, 20 million Americans identified themselves as of German origin. On the 1980 census, though, the figure was 49 million, and by 1990 it had soared again to 58 million, even though there had been no significant immigration from Germany in the interim. Answers to the ancestry question are manifestly not indicators of deep and enduring ethnic identification. Indeed, one study of a representative national sample compared how the same individuals responded to the ancestry question when it was asked of them in 1971 and then again in 1972. One-third of all those who initially said they were German did not report having any German ancestry just one year later!

German-Americans are not unusual in having disappeared into the melting pot. Essentially the same story holds for the other major immigrant groups that arrived in the nineteenth century: English,

Of course, the World Wars turned up the melting pot temp. for Germans! — Duh!

Irish, Scottish, Welsh, Dutch and Scandinavian. The non-English mother tongues they brought with them did not survive for very long; most of their children and almost all their grandchildren spoke English at home as well as at work. And while Horace Kallen expected young people to choose mates whose grandfathers were of the same ethnic background, it didn't happen. Marriage outside the ethnic group was common among American-born second-generation immigrants; by the third generation it was the norm.

The same holds for those groups that arrived in large numbers in the first quarter of the twentieth century: Italians, Poles, Greeks, Hungarians, Slovaks, Russian Jews and others. People of these backgrounds are closer to the immigration experience, of course, so they tend to be less assimilated by some measures. But not much less. Among American-born people who claimed Italian ancestry on the 1980 census, 58 percent of those born before 1920 chose spouses who were of unmixed Italian ancestry; for those born after 1950, only 15 percent did so, and 75 percent picked mates who had no Italian ancestry. Among Poles, 47 percent of the pre-1920 generation married within the group; for the post-1950 cohort it was only 7 percent, and 82 percent wed people who had no ancestral ties to Poland.

The evidence about language indicates the same thing. Although 11 million Americans reported being of Italian ancestry in 1990, fewer than a tenth of those born in the United States said they could speak a language other than English. (And even that small group could include many who had picked up some Spanish or French in school.) The same low proportion was found among the 6 million native-born Americans of Polish ancestry.

Nor is it any longer the case that significant numbers of Americans of European ancestry live in ethnic "ghettos"—Little Italys, Poletowns and the like. Richard Alba's analysis of 1980 census data from the Albany-Troy-Schenectady area of New York found that just 2.3 percent of Italian-Americans resided in neighborhoods with an Italian majority. For the Irish, 1.8 percent lived in areas with a majority of their co-ethnics; for Germans, 0.1 percent. And not a single neighborhood in this huge metropolitan area had a Polish majority.

Further evidence about ethnic identification has been gathered by Alba in a survey described in his book *Ethnic Identity: The Transformation of White America*. For example, he asked respondents to identify their friends by ethnicity. It turned out that only a sixth of them had three or more friends (other than relatives) of the same ethnic origin, and only one in six had ties to an ethnically based organization of some kind.

Even so, Alba concluded that ethnic divisions remained significant in American society at the end of the 1980s because most of those he surveyed had some knowledge of their ethnic ancestry, reported it when asked about it and expressed some attachments to family traditions related to their ancestry. For example, 85 percent of the Italian-Americans in his survey sometimes ate food they considered Italian, and more than 60 percent consumed it at least once a week. (The author failed to report, however, how many non-Italians frequently visit Italian restaurants or cook pasta at home. In the cities of the Northeast, at least, a large fraction of the population regularly patronizes Italian restaurants.) Somewhat more impressive was that half the Poles in his study consumed Polish food on occasion, surely a much higher figure than among the general population.

One wonders, though, if this behavior really matters much, except to market researchers. The traces of ethnicity that Alba found seem little more significant than other lifestyle choices—more like preferring Pepsi to Coke than the behavior Horace Kallen expected in a "federation of nationalities." The crucial point is that it is *voluntary*, not inexorably governed by who your grandfather was. We all have two grandfathers (and two grandmothers, who should also count), and by the 1980s Americans of European ancestry typically had grandparents who fit into different ethnic categories. What Alba found was only "symbolic ethnicity," almost completely divorced from the social structure. It was no longer closely tied to where you lived, what school you attended, what your profession was, who your friends were, or whom you married. The melting pot had not quite been a Cuisinart that produced an absolutely uniform soup. But it had certainly melted away the very large group differences visible a century ago—and in the process, ethnic divisions that were deeply rooted in the social structure were transformed into matters of consumer choice.

WILL THE MELTING POT WORK FOR ASIANS AND HISPANICS?

The 1965 immigration reform act not only opened the door to a sharp increase in total immigration to the United States. It was followed by a dramatic shift in the sources of immigration. By the 1990s, only one out of seven newcomers hailed from a European country, while nearly half were from Latin America, and almost a third from Asia.

Will the post-1965 immigrants melt into American society as successfully as their European predecessors did? Those who doubt that the melting pot really functioned a century ago are even more dubious about the assimilation of recent Asian and Latino newcomers. And some who concede that earlier European immigrants were successfully absorbed maintain that these new groups will face greater barriers because they are not white. They will tend to remain separate and unassimilated because of their inevitable bitter experience of racial discrimination.

From the mid-nineteenth century, when the first Chinese arrived in California, through World War II, Asian-Americans were indeed the object of intense racial prejudice. Immigration from China was barred four decades before European immigration was restricted in the 1920s. Newcomers from Asia were denied the opportunity to become naturalized citizens; a new legal category of "aliens ineligible for citizenship" was invented to keep them apart from the body politic. During World War II, the long tradition of white racial fears contributed to the decision to confine West Coast Japanese-Americans behind barbed wire for the duration of the conflict with Japan.

Since World War II, however, Asian-Americans have been transformed from a stigmatized racial group into a spectacularly successful and rapidly assimilating one. Some Asian-Americans do argue that their race is still a huge barrier. A 1999 article in the *Yale Law Journal* asked "Are Asians Black?" and answered the question in the affirmative. If there had been a competition for the silliest essay published that year, this one would have been hard to beat. Among the crucial facts it managed to ignore were that Asian-American students, though only 4 percent of the population, comprised one-sixth of the student body at Yale College, one-fifth at Harvard College, and one-fifth of all students enrolled in medical schools in the entire United States. Their representation at Yale Law School, the nation's most selective and prestigious, was triple their share in the overall population. Native-born Asian families have median incomes 50 percent above the national average and far outpace whites in rates of college graduation. On many measures of socioeconomic status, they rank about as far above white Americans as whites rank above African-Americans.

An ethnic group can prosper, of course, and still remain quite separate from the larger society. But Asian-Americans are certainly not remaining socially separate. The most telling sign is their very high rate of marriage outside the group. Marriages between "Orientals" and whites were once strongly stigmatized; just 2 percent of the Japanese marrying in Los Angeles County in the 1920s married whites. But today all Asian groups follow the customary immigrant pattern of steep generational increases in marriage outside the group. In the second generation, the 1990 census showed, a third of Asian-Americans married non-Asians; by the third generation, the majority did. In evaluating the claim that Asians are black, it might be noted that the intermarriage rate for blacks at the time was in the single digits.

It is simply absurd to compare the situation of Asian-Americans with the much more difficult one of African-Americans. With Hispanics, there are more grounds for debate. Hispanic-Americans today do superficially resemble blacks in their poverty rate, and they are even less likely than blacks to graduate from high school and from college. Such crude comparisons, though, are worthless, because they lump together all Hispanics, those who arrived yesterday and those whose families have been here for generations. Since 1965, most immigrants from Latin America have come with levels of education and skills far below the American norm. Any judgment about whether Hispanic groups have been assimilating at about the same pace as Italians or Poles a century earlier requires a more detailed and nuanced look at the evidence.

When an immigrant's years of residence in the United States is taken into account, a much more reassuring picture emerges. The 2002 National Survey of Latinos, conducted by the Pew Hispanic Center, indicates rapid generational change in the Hispanic population. For example, the stereotype that Hispanics are much more resistant than other immigrants to learning English is clearly false. The survey found that 72 percent of foreign-born Latinos were "Spanish-dominant," and all but 4 percent of the rest were bilingual. But only 7 percent of the second-generation were Spanish-dominant; by the third generation, the figure fell to zero, while 78 percent were English-dominant.

Similarly, while only a third of first-generation Latino immigrants said that they had ever described themselves as "American," in the second generation the figure jumped to 85 percent, and by the third to 97 percent. Other studies clearly show rising educational attainment and substantial upward occupational mobility for Hispanics from one generation to the next. Data for 1996–1999 reveal that those born in Mexico had an average of little more than eight years of school, while their American-born children averaged nearly twelve years. Only 14 percent of first-generation Mexican immigrants had attended college; for their native-born children the figure was 40 percent. Similarly, second-generation Hispanics typically have better jobs than their immigrant parents and are more likely to own their own homes.

It could still be argued that switching to English, staying in school longer and getting better jobs are not direct proof that an ethnic group is becoming truly assimilated. But the best direct evidence on that point concerns marriage patterns, and here the signs of assimilation are indisputable. In 1990, only one of eight married first-generation Hispanic immigrants had a non-Hispanic spouse. In the second generation, it was one in three. By the third generation, there was a clear majority, 54 percent.

CONCLUSION

All this evidence reveals that the American melting pot is just as strong today as it was in the past. It also shows why it is so unnecessary to worry, as many observers have, about the Census Bureau's prediction that by 2050 the proportion of Hispanics in the U.S. population will double to 24 percent, while non-Hispanic whites will comprise a bare majority at 52 percent and drop to a minority of the total by 2060. Even if such population projections are reliable, their fundamental mistake is that they assume such categories point to socially meaningful differences. Remember today's 55 million Americans of German ancestry—they represent about a fifth of the total population, but who cares? There are no major social cleavages between Americans of German ancestry and any other segment of the population.

Whether the differences between Hispanics and non-Hispanics will be as negligible in 2050 is impossible to say. But this example clearly illustrates the peril of putting individuals into categories based on their ancestry and assuming that those categories will have great social significance far into the future. Given the power and success of assimilation so far in American history, my bet is that by the time we have a "minority majority" in the United States, no one will notice it.

5

ASSIMILATION TODAY: IS ONE IDENTITY ENOUGH?

by Nathan Glazer

T HE WAY WE THINK ABOUT assimilation is still largely determined by
the experience of the great wave of European immigrants that arrived in the United States from the 1880s through the 1920s. Indeed,
a large part of American sociology—including the work of the discipline's University of Chicago pioneers, Robert E. Park, Louis Wirth,
W. L. Warner, Leo Srole and Milton Gordon—was created to analyze
the absorption of immigrants from Southern and Eastern Europe into
American society. Today, we see the assimilation of those European
immigrants, which originally aroused so many fears, as a great success
story: peoples from many nations were molded into one nation. Inevitably, we compare the experiences of current immigrants, who
come mostly from the Caribbean, Latin America, the Middle East,
and Asia, and ask anxiously if they are following the same path, at the
same pace. But today, in the midst of a new and very different wave of
immigration, that earlier experience may no longer be a suitable
guide. In fact, it may lead us to have both false expectations and unnecessary fears about today's immigrants. Immigrants have always as-

similated, and they always will; but the nature of assimilation is significantly different today than in the past.

There are many obvious differences between the last great wave of European immigration and the current wave of Latin American, Middle Eastern, Asian and Caribbean immigration: race, culture, religion, language. But two other important differences have not been sufficiently noted. The first is the effect of two world wars in promoting the rapid assimilation of the earlier European immigrants; the second is the surprising change in American law and practice, starting in the 1960s, that makes multiple citizenship—and by implication, multiple national identities—more common and acceptable. Both factors affect one key element of assimilation: the acquisition of a new and exclusive national identity.

*   *   *

The path to the assimilation of the last wave of European immigrants—the "new" immigration, as it was then called, of Jews, Italians, Poles, Hungarians, Greeks and other Eastern and Southern European peoples—was punctuated by World War I, and further deeply affected by World War II. These wars emphasized and widened the differences between immigrants' old and new countries. Almost all the major European groups, including those who had arrived in earlier immigration waves, were deeply involved in these wars. Their homelands were fighting as allies or enemies of the United States; the fate of their relatives would be affected by the outcome. Yet the intensity of American chauvinism—or, if you will, patriotism—during World War I was so great that many immigrants' loyalty to their former people or country was burned away or buried underground. This was the melting pot in operation, with a vengeance.

Before World War I, German immigrants—the largest of the continental European immigrant groups—demonstrated great pride in Germany and its culture. Cultural, social, and athletic institutions preserved these newcomers' language and identity. German was taught in the public schools of states with large German populations;

indeed, many public schools were conducted in German. What's more, pride in German culture among German immigrants was matched with respect for German culture among native-born Americans (a situation rather different from that which prevails in current bilingual education). A degree of "multiculturalism" prevailed in German communities in the Midwest that would match anything found among new immigrant groups today. ✓

But all this was expunged by World War I and its aftermath. By the time of World War II, Americans were hardly conscious of the fact that one of the largest ethnic groups in the country was in effect, by nature of its origins, allied with the enemy. Nationalism ran high throughout America, among immigrants and nonimmigrants alike. And while from today's vantage point we would almost all abhor the passions that led to the banning of the German language in World War I, or the incarceration of the Japanese population in World War II, these ordeals certainly promoted assimilation, encouraging identification with the American state and people and the suppression of other national loyalties. Admittedly, they could also lead to resentment and anger that would hamper assimilation; but there was surprisingly little of that kind of reaction.

This important difference between the first half of the twentieth century and the second has had significant consequences for the political assimilation of our current immigrant population. There have been no world wars, fortunately, since 1945. Immigration has expanded during a long period remarkably free, by American historical standards, of nationalist passion. Neither the Cold War nor the fighting in Korea and Vietnam did much to stir patriotic fervor. (If we feared subversion during the Cold War, it was not from those who would sympathize with our enemies because of national origin but from those who, whatever their national origins, might sympathize with them out of ideology.) And as a result, today's newcomers have never experienced the wartime pressures that forced the quick assimilation of earlier immigrants.

Of course, the events of September 11, 2001, and the subsequent "war on terrorism" raise new questions. With wars in Afghanistan and Iraq, the Patriot Act, registration of many aliens from Muslim countries and new restrictions on visitors from the Middle East and any country with a large Muslim population, one may ask: will Muslim and Arab immigrants face hostility similar to that encountered by German- and Japanese-Americans? Although we do not classify any group as "enemy aliens" because we have not declared war on any nation, many Muslim and Arab immigrants are now being treated with hostility and suspicion, and some are in detention for what until recently were considered minor derelictions in legal status. Will the impact of these measures lead American Muslims and Arabs to increase the pace of their assimilation, or return to their home countries, or become a permanently aggrieved minority? Right now it is too soon to tell. But since no one expects the war on terrorism to be short, and since there is a sharp discord between some key Muslim values and the evolving pattern of American culture, this war may well have grave effects on the assimilation of Muslims and Arabs in the United States. Still, even in this case, war does not seem to be accelerating assimilation today as it did 100 years ago.

*   *   *

The second major development, which has also received too little notice, is the surprising change in our conception of the claims of citizenship and national identity on the new American. Until the 1960s, dual citizenship was seen as an anomaly to be eliminated as soon as possible so that each citizen owed allegiance to one country only, and each country claimed the full allegiance of every citizen. But today, millions of new Americans remain citizens or nationals of their countries of origin. ("National" is the wider term, and, depending on the country of origin, a national may not have all the rights of citizenship.) It has been estimated that 500,000 children born in the United States each year, who by that fact alone are American citizens, are also legally citizens of their parents' countries of origin.

We might consider this only a technical anomaly that will rapidly be overcome by the forces of assimilation. After all, the European immigrants of the last great wave were also for the most part dual nationals or dual citizens, yet they were expected to, and did, fight against their homelands in two world wars. But the dual nationality of those European immigrants was a very different thing from dual nationality today. Then, it was a passive legal status of which the immigrant might become aware only if he visited his homeland, where he might find, for example, that he was subject to military service. And of course, visits back home were then much less frequent.

Today, dual citizenship is a more conscious and deliberate matter, if only because so many of today's immigrants remain in touch with friends and relatives in their homelands and visit frequently. Many immigrants to the United States are also encouraged by their countries of origin to keep their original citizenship, further promoting identification with and commitment to the homeland. The continuity of citizenship and nationality is, of course, only one of the factors that enhance the ties between immigrants and their homelands; the development of easier and cheaper means of travel and communication are undoubtedly more significant. But taken together, these factors make for a strikingly different attitude towards assimilation among today's immigrants.

*　　*　　*

At the same time, America's expectations of its immigrants have undergone a marked change. At the beginning of the twentieth century, Theodore Roosevelt was a friend of immigration because he thought it increased the strength of the United States. But he had strict views on the duties of new immigrants: no "hyphenated Americanism," a full commitment to English, a complete break with the country of origin. These views were shared by liberals and conservatives alike, and they dominated the Americanization movement during World War I and after. Nor are we to think of this exclusive American identity as being brutally imposed on an unwilling immigrant population. Imposed it was, in the schools, at work, and through the insistence of national figures—liberal and conservative—in a national movement. But it was also embraced by new immigrants fleeing poverty and various forms of discrimination. No hyphenated Americanism, an exclusive and fierce loyalty to the new country: these were the sentiments that became dogma in World War I and its aftermath. It is the weakening of this principle that arouses so much concern today among many observers used to a simpler, more direct route to assimilation.

By the time of World War II, there was already a softening of that norm. To assist in the war effort, America began to call on the old ethnic identities of many of its citizens, identities that had been forced underground by World War I and forceful assimilation. "One hundred per cent Americanism" could now be legitimately supplemented with loyalty to an occupied and oppressed European homeland. The idea that immigrants' loyalty to their original culture was consistent with assimilation, restricted during World War I to marginal thinkers like the philosopher Horace Kallen and the brilliant young journalist Randolph Bourne, now became part of the mainstream. In some popular writing and some school curricula, immigration and immigrant cultures were celebrated. But even so, the aim was to spread tolerance in the service of a greater national unity rather than embrace multiple and complex identities for their own sake.

In the 1960s and 1970s, of course, the way we conceive of national identity and national loyalty altered dramatically. The change in immigration laws, from preferential quotas for certain national origins to a formally equal treatment of all nations and races, was perhaps the most significant evidence of a revolution in American national identity. The shift was also reflected in key Supreme Court decisions that extended rights to noncitizens—for example, the right to welfare—and decreed that an immigrant could not lose American citizenship by identifying with his or her country of origin—for instance, by voting in an election in the home country.

This enormous change was driven by many factors. The civil rights movement and the international human rights movement encouraged and justified ethnic identities and diminished the exclusive claim of national identity. These and other developments, at home and abroad, changed the view the United States had of itself as a paragon among nations, so far above all others that it deserved exclusive loyalty. And inevitably, this sharp decline in what we demand legally of new citizens has affected their approach to assimilation and their understanding of it.

* * *

The traditional concept of assimilation, based on exclusive loyalty to the United States, is enshrined in the oath of citizenship, now taken by 1 million immigrants a year:

> I hereby declare, on oath, that I absolutely and entirely renounce and abjure all allegiance and fidelity to any foreign prince, potentate, state or sovereignty; that I will support and defend the Constitution of the United States of America against all enemies, foreign and domestic; that I will bear arms on behalf of the United States when required by law. . . .

This language goes back to the 1790s, and we would never adopt such an oath today. (In fact, the oath has been somewhat modified to reflect our weaker sense of citizenship: for example, it now goes on to specify that alternative, nonmilitary activities can substitute for the taking up of arms.) On its face, it would seem to make dual citizenship or dual nationality a direct violation. But as a matter of fact, we tolerate the continuation of foreign loyalties, as expressed in the continuation of the new citizen's original national status, and the United States takes no action against any person who maintains dual citizenship. In a sense, the grand oath is a dead letter.

Another example of what exclusive loyalty to the United States once entailed can be found in the language of every American passport:

> Under certain circumstances, you may lose your citizenship by performing any of the following acts: 1) naturalizing in a foreign state; 2) taking an oath or making a declaration to a foreign state;

3) certain service in the armed forces of a foreign state; 4) accepting employment with a foreign government; or 5) by formally renouncing U.S. citizenship before a U.S. consular official overseas.

This too is pretty much a dead letter, killed by a series of Supreme Court decisions and federal regulations. American citizens now can and do take up major posts in foreign governments with no apparent threat to their American citizenship. In one striking example, Valdus Adamkus became president of the newly independent Lithuania while he was an American citizen. (He did eventually give up his American citizenship, but apparently the laws of neither country required him to do so.)

In recent years, constitutional lawyers and others have expressed exasperation with not just the language but also the intent of the naturalization oath because of the way it flies in the face of today's acceptance of dual citizenship. We accept, even praise, sentiments and actions that our laws explicitly condemn; yet we cannot bring our laws into line with our practice. In the year 2001, on Cinco de Mayo, Mexico's national day, President George W. Bush sent a message in Spanish to our Mexican-origin population, in effect recognizing their continuing loyalty to Mexico, and most of us considered it perfectly acceptable. The gesture not only appeared politically astute, but also expressed our current vision of a tolerant and "multicultural" America. But can anyone imagine the president's proposing, or Congress's approving, a change in the oath of naturalization to eliminate its forceful rejection of all previous national loyalties? Similarly, one suspects that the language in the U.S. passport will remain, even though American citizens take up posts under foreign governments, enroll in foreign armies and vote in foreign elections with impunity.

The oath and the language in the passport express the sentiments of the United States of Theodore Roosevelt and Woodrow Wilson, and they were echoed by a president as recent as John F. Kennedy. His views on the matter are reflected in the inscriptions, from the early 1960s, at the entrance to the John Fitzgerald Kennedy Park in Cambridge, Massachusetts: patriotic sentiments, expressed in an elevated language, that no president, Democrat or Republican, would breathe today.

"Now the trumpet summons us again—not as a call to arms, though arms we need—not as a call to battle, though embattled we are—but a call to bear the burdens of a long twilight struggle, year in and year out, 'rejoicing in hope, patient in tribulation'—a struggle against the common enemies of man: tyranny, poverty, disease, and war itself." This was written during the Cold War; but anything of the sort would today sound chauvinistic and grandiose. Some people may regret that a simpler world has passed away, and Americans who grew up under that earlier dispensation may at times be dismayed by the newer and more complex situation that has replaced it. But regret and nostalgia will not resuscitate that earlier era: a world in which emigrants left oppressive homelands with the intention of embracing a new nation, and the United States in its turn demanded a full embrace from them. Although many new immigrants still feel this way, many more maintain pride in the countries they have left, a pride supported by a widespread multicultural sentiment in the schools and in popular culture. Today, the nations these emigrants have left see their nationals in the United States as potential tools of foreign policy, while we on this side celebrate our diversity. Ellis Island matches or surpasses Independence Hall as an icon of our history, and we find it hard to set any limits on the expression of diversity, even when that includes, as it does for millions, the maintenance of dual citizenship.

*　　*　　*

Consider our largest current immigrant group, Mexicans. We commonly refer to all categories of Mexican immigrants—naturalized, not yet naturalized or illegal—as Mexican-Americans, because our historic expectation is that every migrant hopes and plans to become an American. But does it really make sense to use the term "Mexican-American" for immigrants who are not U.S. citizens, or for the 3 to 4 million Mexicans who are here illegally? In fact, the legal status of Mexican immigrants has undergone a striking change in the last few years. The Mexican Constitution was until 1998 as severe as our oath of naturalization in rejecting the possibility of remaining a Mexican citizen when one became the citizen of a foreign country. When Mexicans became American citizens, they were no longer nationals of Mexico, and when they visited home they went as foreigners, needing visas and the like. Perhaps this was one reason fewer Mexicans became American citizens, compared to immigrants from other nations.

But a few years ago, political leaders in Mexico implemented a change in Mexico's Constitution—a process as elaborate as amending our Constitution—that made it possible for Mexicans who became American citizens to remain Mexican nationals and allowed those who had lost nationality because they had become American citizens to regain it. (Nationality, in Mexico, is a status that does not give all the rights of citizenship, such as running for office and voting, but allows the national who returns permanently to Mexico to regain these rights eventually.) With this change, Mexico came into line with many other countries, in Latin America and elsewhere, that do not require the surrender of nationality or citizenship on becoming a citizen of another nation.

All political parties in Mexico supported this change, and many reasons were given for it. It would ease some difficulties for Mexican-Americans in inheriting and buying land in Mexico; it would allow emigrants to protect their interests and rights in the United States by becoming American citizens without losing their link to their homeland; and it would help Mexican-Americans serve as an interest group in defense of Mexican interests in the United States with respect to trade and immigration.

But the full implications of the change did not become clear until the presidency of Vicente Fox. "In his frequent visits to the United States," *The New York Times* reported in 2001, "President Fox regularly meets with migrant workers and Mexican business leaders. Calling himself the President of 123 million Mexicans, 23 million of whom live in the United States, Mr. Fox promises to defend the rights of his constituents regardless of which side of the border they call home." What is noteworthy is how few people in the United States have expressed alarm or outrage that the President of Mexico sees himself as the leader of the Mexican-Americans in this country. Similarly, there was little reaction, in public opinion or in Congress, when Mexico changed its Constitution to enable Mexican-Americans to remain Mexican nationals.

I refer to these developments, not to raise alarm, but to illustrate how much our concept of assimilation—particularly political assimilation—has changed. Today we acknowledge that many immigrants will wish to retain citizenship in their countries of origin and promote those countries' interests, and we accept that. We should note, of course, that these interests are not only "Mexican" interests but also the interests of many non–Mexican-Americans who favor an easier flow of labor and goods across international frontiers. When Mexican-Americans support President Fox's efforts to make life easier for illegal Mexican immigrant workers in this country, or to allow Mexican trucks to travel into the United States, they are also supporting the agenda of pro-immigration Americans from President George W. Bush to *The Wall Street Journal*. Globalization can make it hard to know what national interest means today, and what loyalty requires.

Of course, we don't know just how Mexican-Americans are affected by this vigorous campaign to align them more closely with the interests of their home country. And it is not only Mexico that tries to do so. What President Fox has done hardly compares, as yet, with the close links forged between Israel and American Jews. These ties were once seen as raising questions of dual loyalty among American Jews: the issue was hotly debated in the 1950s, and was seen as cause for great concern. But today, many nations try to enlist the support of their ethnic cousins in the United States in support of their own interests.

*   *   *

What does this all mean for assimilation? Assimilation has many aspects. In its most general sense, we think of it as a process by which an immigrant or his child becomes an American, as recognizably

American as any native-born descendant of pioneers, settlers or earlier immigrants. But perhaps that is too simple a definition—one that needs revising in light of the way the world is changing.

In the United States and the rest of the free developed world, national identity has lost its sharp, exclusive edge. The legal order has shifted, according the immigrant many of the same rights as the native. Forceful assimilation has gone out of fashion. The word "Americanization," with its whiff of narrowness and chauvinism, can no longer be used in polite discourse. Americans' feelings about their affiliations are different, and multiculturalism must be accommodated, whether in schools, in the workplace or in public ceremonies. Plainly, all this has important consequences for our sense of assimilation—what it means and what it requires.

Today, as in the past, there are many empirical tests of whether immigrants have become American: how well they speak English, whether they live among their own group or in an integrated community, how much education they have, the kind of occupations they hold, how much they depend on welfare, whether they become citizens, whether they vote, who they marry and so on. By most of these tests, there is no significant evidence that today's immigrants are much different from yesterday's. They still enlist in our armies and fight in our wars. They still become American citizens. They still learn English, work and pay taxes. But clearly these measures are only an approximation of what we mean by assimilation.

Consider, after all, the situation of American blacks. On some of these measures—residential separation, intermarriage, achievement in standardized tests—blacks are among the least "assimilated" of any group in the United States. Yet there can be no question that blacks are deeply and integrally American. They arrived at the same time as the first English settlers. They were established here long before the coming of the major European ethnic groups. They see themselves as fundamentally American, even though many also maintain another identity that sets them apart from the mainstream. And ultimately this makes nonsense of some of our standard measures of assimilation. It reminds us that, at the deepest level, assimilation refers not to any external measure but to a subjective sense of identity: how one conceives of oneself and one's national community.

What, then, are we to make of the fact that immigrants today maintain so much stronger ties than in the past to their homeland and its people? My conviction is that assimilation still works; but today it works in different ways. More easily than in the past, it accommodates more than one identity and more than one loyalty. Immigrants continue to identify with the old country, its institutions and its politics. But this is not necessarily cause for regret—for they also forge an identity as Americans.

Thus we find Dominicans in New York City waving Dominican flags when a Little League team of young Dominicans wins a world series title for the United States. New Yorkers are at worst bemused when Dominican presidential candidates come to raise money in New York's Dominican community, and we already see candidates for mayor of New York adding the Dominican Republic to their campaign itineraries. Most important, though it may take several generations, eventually the newcomers' connection with their home island will diminish. Thus it was in the past, and thus it will be today—for Dominicans and for other new Americans. The world itself is very different, and assimilation too looks different—a marked departure from what it was during and after the great European immigration. But eventually today's immigrants, like their predecessors a century ago, will most likely become Americans.

6

THE 21ST CENTURY: AN ENTIRELY NEW STORY

by Roger Waldinger

T HE MIGRATIONS OF THE TURN of the twentieth century transformed America and transfixed its social science observers. Immigrants from Eastern and Southern Europe arrived without skills, started at the bottom, and encountered dislike and discrimination at almost every step up the ladder. But at the turn of the twenty-first century, the descendants of those bedraggled newcomers have clearly made it, moving ahead, even beyond, the people who previously held them in contempt.

Does this story have any bearing for today?

Optimists answer yes. In their view, the past provides a reliable guide to the route ahead: remembering that the America of the early twentieth century was deeply exclusionary, optimists emphasize the upside of the newcomers' encounter with today's more open and democratic society. Immigrants, now as then, are strongly motivated by the quest for the better life. Just as they did earlier, immigrants' earnings improve over time, and with economic progress come changes in lifestyles and personal relationships that make ethnicity purely optional. Just as their predecessors did, today's newcomers and their descendants will move from ethnic ghetto to suburb, and from a spe-cialized ethnic niche into the general economy. Gradually they will drop old country ties and take their children to communities where friends, and eventually mates, come from various ethnic backgrounds.

Pessimists, by contrast, look at the same history and see irrelevance. In their view, Italians, Poles and Jews shared a common European heritage with America's ruling WASPs, while the contemporary immi-grants from Mexico, Central America, Asia and elsewhere have no such connection. As "people of color," today's newcomers are said to en-counter resistance that is far more entrenched. Moreover, the old factory economy allowed for a gradual move up the totem pole. Immi-grants' children could drop out of high school and still find blue-collar jobs that paid well, and the grandchildren could then progress from this solid, if modest, base. By contrast, today's knowledge economy gives immigrant offspring no time to play catch-up. To get ahead, the second generation, which generally starts out in deeply troubled, big-city school systems, has to do well in school and stay enrolled through college. Some will surely make it; many, however, will fail.

In fact, neither optimists nor pessimists get it right. Ironically, since both subscribe to the same story about the past, both fail to de-tect how different things are today when it comes to politics, ethnic-ity and group mobilization.

First, politics. The conditions for membership in the American people changed in the decades after the last mass migration ended. The United States was then an ethnocracy, dominated by one ethnic group; it has since been transformed into a democracy. Politically, civil rights have been extended to all citizens; culturally, the bound-aries of "we, the people" have been enlarged to encompass everyone in the United States, origins notwithstanding.

Second, ethnicity: the group affiliations newcomers bring take a different form. New immigrants now arrive with broad, politicized group identities, which, in turn, make them more confident con-tenders for a piece of the American pie.

Third, group mobilization: mobilizing on an explicitly ethnic basis is currently accepted today as it has never been before. In the past, ethnicity often competed unsuccessfully with other forms of allegiance rooted in class or religion. These alternatives have since lost influence, replaced by a minority-group model that gives new immigrants a much more effective means of making their claims heard.

Taken together, these three changes make it easier than ever before for new immigrants to become full-fledged Americans.

MEMBERSHIP IN THE AMERICAN PEOPLE: THEN AND NOW

The first change involves the politics of belonging: how can a foreigner become one of "us"?

America's answer to this question has fluctuated significantly over the last two hundred years. Yes, America has seen itself as uniquely fluid, always in the process of being forged from peoples of many different kinds. But this expansive notion has also competed with a narrower conception in which true "American-ness" was defined restrictively—on the basis of ancestry. The arrival of vast numbers of new immigrants between 1880 and 1920 provoked such a narrowing of the definition of American identity, redefining membership in ways that made it much harder to belong.

In the early twentieth century, immigrants to the United States encountered a nation that was, as the historian Alexander Saxton put it, a white republic—though the definition of "whiteness" itself remained a matter of debate and contention. Until the late nineteenth century, the formation of American identity mainly involved distinguishing whites from domestic "outsiders": African-Americans and American Indians. With the upsurge of immigration, however, the ethnic majority increasingly defined the national community in opposition to the newly arriving "aliens." Immigrants born in Asia were legally barred from naturalizing as U.S. citizens—discrimination that paved the way for further discrimination and, eventually, the internment of Japanese-Americans during World War II. Similarly, German Jews, previously well accepted in America, experienced ostracism after the arrival of Russian Jewish immigrants who were not as wealthy or well educated. In the end came immigration restriction: the National Origins Act of 1924 spelled out the American reaction against people seen to be unacceptably different and foreign.

Things were very different by the time mass migration began again at the end of the twentieth century. Most important, the immigrants of the late twentieth century entered an America democratized by the civil rights revolution: one in which racial and ethnic origins were formally irrelevant to both membership and citizenship. Likewise, racialized conceptions of American identity have become almost entirely things of the past. As sociologist Nathan Glazer has powerfully argued, we are all multiculturalists now: the boundaries of the American "we" have been enlarged, and its definition relaxed. The terms of belonging aren't fixed but are the subject of continuing discussion in which the range of participants continues to grow. The prevailing view is increasingly expansive: America is a nation made and remade by people who may come from any part of the globe, but who all wish to be Americans.

Not all the foreigners living in the United States find acceptance as Americans, of course. The millions of illegal immigrants who work hard and play mainly by the rules are explicitly excluded from the club. Even legal immigrants often find the road to citizenship difficult: an America less ambivalent about immigration and more committed to assimilation would be making citizenship easier, not harder, to obtain. And the stigma associated with the low-status jobs that so many newcomers fill provides longer-established groups with additional reason for thinking that immigrants are not fully respectable.

But making it in America has never been easy or automatic. Now, as in the past, it involves a complex, protracted negotiation between newcomers and established groups. Yet today's more open vision of American nationhood gives contemporary immigrants a kind of cultural leverage that they can use to claim membership in the national club. Thanks to the democratization of the American people, contemporary immigrants enjoy a significant advantage unavailable to their predecessors of a century ago.

GROUP IDENTITY, YESTERDAY AND TODAY

Today is also different from the past in a second way. Migrants' backgrounds and experience are different and, as a result, ethnic affiliations take very different forms.

The last great wave of immigrants came mostly from peasant societies not yet transformed into nation-states. Eastern Europeans came mainly from the multiethnic empires of Russia and Austro-Hungary, in which nationality and ethnicity rarely converged. Italian immigrants came from a newly founded state that had made little progress in turning its various regions into a unified country. Thus, before their arrival on American shores, Italians and Slavs knew almost nothing of the "nation" to which they were supposed to belong. Instead, the relevant homeland was local, a place with its own dialect, customs, clothing and cuisine, all different from those on the other side of the valley. Immigrants' local ties were so strong that moving across the Atlantic often meant re-creating their original village on New York's Lower East Side or some similar neighborhood.

Yet because such local cultures were largely taken for granted and were rooted in local custom and routine, they were hard to transmit to children who had not shared the same experience. Nor did these "migration chains," as scholars call them, necessarily produce a sense of connection to immigrants from some other place in the old country—how could they, if the transplanted villagers spoke mutually unintelligible dialects? What's more, since many migrants came to America only temporarily—a pattern reflected in rates of re-migration far higher than those known today—it was easy to break the ties formed during a stint of labor in the United States.

So in speaking of the assimilation of ethnic groups, the classical literature is misleading. Immigrants came to America as members of small-scale local communities that evolved into ethnic groups only after settlement in the New World. Outsiders, who could not tell Neapolitans from Sicilians, or Galician Jews from Lithuanian Jews, unwittingly taught immigrants that they shared an identity with people they had once viewed as very different. Ideologues and intellectuals in the immigrant community tried to impart a similar view, creating allegiances and kindling connections to a national ideal often first encountered in the United States. But the process took a long time. Regional and hometown loyalties and jealousies remained strong until well after the end of the great immigration. Local attachments faded only with the second generation, by which time knowledge of the mother tongue and other aspects of the parental culture were also usually discarded.

Today's immigrants face far different circumstances. They come mainly from established nation-states, which means that they arrive with identities that extend far beyond the local village. They are already fully equipped to understand themselves as members of an ethnic group. As in the last era of mass migration, ties to particular places back home and to hometown contacts already living in the United States remain significant: these are the connections that immigrants use to get started in the new land. But unlike in the past, these aren't the only loyalties that count. And if some of today's newcomers haven't fully absorbed the ethnic ideal—remaining more attached to their village or region than to the nation from which they came—there are intellectuals in almost all immigrant communities ready to teach their peers how to think about identity.

The result is that immigrants find their ethnic identities more significant today, in part because such local differences are so much less important than they were a century ago. Paradoxically, such ethnic mobilization is encouraged by the very openness of American society to today's immigrants. It is often assumed that increased contact between immigrants and the native-born breeds acceptance. But the opposite can also be true: exposure to the American mainstream makes immigrants sensitive to deprivations they wouldn't have noticed from a greater distance. And today more than ever before, newcomers can respond to the divergence between the promise of America and its reality by taking recourse in their ethnic identities. Ironically, then, such identities are often forged not from the elements of traditional culture—which have been lost or jettisoned in the transition to America—but out of entirely new notions of ethnicity, learned in the United States.

ETHNIC "MINORITIES" THEN AND NOW

We used to think about immigrants as "the uprooted," a term coined by historian Oscar Handlin in a famous study four decades ago. Now we describe them as "the transplanted," a term from a slightly less celebrated but no less influential history produced twenty-five years later. These shifting metaphors convey the essence of what is different today: we now understand that immigrants aren't lonely adventurers but members of a community whose ties guide the transition from the old country to the new. And this institutional context provides yet another point of contrast between immigration today and in the past. The strong institutions that once helped form immigrants' religious and class identities have changed radically, removing what were once significant incentives to replace old ethnic identities with new identities of a different sort.

One of the most important such institutions is the Roman Catholic Church, once a major force in detaching immigrants from their Old World loyalties. Today's immigrants are introducing unparalleled religious diversity into American life—and entering a society characterized by unusually high levels of religious innovation. Religious diversity was not unknown in the past: the immigrants of the 1880–1920 period gave Judaism and Eastern Orthodox Christianity far higher profiles on the American scene than ever before. But the main challenge posed by immigrants to the American religious establishment involved their imported versions of Catholicism. Italian and Polish Catholics arrived in cities where earlier Catholic migrations, from Ireland and Germany, had already created powerful institutions. These older Catholic hierarchies strove to remake the new immigrants' religious practices and loyalties.

This encounter between immigrants and the American Catholic Church was deeply conflicted; but in the end, the Church always won.

In the short term, immigrant preferences for rituals performed as in the old country, and for parishes organized along the lines of national origin, often prevailed. In the long term, however, such preferences and traditions gradually withered. As immigrants and their children moved up the occupational ladder, they also moved out of the neighborhoods where they had first settled, heading for more comfortable areas with more diverse parishioners. In the process, the institutional influence of American Catholicism took hold. The Church sought to replace ethnic loyalties with an identity rooted in its own universal teachings. And in the long run it succeeded, using the local priest and the parish school to consolidate ethnic loyalties in a broader religious community.

Nor was religion the only force working to weaken ethnic attachments among early twentieth-century immigrants and their descendants. The former peasants, artisans, and petty shopkeepers who arrived in the United States at the turn of the last century held jobs a good deal more modest and less varied than those held by immigrants today. These immigrant workers' shared attributes and interests frequently led them to identify as members of a working class, regardless of differences of nationality or ethnicity. Although ethnic solidarity often provided the cohesion required by the picket line, the picket line stood only if it encompassed workers of all ethnic types. What's more, unions and influential labor radicals—many of them foreign-born themselves—saw the labor movement as a means by which newcomers could escape the cramped quarters of immigrant life—in effect, promoting a strategy of "Americanization from the bottom up." When they joined the labor movement, immigrant workers thus found their allegiances reshaped, class loyalties gradually replaced ethnic attachments.

Today, all this has changed. Contemporary immigrants work and worship in a much less organized and more diverse environment than in the past. Religious institutions, already used to compromise with the forces of modernity, are far more ready to accommodate themselves to immigrants' practices and preferences. Similarly, the working-class ethos and institutional life of the first half of the twentieth century have largely disappeared; unions survive only in an embattled and bureaucratized form.

While religion and class exercise a weakened influence on immigrants' allegiance, ethnicity has become more potent. The immigration of the late twentieth century occurred in an America whose politics and culture had been transformed by the civil rights movement. And, as a result, ethnicity has now emerged as the accepted and expected way of mobilizing to advance group interests.

Earlier in the century, immigrants were stigmatized for their foreign origins and old-country ways; Americanization convinced the newcomers and their children to accept this view themselves. But the dynamic altered once the Black Power movement persuaded the rest of America that black was beautiful. Not only did ethnicity then become a value to be preserved rather than discarded, it became a matter of strategic interest. Membership in a minority group served as a source of pride and a tool for achieving redress—a way to force white Americans to confront the shame of their own bigoted attitudes and discriminatory ways.

Changes in the political realm pushed matters even farther. The policy innovations described by sociologist John Skrentny as the "minority rights revolution"—affirmative action, bilingual education, voting rights and a more liberal immigration code—took ethnicity out of the private realm of neighborhoods, friendship networks and even self-help organizations and gave it institutional form. Starting in the public sector but spreading to the private sector, these policies acknowledged that certain, though not all, ethnic minorities had experienced collective discrimination. Since those groups were entitled to targeted efforts designed to undo the adverse effects of past and present unfairness, the incentives that had earlier led immigrants to abandon ethnicity suddenly altered. Immigrant political leaders realized that they could gain access to resources by organizing themselves as members of a minority—a message relayed to the immigrant rank and file through the process of acculturation and its eye-opening lessons in how to "make it" in the United States. What's more, because ethnicity became the basis for distributing public and private benefits, immigrants found reason to adopt a broad, officially recognized ethnic category, such as "Asian-American" or "Latino," regardless of how it corresponded to the identities and self-definitions current back home.

Thus, history made all the difference—though not in ways that most observers think. Arriving in the aftermath of the civil rights movement, the immigrants of the turn of the twenty-first century encountered a transformed political culture, one that supported the assertion of ethnicity, not its abandonment, as had been the case at the time of the earlier great migration. Not only did the class and religious attachments that had earlier competed for immigrants' loyalty lose sway. But the potential to accumulate political and social power by acting as members of minority groups provided newfound motivation to organize along ethnic lines.

CONCLUSION

The history of immigration in the United States certainly offers reasons for discouragement. But that history also teaches us that even the weak have weapons. In everyday life, immigrants have always fought for dignity and a place in American society, and they continue to do so today. What's more, in the United States, insiders have never been quite as strong as they think, nor are outsiders as powerless as they might imagine.

Today, even more than in the past, immigration is forcing Americans to debate the boundaries of our national community. Past immigrants entered this discussion in a position of weakness. They faced a native population that equated American-ness with whiteness; they lacked the cultural and intellectual resources needed for self-conscious ethnic assertion; and they were linked to institutions that diluted the loyalties and allegiances they brought with them from their home countries. By contrast, today's newcomers have the good fortune of encountering a society transformed by the civil rights struggle and its expanded understanding of what it means to be American. Contemporary immigrants also defend their own interests more effectively: they arrive with an established ethnic identity and can benefit from a highly effective new model of group mobilization. For all these reasons, today's immigrants and their descendants are going to remake the United States in ways more fundamental and far-reaching than their predecessors ever imagined. And that is good news for all Americans, whether their ancestors came to these shores in the seventeenth century or the twenty-first.

7

TOWARD A NEW DEFINITION

by Victor Nee and Richard Alba

A HUNDRED YEARS LATER, nobody doubts that the descendants of
the great wave of immigrants from Southern and Eastern Europe
succeeded in assimilating into American life. But things are different, many observers say, for today's newcomers. For one thing, most
contemporary immigrants come from Asia, Latin America and the
Caribbean; since the passage of the Immigration Act of 1965, more
than 20 million legal immigrants have made their way to the
United States, 80 percent or more of them from countries outside
Europe. What's more, such critics argue, racism is an incorrigible
feature of American society, and these new, nonwhite immigrants
and their children are at risk if they sacrifice their cultural identity
in an ill-fated attempt to assimilate. Instead, they are better off remaining in their own protective ethnic communities. Thanks to this
view, many people, social scientists and the general public alike,
now see the very idea of assimilation as an unattainable, even misguided goal.

But this pessimistic assessment is based on a narrow and misleading conception of assimilation. The differences between today's immigrants and those of a century ago are smaller than people think and

there is no reason to doubt that many in the second and third genera-tions of today's newcomers will assimilate successfully. To understand why, we need to rethink our understanding of assimilation and the forces that produce it. In short, we need a new theory of assimilation.

OLD AND NEW CONCEPTIONS OF ASSIMILATION

For the past half century, the standard view of assimilation has been simple and one-directional: immigrants and their children shed their Old World identities to adapt to the cultural and social norms of an idealized Anglo-American mainstream. This view emphasized the need for immigrants to "unlearn" their inherited cultural traits in order to "successfully learn the new way of life necessary for full ac-ceptance," to quote the mid-century sociologists W. Lloyd Warner and Leo Srole. And it tacitly embraced beliefs about the superiority of Anglo-American culture. Ethnic identity was seen as merely a tempo-rary phenomenon, destined to disappear on the road to eventual as-similation.

Instead, we propose a new conception of assimilation—one that recognizes that the mainstream into which immigrants assimilate is itself changed in the process. American society is not a monolithic whole but rather a composite that has been built up over the years from the contributions of many groups, with complex variations based on culture, class and region. And today, as in the past, this mainstream is porous, capable of incorporating elements of other cul-tures. This assimilation can occur through changes in the newcomers, but also in the mainstream.

Nor does assimilation as we define it require the eradication of ethnicity. In our view, ethnicity is a social boundary: a distinction that individuals make in their everyday lives and that shapes their ac-tions and attitudes towards others. This boundary is given concrete significance by the social and cultural differences between groups—differences that allow members of one group to think "they are not like us." Assimilation is best understood as the fading of such boundaries, i.e., individuals on both sides of the line come to see themselves as more and more alike. Thus, at one time an ethnic distinction may be relevant for most if not all the life chances of members of two different groups—where they live, what kinds of jobs they get, and so forth—while at a later time it may recede to the point that it is observed only in occasional family rituals.

At the same time, we do not assume that assimilation is a universal outcome—or one that occurs in a straight-line trajectory from the time of arrival to the time of entry into the middle class. Many of today's newcomers are concentrated in poor, urban enclaves, and many of their descendants may become trapped in concentrated poverty, much like many poor African-Americans. Thus, incorporation is likely to happen in a "segmented" fashion, with different outcomes for different groups and with descendants of poor nonwhite immigrants at considerable risk of merging with the underclass in central cities.

MECHANISMS OF ASSIMILATION

The pace and success of assimilation depends on three factors or mechanisms. The first is the crucial effect of institutions—law and government policy—in removing blatant racial barriers and creating a setting in which assimilation is possible. Second are the workaday decisions of individual immigrants—which often lead to assimilation not as a stated goal but as an unintended consequence. And third is the role of immigrant communities and networks, which shape the particular ways in which their members adapt to American life.

Institutional Mechanisms
The most dramatic changes affecting assimilation in the last half century were changes in law and public policy. Immigrants from Southern and Eastern Europe encountered discrimination, but there were few formal legal obstacles to assimilation and—unlike in the case of blacks—the newcomers' rights were fully enforced. By contrast, for

nonwhite minorities prior to World War II, both the law and its enforcement bolstered the racism that excluded them from civil society. Thus, for example, Asian immigrants were ineligible for citizenship until 1952, and they faced many discriminatory local and regional laws that restricted their property rights and civil liberties.

But these obstacles eventually yielded as a result of the legal changes of the civil rights era, which extended fundamental constitutional rights to racial minorities. These changes have not been merely formal; they have been accompanied by new institutional mechanisms for monitoring and enforcing the law. For instance, Title VII of the Civil Rights Act of 1964 allows the Equal Employment Opportunity Commission to intervene in private bias lawsuits when it deems that the case is of "general public importance." Although enforcement of Title VII has been inconsistent under different administrations, corporations and nonprofit firms have become more attentive in observing its guidelines. Increasing numbers of firms offer diversity training for managers and employees; others have instituted company rules and grievance procedures against racial and gender discrimination. Meanwhile, landmark settlements of federal discrimination lawsuits, such as that against Texaco in 1997, have raised the cost of discrimination, encouraging corporations to obey the law so as to insulate themselves from litigation that would harm their public image.

These changes cannot be effective in a vacuum; economic growth is also a necessary condition for assimilation on a wide scale. But growth alone is not enough. During the nineteenth and early twentieth centuries, the sustained economic expansion sparked by the Industrial Revolution was accompanied by the rise of Jim Crow in the South and the informal but no less rigid segregation of blacks in the North. It is only in combination with institutional changes that growth can make an important difference in promoting assimilation.

Of course, implementing the formal rules of civil rights is not the same as the effective realization of their intent. A wealth of research in the social sciences has documented the persistent effects of racism in limiting the life chances of minorities, especially African-Americans. Nevertheless, changes since the civil rights era have altered the character of racism, which is now more covert and subterranean, and can no longer be advocated in public without sanction.

Institutional changes have increased the cost of discrimination and indeed have gone hand in hand with changes in mainstream values. One of these is the remarkable decline in the power of racist ideologies since the end of World War II. More than half a century of survey data demonstrates unequivocally that the beliefs in racial separation—endorsed by a majority of white Americans at mid-century, when only a third of whites believed that "white students and black students should go to the same schools"—have been steadily eroded. Americans today generally embrace the principle of racial equality even if they are also ambivalent about policies, such as affirmative action, intended to bring about equality as a matter of fact. Hence, despite continuing problems in black-white relations, many contemporary immigrants and their children face a largely unblocked path into the mainstream.

Individual Action
Important as broad institutional mechanisms may be, individual immigrants are not moved by abstract social forces, and indeed they often enter the American mainstream only as an unintended result of the private choices they make in the pursuit of self-interest.

In adapting to life in the United States, immigrants generally choose between two paths: "ethnic" strategies (which rely on opportunities available in their own communities) and "mainstream" ones (which involve the American educational system and the open labor market). Newcomers don't always have a choice. Those who are poor, uneducated or undocumented are often limited to jobs located through ethnic networks, and they usually live in segregated ethnic areas. But most immigrants use a mixed strategy built from both ethnic and mainstream elements. For example, a second-generation young adult might get a job through family and ethnic networks while continuing his or her formal education.

Individuals striving for success in American society often do not see themselves as assimilating. Yet the practical strategies they pursue to achieve their goals—a good education, a good job, a nice place to live, interesting friends and acquaintances—often result in assimilation as an unintended consequence. It is not uncommon, for instance, for first- and second-generation Asian parents to raise their children speaking only English—not out of a desire for them to "become American" but to improve their chances for success in school. Likewise, the search for a desirable neighborhood—one with good schools and positive influences for children—often leads immigrant families to ethnically mixed suburbs. The consequence, whether intended or not, is a greater interaction with families of other backgrounds, and such increased contact tends to encourage acculturation, especially for children.

Network Mechanisms

The immigrant community also plays a critical role in facilitating assimilation. Most newcomers do not arrive alone or in a vacuum, and most turn to relatives and friends for assistance in meeting practical needs, from help with the adjustments of the first weeks to finding jobs and residences. These friends and relatives constitute an informal network that not only orients the newcomer but also enforces informal rules that help individuals improve their chances through cooperation with others in the immigrant community. The expanding chains of labor migration that link small communities in Mexico to destination points in California and the Southwest are a typical example. For labor migrants from south of the border, these networks lower the risks of international migration and increase the likelihood the newcomers will make the transition to settled lives in America.

Networks become especially critical when discriminatory barriers prevent individual immigrants from succeeding on their own. When individual mobility is blocked, assimilation depends on collectivist strategies—and indeed most ethnic groups in America have relied on such strategies to some extent. Irish-Americans, for instance, in their effort to shed the stereotype of "shanty Irish," socially distanced themselves from African-Americans and ostracized those of their own who intermarried with blacks—a group strategy designed to gain acceptance from Anglo-Americans. Likewise, assimilated German Jews used their charitable activities in the immigrant neighborhoods of New York City to encourage the acculturation of Eastern European Jews, lest these impoverished co-religionists blemish the favorable image of the entire Jewish community. More recently, Punjabi farmers who settled in the agricultural towns of northern California discouraged their children from having contact with local whites with limited academic ambitions, and they pressed their young to succeed even if it meant leaving the ethnic community. In all three cases, the immigrant community facilitated assimilation, primarily by influencing the values and expectations of its individual members.

FORMS OF CAPITAL

A century ago, most immigrants were European peasants with no money and very low levels of education. Today, by contrast, immigrants bring a wide range of resources: not just financial assets, but also skills, values, education and social connections—both here and abroad—that they can draw on in adapting to life in America. Social scientists call all of these resources "capital."

Different groups of immigrants bring different kinds and different amounts of capital. At one end of the continuum are Indian, Korean and Filipino immigrants, many of them professionals and technical workers with advanced degrees. At the other end are low-wage laborers from Mexico, most of whom have only a primary-school education. Still other groups bring financial capital, which can be important in easing the transition to the American economy. Many middle-class Korean immigrants, for example, sell their homes and assets before they emigrate, and the money they bring helps to explain the high rate of Korean small-business ownership. By contrast, laborers who have to borrow money to cover the cost of undocumented immigration often end up trapped in a modern form of indentured servitude, working for ethnic entrepreneurs who exploit them as cheap labor.

The mix of social, financial, human and cultural capital that immigrant families bring strongly influences the decisions they make in adapting to the United States, and not surprisingly their patterns of adaptation vary widely. For example, Indians and Filipinos—most of whom speak English upon arrival—tend to find jobs in the mainstream labor market and live in mixed residential neighborhoods, and they show little proclivity for self-employment or building an ethnic enclave economy. By contrast, Korean immigrants, who do not come from a culture where English is widely spoken, make the most of their cultural and financial capital by investing in small businesses and developing an ethnic economy. But all three of these Asian groups appear to be on the path to assimilation. Their children adapt to American cultural norms, they frequently go beyond secondary school to attend four-year colleges followed by professional and graduate schools, and they often marry outside the ethnic group.

Professional immigrants like these tend to be family-based. They generally intend to immigrate permanently rather than merely sojourn in the United States for a time. They hope to reestablish their middle-class lifestyles; even if they are unable to secure jobs in their area of training, they often build careers as entrepreneurs or technical workers. In such families, the parents are determined to hand their own prosperity and education on to their children. And for many, this entails moving to the suburbs, where the schools are better, and learning how to mix socially with neighbors who are not of the same ethnic group—decisions that ultimately lead to assimilation.

Labor migrants, on the other hand, generally lack human, cultural and financial capital. Immigrants from Mexican villages, for instance, are often barely literate. Many come to America merely for a temporary stint of work—though over time, and after several return visits to marry and establish families in Mexico, most eventually settle permanently in the United States. The most valuable capital these immigrants bring is their social capital: the network ties that connect their home villages to the United States. Yet reliance on this form of capital can give rise to dependence on the ethnic community and ultimately hinder assimilation.

CONCLUSION

The new theory of assimilation presented here is intended to remedy the deficiencies in earlier conceptions. One of the most important of these defects is the way absorption is usually viewed as a one-way process. In this view, the minority must make itself more like the majority, whose role is limited to accepting or rejecting the minority "petition" to be allowed into the mainstream. But the historical reality is that the majority changes, too, and the American mainstream has been continually reshaped by the incorporation of new groups.

Another problem was that earlier conceptions lent themselves too easily to the view that assimilation was inevitable. Critics of assimilation theory have correctly pointed out that immigrants follow a variety of paths into American society. In the past, some people from some groups assimilated almost entirely. In other groups, most assimilated, but a small number remained in the ethnic enclave, living out lives that were still determined, generations later, by inherited Old World customs. Still other groups—like the Chinese and Japanese in the late nineteenth and early twentieth centuries—became racial minorities with no possibility of assimilating. And many argue that today's immigrants are more likely to remain in some fashion apart— either blocked from assimilating or only partially integrated.

But such arguments do not take account of the major institutional changes that have occurred since World War II, largely removing the barriers that once kept racial minorities out of the mainstream. Problems remain, but America today is a less racist place than it once was, and all newcomers, of all colors, benefit from opportunities that did not exist in the past. To be sure, other options also exist—options to cultivate and celebrate one's ethnic heritage—and thorough-going assimilation may not prove the nearly universal pattern that it was for Europeans. Nevertheless, we believe, assimilation will continue to be a powerful force in the lives of post–1965 immigrants. Today is more like the past than it is different, and most of the newcomers arriving on our shores today will continue to join—and reshape—the mainstream, just as others have throughout our history.

PART THREE

THE IMMIGRANT BARGAIN

8

THE ASSIMILATION CONTRACT: ENDANGERED BUT STILL HOLDING

by Peter D. Salins

A NATION APART

One of the most important things that sets the United States apart from other nations in the post–Cold War era is its unique success as a multiethnic society. In Eastern Europe and the developing world, ancient ethnic hatreds repeatedly dissolve into bloodshed. Even our democratic allies in Western Europe are roiled by ethnic conflict as their immigrant populations grow. Against this backdrop, we can appreciate how remarkable it is that the United States has forged one of the world's most unified and prosperous societies from a blend of peoples differing sharply in national ancestry, language, race and religion.

But Americans should not take this tranquility for granted. The most important lesson we can learn from the social and political instability of other nations today, and especially from the scourge of terrorism spanning the globe, is that the institutional foundations of ethnic harmony are fragile and need to be continuously nurtured and reaffirmed.

In any ethnically diverse country, conflict arises when citizens place their ethnic identities ahead of identification with the nation. The most common basis of ethnic division is religion (Ireland, India, Bosnia, Lebanon), but it can also be race, language (Canada, Belgium), national origin or even geographic location. Such conflicts are sharpened when an ethnic group tries to capture the institutions of the state and implement policies that favor its interests and discriminate against other groups: for example, Islamic fundamentalists in Iran and Afghanistan, Francophones in Quebec and Orthodox Jews in Israel.

Historically, as the central governments of nation-states consolidated their authority, most dealt with the tensions between ethnic groups by means of repression. In many places, this is still common practice today. But as nations have become more democratic, especially since World War II, the strategy of repression has generally given way to negotiated power sharing—a concept I refer to as "ethnic federalism." At first, that may seem like an improvement, but in practice it rarely if ever works because the resulting jockeying for power among groups invariably leaves the most radical elements dissatisfied. When repression and ethnic federalism both fail, the result is perpetual conflict, and in an increasingly common scenario, secession or the threat of secession: for example, the shattering of Yugoslavia, Slovakia's withdrawal from Czechoslovakia and Eritrea splitting off from Ethiopia.

Only the United States has come up with a better paradigm. From the very beginning, the Founders proposed to resolve the potential problems created by ethnic diversity by decisively repudiating both repression and ethnic federalism. Instead, the American model is grounded not only in a conception of individual liberty but also in constitutional protections and in a fundamental respect for individual achievement rather than group membership. That is both the meaning and aspiration of the slogan on the great seal of the United States, *e pluribus unum* (technically, "from many, one," but perhaps better translated today as "out of diversity, unity"), coined in 1782, six years after the Declaration of Independence and seven years before the installation of the new country's first formal government. The United States Constitution forbids the government to discriminate among citizens on the basis of sectarian affiliation.

The clearest example of this principle is the firewall of separation between church and state. Over time, through constitutional amendments and judicial interpretation, this firewall has been extended to cover other potentially divisive issues, forbidding the government to favor or harm individuals on the basis of national origin, race or language. Obviously, our country's history is marred by egregious violations of this principle—most notably in its treatment of African-Americans both before and after slavery was abolished. But even though the United States has at times honored the principle only in the breach, it has been the one nation that always explicitly affirmed a strict separation of political entitlement from any kind of sectarian affiliation. The nation's civic institutions have encouraged Americans to judge others by their individual character and accomplishment rather than their ethnic characteristics. More broadly, they have fostered a culture of tolerance.

This is how the United States came to be not only a "nation of immigrants" but more remarkably a nation of *assimilated* immigrants. An honest look at our history shows that assimilation was never painless, and every immigrant group—even Germans and Scandinavians—initially faced discrimination at the hands of "native" Americans (who were usually recent immigrants themselves). But over time, every wave of immigrants did successfully assimilate, and Americans were highly conscious of this. At the turn of the twentieth century, otherwise all-but-forgotten playwright, Israel Zangwill, wrote a drama whose title to this day seems to epitomize our view of assimilation: *The Melting Pot.* The metaphor was so appealing that it was adopted by everyone from President Theodore Roosevelt to the man in the street.

But while the metaphor was compelling, the truth is that the United States has never really been a melting pot, and that has been the key to the successful assimilation of wave after wave of new immigrants. Americans never asked immigrants to shed their distinctive ethnic, cultural or religious identities—never sought a "blended" American, a human alloy. Indeed, Americans have been remarkably indifferent to the surface trappings of cultural assimilation (what sociologists call "acculturation"), focusing instead on common values and strong institutions built upon those values. Immigrants were expected only to abide by the basic tenets of an unspoken "assimilation contract": allegiance to the nation's democratic principles, respect for individualism and hard work and—yes—willingness to learn English and use it outside their homes. Beyond that, they were free to indulge ethnic, cultural or religious preferences and practices to their hearts' content.

Sealing the assimilation contract, America has always made it easy for immigrants to become citizens. When first adopted in the late eighteenth century, the United States' naturalization laws were more lenient than those of virtually any other nation. Even today, a majority of nations give immigrants only residency privileges, not full citizenship—if they allow immigration at all. And while U.S. rates of naturalization waxed and waned over the years, until recently the vast majority of immigrants became citizens as quickly as the law allowed.

America's committed but liberal approach to assimilation is in marked contrast to much of the rest of world. To blunt the political consequences of cultural diversity, most countries either forcibly acculturate immigrants (as in France, for example), or segregate and marginalize them to minimize their political impact (as in Germany). Both approaches inevitably breed resentment and strife, which is intensifying in France, Germany and other European countries as their immigrant populations grow. By contrast, America's tolerant, individualist approach to assimilation has led, over time, to unprecedented levels of intermarriage and to the creation of a common American culture that draws on all the nation's different ethnic traditions.

ARE WE LOSING OUR WAY?

Now, in the shadow of September 11, 2001, as we regain our prosperity and confidence and prosecute the war on terrorism, we need to reaffirm our commitment to the American concept of assimilation, an idea that has allowed the United States, uniquely among the world's nations, to flourish as a unified multiethnic society. Looking around us, we can take great pride in the extent to which the nation-building design of the country's Founders has been fulfilled. But it's also true that America's historic ability to join high immigration with effective assimilation has been eroding for some time. As a result, Americans in recent years are not quite sure how they feel about immigration, and they have been made to feel guilty about aggressively promoting assimilation.

The events of 9/11 have only deepened this confusion and ambivalence. Because the attackers were immigrants, Americans have become more suspicious of immigrants generally. Because the attackers were Muslim, Americans are more willing to compromise our culture-blind universalism. Because the attackers took advantage of our freedom and civic openness, Americans are willing to consider curtailing our most jealously guarded civil liberties.

A better response would be to address and arrest the trends that have been eroding our traditional unifying practices and institutions for some time now. At a time when the United States is admitting immigrants at a rate last seen one hundred years ago, the most urgent priority is to restore the successful paradigm that turned previous generations of immigrants into loyal and contented Americans. That sounds easy enough—who could object?—but in fact it is highly contentious, and provides the subtext of vigorous policy debates currently being waged on a number of important issues.

One of the most bitter is the dispute over bilingual instruction in public schools. Proponents and critics of bilingual education both pose the issue mainly as one of pedagogical effectiveness. Supporters of bilingual education claim that it is the only way for immigrant children to be acclimated to English without experiencing psychological trauma or losing ground in subjects like math and science. Opponents argue that bilingual education is unnecessary and that it needlessly delays students' mastery of English, recommending instead that schools combine English immersion with English-as-a-second-language (ESL) instruction. But behind this practical disagreement are well-documented agendas for and against America's longstanding approach to assimilation. Bilingual instruction advocates (the majority of whom are Hispanic) have conceded that one of their primary objectives is to keep Hispanic cultural attachments alive and to slow assimilation. Likewise, opponents of bilingual programs make no secret of their strong belief in the need to promote the assimilation of recent immigrants and their children.

Disagreement about America's approach to assimilation is also clearly at the root of the fierce national debate over racial preferences in college admissions. In this case, the debate is ostensibly about what is just. Proponents of affirmative action cite the benefits of greater diversity on campus and buttress their arguments with evidence that minority students admitted under such policies gain immeasurably more than white students lose. Those that challenge these policies do so primarily with appeals to fairness and equal treatment under the law. In the background, however, rages a divisive quarrel about the desirability of ethnic federalism. Proponents of preferences see such measures as corrective actions that redress centuries of grievance. Opponents see capitulation to powerful ethnic constituencies and an erosion of America's constitutional commitment to individual, as opposed to group, rights.

But immigration is the policy issue that most directly tests the strength of our continuing commitment to assimilation: who we admit, what we do about those who enter illegally and how we feel about citizenship. Throughout the nineteenth century, immigration was not restricted by national origin, class, religion or any other discriminatory variable. Thus the United States attracted an unusually diverse immigrant pool. This in turn confirmed the universalist basis of our immigration policy and eased assimilation by reducing the kind of polarization between "natives" and "foreigners" that arises when immigrants are drawn from just a few national or ethnic backgrounds.

In the twentieth century, the very desirability of immigration became much more controversial, leading to policies designed to curtail the flow and to favor immigrants with particular ethnic backgrounds. The restrictive immigration laws of the 1920s set numerical quotas favoring applicants from Northern European countries. Post-1965 immigration policy abandoned this indefensible bias, but the new rubric that replaced it preserves many of its problematical aspects. The primary criterion for eligibility today—accounting for 60 percent of all those admitted—is "family sponsorship," which accords preference to relatives of immigrants already resident in the United States. While not explicitly bigoted, this basis for favoring immigrants from some countries over others is hardly more universal than the 1920s "national origins" concept.

In this instance, too, the public debate about practical issues conceals a profound disagreement over America's civic design and assimilationist ethos. Admitting relatives of current residents is politically smart, and it appears compassionate. But it results in the emergence of geographically concentrated immigrant clusters—Cubans in Florida, Mexicans in California and Texas, Dominicans and other Caribbeans in New York—whose inevitable mobilization behind an ethnic agenda (issues such as bilingual education) directly threatens our nonsectarian assimilationist values. Reducing the strong bias toward family sponsorship in our current immigration policy might be politically difficult, but the universalist basis of immigration would be strengthened if the proportion admitted under this category were reduced in favor of legitimate refugees (currently only 15 percent), applicants drawn by lottery from all nations (the "diversity" pool, currently 7 percent), and those admitted to work in designated "labor-short" occupations (currently 17 percent).

But arguably the most important of our current disputes about immigration concerns those foreigners who arrive illegally and live for years outside of the law. While immigrant advocacy organizations, and most politicians, favor a "don't ask, don't tell" indulgence of illegal immigration, we should all be troubled by this growing class of newcomers who cannot really assimilate, even if they wanted to. To survive, its members must disregard much of our law. They do not participate fully in our social or economic life, and they dare not come out of the shadows to claim the normal civic and economic rights of Americans without risking deportation. The fact that the 9/11 terrorists were mainly undocumented recent migrants sheds new light on the terrorist threat that illegal immigration might pose. But at least as serious a threat is the long-term polarization sure to ensue in the two-tier society we are creating. Unfortunately, the media—and liberals generally—invariably characterize policies aiming to curtail illegal immigration as anti-immigrant, conflating them with the discriminatory restrictions of the 1920s or the neo-nativism that roiled California and other high-immigration states in the early 1990s. But in fact, turning a blind eye on this group of permanently disenfranchised American residents is harmful not only to the nation's civic aspirations but also to the individuals and families thus marooned in this legal and civic limbo.

A less visible, but profoundly important, tear in our assimilationist ethos concerns citizenship—and the need to encourage today's immigrants to become citizens, as generations of their predecessors did. Attaining citizenship not only cements the national bond between immigrants and other Americans; it is the only way immigrants can fully participate in the American political process, as voters and as candidates for office. Sadly, the rate at which immigrants have chosen to become citizens has declined dramatically during precisely the period that immigration itself has increased. Naturalization rates of legal immigrant adults, which had been as high as 80 percent in 1950, fell to 44 percent in 1990. Even discounting the impact of continuing immigration, this is the lowest rate in a hundred years—the previous low point being 1920, just before the restrictionist ax fell, when the rate was 52 percent.

Meanwhile, for many immigrants who do choose to become citizens, the significance of the act has been severely undermined. Thanks to legal changes in their native countries, many new citizens no longer need to relinquish citizenship in the place they left behind. And worse yet, several recent American judicial rulings support this shift, even though our citizenship protocols clearly indicate that maintaining dual citizenship violates the spirit of becoming an American citizen. (Naturalization applicants are still explicitly advised in the U.S. citizenship manual: "When you take the Oath of Allegiance to the United States, you are promising to give up your allegiance to other countries. . . .") This provision is now impossible to enforce, but, unlike the issue of illegal immigration, it no longer even arouses concern.

COUNTING OUR BLESSINGS

As these debates show, Americans' commitment to the civic paradigm that sustains our remarkable unity may be fraying. We could profit from a more forthright discussion of what needs to be done to sustain *e pluribus unum* for the generations to come. Nevertheless, in their day-to-day behavior and attitudes, most Americans demonstrate that despite these disputes, the nation's assimilationist dynamic remains robust and ethnic federalism has not yet gained an insurmountable foothold.

Except for scattered and isolated incidents, 9/11 has not impelled Americans to the kind of xenophobia and nativism—even toward Middle Easterners and Muslims—that followed previous attacks on the United States. Just contrast the generally mature attitudes of Americans today with their forebears' behavior toward German-Americans after the United States entered World War I, or the internment of Japanese-Americans after Pearl Harbor. Further, support for continued high levels of legal immigration appears unabated; neither government leaders nor the public are demanding that the nation pull up the immigration drawbridge.

Another heartening development is the restored respectability of unabashed patriotism. After several decades during which educated Americans ridiculed expressions of patriotism as the province of bumpkins or rednecks, it is no longer politically incorrect to display the flag on one's lapel or bumper sticker. Indeed, the revival of patriotism is even finding its way into the classroom.

Perhaps most encouraging, ordinary social interaction among Americans of diverse backgrounds is as common and vigorous as it has ever been. Recent demographic data show that intermarriage among individuals of different races, religions and national origins is at record levels, and growing. Within a few decades, it is estimated, 21 percent of all Americans will be of mixed black, white, Hispanic or Asian heritage. Other data point to increasing heterogeneity in our colleges, our workplaces and even a growing number of residential neighborhoods.

The internal harmony of the United States is a blessing in itself, but it will also be indispensable to our success in fighting the war on terrorism. Our first instinct in prosecuting this new war, as in wars past against more conventional enemies, has been to assume that the only terrorists we need to fear will come from abroad. This is not entirely wrong: the nineteen perpetrators of the 9/11 attack were all recently arrived visitors, and perhaps tighter monitoring of temporary and student visas, or other border control measures, might have kept some of them from carrying out their demonic plans. But the experience of other countries, from Northern Ireland to northern India, demonstrates that the greatest threats are often posed not by imported terrorists but by disaffected residents of the homeland. And the most common source of that disaffection is sectarian grievance, whether ethnic or religious or some other kind. Whatever geopolitical objectives may be motivating Al Qaeda, most terrorism in most parts of the world—whether involving Basques in Spain, Catholics and Protestants in Northern Ireland, the assorted shards of what once was Yugoslavia, or Hindus and Muslims in Kashmir—is driven by intergroup hatred and intolerance within a nation-state.

Yet as we guard against internal disunity, it would be a great mistake to conclude that it is mainly individuals of Muslim or Middle

Eastern backgrounds that we need to worry about. Stigmatizing or isolating any group undermines the values that inoculate all Americans—including those of the Muslim faith—against letting their ethnic or religious identities overwhelm their bonds to country and countrymen. Indeed, only because we can still count on the loyalty of the overwhelming majority of ethnic Americans, irrespective of religion or race, are we able to root out potential terrorist cells in their midst. One of the most frequently heard sentiments after 9/11 was that if terrorism leads us to engage in "ethnic profiling" or to trample civil liberties, it will mean "that the terrorists have already won." Not only is this true, it is especially gratifying that so many Americans express it.

The still-fresh trauma of 9/11 has brought Americans together, in a way not seen since World War II, to appreciate our precious national legacy. In the years ahead, when we have prevailed against the immediate dangers that preoccupy us today, we face the unending task of preserving that legacy. It is over the long haul that we will discover whether America's diversity continues to be its most vital source of strength or, as in much of the rest of the world, the source of growing disunity and conflict.

9

THE AMERICAN SIDE
OF THE BARGAIN

by Douglas S. Massey

B ETWEEN 1980 AND 2000, 15.6 million legal immigrants came to the United States, and another 5.5 million entered the country illegally. The vast majority of these people—85 percent of documented migrants and 95 percent of those without documents—were non-Europeans, mainly from Asia, Latin America and the Caribbean. The large number and nonwhite origins of these new immigrants have unnerved many observers, who worry about the newcomers' ultimate ability to assimilate—socially, economically, and culturally—into the social fabric of United States, and how the country might change as a result.

Nothing about the new immigrants suggests, however, that they will be any less assimilable than those who arrived in the past. Just as before, today's immigrants come to the United States to work hard, get ahead and enter the American mainstream. They don't expect much from the government and they generally stay out of trouble. To the extent that difficulties appear on the horizon, they have less to do with the immigrants themselves than with our own shortfalls as a host society. Assimilation is a two-way street, and while immigrants have held up their end of the bargain, in very significant ways America has let them down. As a result, the future of assimilation is generally sunny, but with some dark clouds on the horizon.

THE SUCCESS OF IMMIGRATION

Like the U.S. economy itself, immigration has increasingly divided into a high end and a low end. No matter how they enter the United States—legally, for purposes of family reunification or employment, or surreptitiously and without documents—immigrants generally come to work. In the upper echelons of the labor market, globalization has increased the demand for capital in all its forms, including "human capital"—that is, people with advanced education and valuable technical skills. As human capital has become crucial to sustaining the growth of knowledge-based economies, developed nations have found themselves competing for qualified workers. Rather than trying to exclude skilled immigrants, countries have been working to attract them, and their earnings have risen as a result.

At the bottom of the economic pyramid, on the other hand, unskilled immigrants take low-paying jobs that provide poor working conditions and few opportunities for advancement. Nearly all jobs in agriculture fall into this category, as do many positions in construction, nondurable manufacturing, custodial services, hotels, restaurants and domestic employment. Even during periods of relatively high unemployment, demand for unskilled immigrant workers remains steady because the benefits of the modern welfare state raise the expected wages of native workers well above what most employers can pay, making it difficult to recruit them. It is no coincidence that by the end of the twentieth century all developed nations had become labor-importing societies.

As a result, while the average education of immigrants to the United States is slightly above that of natives, this outcome represents a balance between many immigrants with educations above the

U.S. average (over half have gone to college) and many others with educations below it (more than a third did not graduate high school). And this split carries over to employment. Among legal U.S. immigrants in 1996, 38 percent were professional, technical, executive or managerial workers, while 42 percent were unskilled laborers, operatives, farmworkers or service workers. The remaining 20 percent worked in the lower reaches of the white-collar or the upper segment of the blue-collar workforce.

There is little evidence that immigrants with high levels of skill or education or both—nearly half the legal flow—experience significant difficulty in assimilating to life in the United States. Owing to their advanced education, most are familiar with English; indeed, many are already fluent, and those who are not are generally in a position to learn quickly. Although well-educated immigrants may experience a decline in occupational status—from, say, a professor to a taxi driver—when they enter the U.S. labor market, they nonetheless gain a substantial increase in earnings, and both occupational status and income tend to rise quickly over time.

Educated immigrants also experience substantial residential integration within American cities. Unlike the earlier waves of European immigrants, they are quite unlikely to settle in segregated ethnic neighborhoods; most proceed directly to the suburbs, where their children are now among the nation's highest school achievers. And education provides access to the same institutional and residential settings as the children of Euro-Americans, yielding regular contact and intimate associations that inevitably raise the odds of intergroup friendship and romance. As a result, intermarriage with European-origin whites may be expected to be very high in the second generation, and a near certainty in the third.

At earlier points in U.S. history, the arrival of large numbers of nonwhite immigrant professionals might have raised serious concerns about social friction. Before 1960, racial discrimination was common throughout the United States: schools were segregated, job discrimination was legal, intermarriage was forbidden, access to citizenship was restricted, and ethnically biased deportation campaigns were all too common (the last occurred in 1954). Despite their credentials, immigrant professionals in this period would likely have been relegated to an embittered underclass.

Since the 1960s, however, the costs of discrimination have risen dramatically, and open expressions of racism have become a source of embarrassment and public opprobrium. As a result of the civil rights revolution, but also thanks to thirty years of ethnically diverse immigration, mainstream American society has become more open. Today, we are far from the rigid model of "Anglo conformity" that prevailed in the 1940s and 1950s. Whereas Victoria Carranza and Ricardo Valenzuela had to become Vickie Carr and Richie Valens to ensure mainstream success in the 1950s, Gloria Estefan and Christina Aguilera found easy acceptance as Latinas in the 1990s. And whereas Charlie Chan movies in the 1930s and 1940s featured a white actor in heavy eye make up, Jackie Chan is now an international superstar, and martial arts idol Chow Yun Fat scored a major hit in the United States with a Mandarin-language movie set in imperial China. Before the 1960s, such things would have been inconceivable. Although nativism may not have disappeared, it is increasingly marginal, and generally takes the form of empty symbolic gestures, such as the passage of English-only referenda.

Skilled and educated immigrants have been especially well placed to profit from this new dispensation. But immigrants on the lowest rungs of the occupational ladder also benefit. Despite their modest educations and incomes, working-class immigrants are generally doing all that could be reasonably expected to support themselves economically and assimilate culturally. In time, most of them acquire facility in English, often through considerable personal effort; and while movement toward English may be slower in areas where immigrants concentrate, by the second generation the vast majority primarily use English, and by the third generation nearly all speak English exclusively. If anything, recent studies have shown how difficult it is for later generations to remain bilingual, something that is only achieved on purpose through expensive private schooling. The United States seems in no danger of losing its reputation as "a graveyard of languages." According to a recent survey conducted by Alejandro Portes and Rubén Rumbaut in San Diego, for example, roughly 40 percent of the children of Mexican-born parents prefer using English rather than Spanish, and if at least one parent is native-born, the figure rises to 75 percent.

Despite recent alarmist claims, there is little danger of any "balkanization": the United States is not fragmenting into ethnically distinct regions. Historically, the vast majority of new immigrants have gone to just six states (California, Texas, New York, New Jersey, Florida and Illinois), but this pattern changed dramatically in the mid-1990s. Whereas 86 percent of all immigrants went to the "big six" in 1990, the figure had dropped to 66 percent by 1998 and was falling rapidly. Among Mexican immigrants, the shift was even more dramatic. Whereas 63 percent went to California during the period 1985–1990, only 39 percent did so in the first half of the 1990s. Over the past decade, immigration has become a truly national phenomenon, affecting all regions of the country. Even well-established immigrants already settled in gateway states were pulling up stakes to follow opportunities in places that had never before experienced significant immigration. As immigrants and their children gravitate to new regions, every state will increasingly come to resemble the United States as a whole.

In metropolitan areas, levels of racial and ethnic segregation have remained low or moderate for working-class immigrants, despite their recent arrival and meager financial resources. On average, levels of Hispanic and Asian segregation from native whites remain far below that typical of African-Americans. Indeed, the poorest Hispanics and Asians are generally less segregated than the richest African-Americans. Moreover, there is a very clear decline in residential segregation as Latinos and Asians move from the foreign-born to the native-born generation, and from low to high income.

Obviously, the ultimate extent of assimilation will depend on the socioeconomic progress made by immigrants and their children. Among Hispanic and Asian immigrants, studies generally reveal that earnings rise with time spent in the United States. Although the rate of economic improvement varies from group to group, and the ascent is more rapid for those with education than without, the clear pattern is one of steady upward mobility.

The acid test of assimilation, of course, is intermarriage, and here too there is striking evidence of ongoing integration. Among Latinos and Asians in the second and third generations, there is a high rate of marriage outside the ethnic group, irrespective of socioeconomic status. Already, in California and other states, persons of multiple ancestry—the ultimate product of intermarriage—are rapidly growing in number. In the future, the ethnic composition of the United States will be a mixture of European, Asian and Latin American origins. By the year 2050, the National Academy of Sciences projects that the percentage of people with ethnically mixed ancestry will be 21 percent among all those of European ancestry, 36 percent among those of Asian ancestry and 45 percent among those of Latino ancestry. In other words, by the middle of the next century a large and growing number of people claiming at least some European, Asian or Latin American ancestry will, in fact, be some mixture of two or more of these categories.

This blending will bring a significant redefinition of ethnic group boundaries and identities, as happened with Southern and Eastern European immigrants in the second half of the twentieth century. Italians, Jews and Slavs were once considered to be racially distinct from Americans of British, German and Scandinavian ancestry. In 1910 it would have been difficult for native observers to conceive of a day when last names such as "DeNiro," "Rostenkowski" or "Seinfeld" would be accepted as "American." With the passing of the generations, however, thanks in large part to intermarriage, boundaries blurred and the social categories of race and ethnicity were redefined. It is likely that the same thing will happen with the children and grandchildren of today's Asian and Latino immigrants.

CLOUDS ON THE HORIZON

Assimilation should be viewed as part of an implicit social contract between immigrants and American society. The obligation of immigrants is to work hard, stay out of trouble, learn English and not become a public burden. America's responsibility, in turn, is to provide immigrants with the opportunity to improve their lot, protect their equal rights and support the health, education and general welfare of their children. Immigrants have generally held up their part of the bargain, but in important ways the United States has let them down—by underfunding public schools, blocking access to basic social supports and erecting needless obstacles to economic mobility. We must remember that it is not only our moral obligation to hold up our end of the social contract; it is very much in our national interest to do so.

While racial and ethnic discrimination have been outlawed, and wage and employment discrimination have declined markedly as a result, significant discrimination still prevails in one key market: real estate. Numerous studies show a remarkable persistence of prejudiced behavior in this realm. In general, darker-skinned people of all ethnic groups experience greater discrimination in the rental and sale of housing. Although this pattern affects Asians and mestizo Hispanics (those of mixed Indian and European origins), it is particularly severe for people of African origin, immigrant and native alike.

Somewhere around 15 percent of the new immigrants to the United States are of African origin, coming either directly from Africa or from the Caribbean, and for these immigrants, the implicit social contract has broken down. Like U.S.-born blacks, immigrants of African ancestry are subject to a high degree of discrimination in the housing market. As a result, they experience a high degree of residential segregation, a situation that fails to improve even for later generations with higher socioeconomic status. Patterns of segregation for black immigrants more closely resemble those of African-Americans than those of Asians or mestizo Hispanics.

Because where one lives is so important in determining life chances, residential segregation has profound implications for all aspects of assimilation. The concentration of poverty in certain areas creates a supremely disadvantaged social environment characterized by high levels of violence and social disorder. For immigrant children coming of age in such a neighborhood, assimilation is likely to be into an oppositional "street culture," which challenges the core American values of education, hard work and personal responsibility, rather than into mainstream society. To capture this reality, sociologist Alejandro Portes developed the concept of "downward assimilation." Although the children of Asian and Latino immigrants generally seem launched on the path of productive assimilation, second-generation African immigrants are at considerable risk of being stranded in an oppositional culture.

A second major factor undermining the prospects for assimilation is the quality of public schooling. Segregated inner city schools offer some of the poorest instruction to be found in the United States; even if they are not highly segregated, they are chronically underfunded and suffer from a lack of public support. While the children of well-educated immigrants generally attend good private or suburban public schools, the children of working class immigrants overwhelmingly concentrate in the public schools of the inner city. In many states, the situation was exacerbated by the tax revolt of the 1980s, which capped public spending and led to a sharp decline in per capita school funding precisely when the number of immigrant-origin children was rising rapidly. The education of children from poor, non-English-speaking families requires more in the way of resources, not less.

A significant problem in properly supporting immigrants and their children is the geographic mismatch between immigration's costs and benefits. Although the benefits of immigrants—lower inflation, cheaper goods and services, higher tax revenues—generally accrue to the nation as a whole, the costs of absorbing them—maintaining their health, educating their children, safeguarding their welfare—are all borne locally. Federal authorities make decisions about the number and kind of immigrants to accept, but state, county and municipal authorities pick up the costs of absorption. As of 1998, a third of the new immigrants went to just four metropolitan areas: Los Angeles, New York, Chicago and Miami (although this was down from 43 percent in 1990). Can we blame residents and officials in these cities for feeling put upon? They have no say about who comes to their municipalities, yet they must pay the bills for schooling, health care and whatever other social supports immigrants need.

Governor Pete Wilson of California drew upon this sense of grievance in his campaign for reelection in 1992. But rather than mobilizing voters to demand that the federal government relieve the state of its disproportionate burden, he perversely turned voter anxiety against the immigrants themselves. He threw his support behind a proposition to bar undocumented immigrants from using public services, including education. Such ugly nativism could be substantially avoided if only the federal government would transfer additional funds to gateway states and counties to offset the extra costs they must bear to incorporate immigrants on the nation's behalf.

The California episode revealed the fundamental problem with America's attitude toward immigration: we wish to enjoy the benefits without paying the costs. Politicians and the public seek to extract the labor of immigrants, while refusing to acknowledge their claims as human beings, with families and communities, who require a share of the nation's resources. The result is a self-contradictory immigration policy that is doomed to failure.

The purest institutional mechanism for extracting immigrants' labor without social claims is the guest-worker program, in which able-bodied workers are admitted only for purposes of paid labor. Guest workers are allowed to stay in the United States only as long as they are gainfully employed, and they are not under any circumstances allowed to bring dependents with them. From 1942 to 1964, the Bracero program brought 4.6 million Mexicans to the United States for such temporary labor. The civil rights movement forced it to be shut down, but since then, guest-worker migration has been slowly and quietly creeping back. In 1998, 430,000 persons were admitted for temporary labor, up from 145,000 in 1990; and by 2001 the number had reached 816,000.

A still greater blow to the rights of immigrants came in 1996, when Congress restricted the eligibility of legal immigrants for federal means-tested benefits and authorized state and local authorities to do the same. At the same time, it increased the household income necessary for an affidavit of support, which is required of anyone seeking to sponsor the legal entry of a family member. Undocumented migrants, meanwhile, were explicitly barred from receiving federal, state and local public benefits, and the right of children of legally admitted foreigners to attend public schools was curtailed. But instead of curtailing the number of newcomers, as intended, these changes simply forced more adult immigrants to work longer hours, meaning that they had less time to invest in the care and education of their children or in learning English. The net effect has been to make it more difficult for the children of immigrants—documented as well as undocumented—to stay healthy and get a good education.

There is one last way in which America has let down its immigrants. In its zeal to control illegal immigration, the 1986 Immigration Reform and Control Act (IRCA) criminalized the hiring of undocumented workers in an effort to eliminate labor demand as a magnet for immigration. In practice, however, the act has had no such effect: in the ensuing years, undocumented migrants continued to enter the United States in large numbers and to find work. What the legislation did was to encourage wage discrimination against immigrants in general and undocumented migrants in particular, and to push employers toward labor subcontracting and outsourcing. The law, in essence, imposed a "tax" on the hiring of undocumented workers, which employers extracted from the workers themselves in the form of lower wages. As a result, after 1986, immigrants—both legal and illegal—found themselves working longer hours for lower pay.

Other employers took a different route to insure their continued access to undocumented labor. Before IRCA, employers generally hired undocumented workers directly, but afterward they shifted to a pattern of indirect hiring through labor subcontractors. Under a subcontracting arrangement, a U.S. citizen or resident alien contractually agrees with an employer to provide a specific number of workers at a fixed rate of pay per worker. In return for giving employers a legal buffer, the subcontractor retains a portion of the workers' wages as income. Such arrangements quickly became standard across industries characterized by high turnover. Moreover, it was imposed on all workers regardless of legal status or citizenship. Thus, employer sanctions not only lowered the wages of undocumented migrants, but undermined economic mobility for legal immigrants as well.

RENEWING THE SOCIAL CONTRACT

Immigration policies like these not only renege on our side of the assimilation bargain. Still worse, they represent a short-sighted failure to invest in our own human capital. Money devoted to the support of immigrant families and the education of immigrant children should not be viewed as an expense but as an investment that is essential for the nation's economic growth and future prosperity. In the new century, as massive immigration continues to transform our economy and culture, America must remember that assimilation requires effort on the part of both immigrants and the host society. Immigrants of all socioeconomic backgrounds generally work hard, learn English, stay out of trouble and participate in American society to the extent that their social and economic circumstances allow. Rather than worrying about what immigrants are doing to assimilate, we would do better to think about what we are doing to make their lives difficult, and what we might do instead to help them along. At a minimum, the United States owes immigrants access to fair and open markets and a social infrastructure sufficient to ensure the health and education of their children. It is in these areas that we have fallen short.

PART FOUR

WHAT WORKS

10

MEXICAN-AMERICANS AND THE MESTIZO MELTING POT

by Gregory Rodriguez

WHILE VISITING ELLIS ISLAND at the turn of the twentieth century, Henry James wondered how the sweeping tide of immigrants would ultimately affect "the idea of" America. Comparing the incorporation of foreigners to sword- and fire-swallowing feats at a circus, James was disturbed by the thought that America was sharing its patrimony with those "inconceivable aliens."

But as we can see from our vantage point at the turn of the twenty-first century, the immigrants that Henry James worried about were entirely successful at assimilating. Today, "the idea of" America includes Italians, Poles and Jews just as much as Anglo-Americans. In fact, throughout American history, immigrants and minority groups, in seeking to make room for themselves, have broadened the definition of America.

In the first half of the twentieth century, Jews were the paradigm of immigrant assimilation, the American minority by which all other minority experiences were understood. In the second half, African-Americans—the descendants of a forced migration—set the course of a racial debate that altered the nation's vision of itself. And today, with Hispanics poised to become the largest minority group, Mexican-Americans—who make up two-thirds of all Latinos in the United States—are poised to take over that pioneering role. More than any other immigrant group, Mexican-Americans are changing how America sees itself in the twenty-first century.

Mexicans' unique perspectives on racial and cultural synthesis will fundamentally alter the nation's attitudes. The second largest immigrant group in American history—they will become the largest within a decade—Mexicans are themselves the product of the clash between the Old and New Worlds. As their heritage becomes more infused into the American mainstream, they will shift America's often divisive "us versus them" racial dialogue.

Instead of simply adding one more color to the multicultural rainbow, Mexican-Americans are helping to forge a unifying vision. With a history that reveals an ability to accept racial and cultural ambiguity, Mexican-Americans are broadening the definition of America unlike any earlier immigrants.

✳   ✳   ✳

While most waves of immigration have a beginning and an end, Mexican immigration has been virtually continuous for the past century. During the last hundred years, American groups of European origin gradually stopped thinking of themselves as immigrants and developed an identity as ethnic Americans. But Mexican-Americans have always had to contend with the presence of unassimilated newcomers. This has made Mexican-Americans' integration into American society a perpetual process, with no clear end-point in sight.

This dynamic hasn't slowed the acculturation of Mexican-Americans, but it has made the formulation of their political and cultural identity a more confusing process. It has also made the Mexican-American experience notoriously easy to misinterpret. The constant influx of new immigrants has long complicated the task of gauging Mexican-American social mobility. High poverty rates among new immigrants tend to weigh down the statistical average and obscure the advances of latter-generation Mexican-Americans. High intermarriage rates for the most assimilated children and grandchildren of immigrants also contribute to a peculiar form of Mexican-American statistical attrition.

The first sizable group of Mexicans to become Americans did so through the conquest and annexation of the Southwest in the mid-nineteenth century. For that reason, the 1960s generation of Chicano activist scholars, heavily influenced by Marxism, black separatism and the colonial independence movements of the day, sought to characterize Mexican-Americans as a conquered people, "an internal colony" whose ancient homeland was being occupied by invading Anglos.

In portraying Mexican-Americans as conquered people, activists sought to highlight their ancestral rights to the Southwest, as well as to claim the additional "protected status" of a colonized ethnic minority. To do so, they had to make the very real abuses Mexicans have sometimes suffered at the hands of Anglos the central, overriding theme of Mexican-American history. They were also obliged to misconstrue Mexican migrants' motivations for crossing the U.S.-Mexico border. Activist historian Rodolfo Acuña was among the first to contend that Mexicans did not come to the United States to improve their economic prospects. Instead, he wrote, "most Mexicans became part of the United States either because of the Anglo conquest or because they were brought here by economic forces over which they had little control. The uprooted Mexican was torn from his homeland 'like a nail torn from its finger.'"

The Marxist leanings of so many of the first generation of Chicano Studies professors made it difficult for them to admit that millions of Mexicans came to the United States voluntarily, hoping to one day lift their families into the middle class. Instead, activist scholars and writers have for years insisted that Mexican immigrants were primarily concerned with cultural and political "resistance" to the American mainstream. But just as no biographer can understand his subject without first comprehending what makes him tick, no writer can adequately explore the dynamics of an ethnic group if he refuses to consider the myriad hopes, dreams and fears that motivate its members.

The intellectual byproduct of this skewed understanding has been volumes and volumes of what might be called Chicano history by acronym. The Mexican-American experience has largely been interpreted through the actions of advocacy groups such as the League of United Latin American Citizens (LULAC) or the United Farm Workers of America (UFW). No matter that surveys find that Mexican-Americans are less likely to join civic groups than, say, Anglos. Most writers and journalists still adhere to the rule that collective, organized activity is the only minority behavior worth writing about. No matter how tiny, fringe activist groups were presumed to represent the entire Mexican-American experience. Ironically, this bias has made left-wing Chicano history anything but populist. With some exceptions, the history of an organized few has obscured the more revealing story of the lives and daily struggles of the unorganized majority.

In fact, even a brief look at the experience of Mexicans in the United States shows that the model of colonization and resistance doesn't capture the real story. While the Southwest became Spanish territory in the sixteenth century, and the presence of Spanish-speaking people has been continuous since the eighteenth century, the vast majority of today's Mexican-Americans are not descendants of early settlers. There were only an estimated one hundred thousand Spanish speakers in all of California and the Southwest at the time of the signing of the Treaty of Guadalupe Hidalgo in 1848, which ended the Mexican-American War and ceded the region to the United States.

Instead, the overwhelming majority of Mexican-Americans are descended from the twentieth century's two great waves of Latin American immigration. The first occurred amidst the chaos of the Mexican Revolution of 1910–1919, which drove thousands of Mexicans northward well into the 1920s. The second wave—several times larger than the first—came during the 1970s, 1980s and 1990s.

This is not to deny that, no matter when they arrived in the United States, Mexican immigrants have often encountered bigotry and mistreatment. Unlike most other immigrant groups, who faced prejudice mainly during the early stages of assimilation, Mexican-Americans have weathered recurrent waves of anti-Mexican sentiment. Because Mexican labor has been recruited into the United States during boom times and expelled during busts, native-born Mexican-Americans have suffered the fallout from campaigns ostensibly aimed at their foreign-born cousins. In the 1930s, the fear that Mexicans were taking jobs and benefits from "real" Americans led to a deportation and repatriation campaign. Countless numbers of United States citizens were caught up in the sweeps.

Similarly, in 1994, the campaign for Proposition 187—the anti-illegal immigrant ballot initiative in California—degenerated into a racially charged referendum on the state's demographic evolution. While early polls indicated that the heavily American-born Latino electorate didn't feel much solidarity with the illegal immigrants, a growing belief that the initiative's supporters were not distinguishing between illegal and illegal immigrants—or foreign- and American-born Latinos—led Mexican-American voters to soundly reject the measure.

This type of recurring scapegoating has reinforced the notion that Mexican-Americans are permanent foreigners, and for decades it induced many to conceal their ethnic backgrounds. Upwardly-mobile Mexican-Americans were reluctant to call attention to a heritage that could impede access to the middle class. A generation ago, when Mexican-Americans were politically, socially, and culturally marginalized, and there was yet no Latino middle class to speak of, it was not uncommon for Mexicans to claim Italian or Spanish heritage.

But massive contemporary immigration, combined with the emergence of a Latino middle class, have forced Mexican-Americans and other Latinos to rethink their place in America. Both political and commercial marketers are trying to increase their appeal to this once "forgotten minority." At the same time, an unprecedented array of political and pop cultural figures—such as politician Henry Cisneros and comedian George Lopez—have helped normalize the image of the Latino in the mainstream imagination. As a result, Latinos are asserting their ethnicity more confidently than ever before.

*   *   *

As a result of this newfound prominence, Mexican-Americans are taking the lead in shaping our understanding of what it means to be an immigrant and a minority in America today. The early twentieth-century debate about the "melting pot" evolved as Jewish writers envisioned an America that might better accommodate Jews. Their historic experience as a minority prompted them to take the lead in re-imagining America for an entire wave of immigrants. The playwright Israel Zangwill, in his 1908 drama *The Melting Pot,* gave a name to the optimistic American civic faith that a fusion of white ethnicities will create a stronger nation. For Zangwill, the United States was both a safe harbor and a crucible that melted Old World ethnics into a distinctly new American culture. The problem was that the melting pot model generally excluded nonwhites.

By the 1960s, America's exclusion of African-Americans from the mainstream provoked a new vision based on multiculturalism. Those whom assimilation rejected had come to reject assimilation. Though it encompassed other minority groups, including women and gays, blacks gave the multicultural movement its key moral impetus. The civil rights movement had begun by advocating racial integration, but by the late 1960s its message had fused with a reemergent black separatism. Multiculturalism—the ideology that promotes the coexistence of separate but equal cultures—essentially rejects assimilation and considers the melting pot concept an unwelcome imposition of the dominant culture. Race became the prism through which all social issues were perceived.

Today, Mexican-Americans are the paradigm for minorities in America, and they are changing the multicultural consensus. Because their past and present is characterized by a continual synthesis, a blending of Spanish and indigenous cultures, Mexican-Americans are inventing their own melting pot vision for America. Rather than upholding the segregated notion of a country divided into mutually exclusive ethnic groups, Mexican-Americans are using their experience to imagine an America in which racial, ethnic and cultural groups collide to create new ways of being American.

It was never clear where Mexican-Americans belonged on the American racial scale. In 1896, two white politicians in Texas grew worried that more Mexican immigrants would naturalize and vote. They filed suit against a Mexican-born citizenship applicant, Ricardo Rodriguez, claiming he was not white, and so—like Asians and American Indians—not eligible to become a citizen. Then, in the 1920 census, Mexicans were counted as whites. Ten years later, they were reassigned to a separate Mexican "racial" category; in 1950, they were white again. Today, Mexican-Americans and Hispanics as a whole are commonly viewed as a monolithic racial, linguistic and cultural category in a country of competing minorities.

But Mexican-Americans do not share the self-defining ethnic narrative of Jews—a narrative that establishes Jewish continuity through history—or the shared history of suffering that has united African-Americans. For all the discrimination and segregation that Mexican-Americans suffered in the Southwest, that region was never the Deep South. In any case, as memoirist John Phillip Santos has written, "Mexicans are to forgetting what the Jews are to remembering." And in fact, most Mexican-Americans have done just that, using their growing political power to enter the American mainstream, not to distance themselves from it.

Nonetheless, assuming that Mexicans would (or should) follow the organizational model of Jews or African-Americans, foundations based on the East Coast contributed to the founding of national ethnic-Mexican institutions. The New York-based Ford Foundation was instrumental in creating three of the most visible national Mexican-American organizations, all modeled after similar black organizations: the National Council of La Raza, Mexican American Legal Defense and Educational Fund (MALDEF) and the Southwest Voter Registration Project.

But with the exception of some scattered homegrown social service organizations and political groups, Mexican-Americans have developed little ethnic infrastructure. One national survey has shown that Mexican-Americans are far more likely to join a nonethnic civic group than a Hispanic organization. There is no private Mexican-

American college similar to Yeshiva University or Morehouse College. In Los Angeles, which has the largest Mexican population in the country, there is no ethnic-Mexican hospital, cemetery or broad-based charity organization. Nor does Los Angeles have an English-language newspaper for Mexican-Americans similar to the black *Amsterdam News* and the Jewish *Forward* in New York.

Though the Spanish-language media is often referred to as the "Hispanic media," it generally serves first-generation immigrants and not their English-dominant children and grandchildren. While sheer numbers indicate that their ethnic identity will not fade away, it is unlikely that second- and third-generation Mexican-Americans will be content to live within the confines of a segregated ethnic market.

*　　*　　*

In the late 1920s, Representative John C. Box of Texas warned his colleagues on the House Immigration and Naturalization Committee that the continued influx of Mexican immigrants could lead to the "distressing process of mongrelization" in America. He argued that because Mexicans were the products of mixing among whites, Indians and sometimes blacks, they had a casual attitude toward interracial unions and were likely to mix freely with other races in the United States.

His vitriol notwithstanding, Box was right about Mexicans not keeping to themselves. Because Mexican identity has always been more fluid and comfortable with hybridity, assimilation has rarely been an either/or proposition. For example, Mexican-Americans never had to overcome a cultural proscription against intermarriage. Just as widespread Mexican-Anglo intermarriage helped meld cultures in the nineteenth-century Southwest, so it does today. In fact, two-thirds of intermarriages in California involve a Latino partner. As a result, according to one study, by 2050 more than 40 percent of United States Hispanics will be able to claim multiple ancestries. Another study projects that by 2100 the number of Latinos claiming multiple ancestries will be more than twice the number claiming a single background.

These figures reflect Mexican-Americans' distinctive contribution to our understanding of race: *mestizaje,* or racial and cultural synthesis. In 1925, the romantic Mexican philosopher José Vasconcelos wrote that the Latin American mestizo, or mixed-race person, heralds a new postracialist era in human development. More recently, the preeminent Mexican-American essayist Richard Rodriguez stated that "the essential beauty and mystery of the color brown is that it is a mixture of different colors."

"Something big happens here at the border that sort of mushes everything together," said Maria Eugenia Guerra, publisher of *Lare-DOS,* an alternative monthly magazine in Laredo, Texas, a city that has been majority Latino since its founding in 1755. As political and economic power continues to shift westward, Mexican-Americans will increasingly inject this mestizo vision into American culture. "The Latinization of America is so profound that no one really sees it," asserted Kevin Starr, the leading historian of California.

Some observers have worried that this rise in Mexican-American ethnic confidence will inhibit their full assimilation into the U.S. mainstream. Yet contrary to myth, assimilation has never required the obliteration of ethnic identity. Throughout American history, assimilation was never about people of different racial, religious and cultural backgrounds becoming homogenous. Instead, as pioneering sociologist Robert E. Park wrote in 1930, assimilation is the process by which people of diverse origins achieve a cultural solidarity sufficient for national coherence. Ethnic pride has never prevented people from becoming part of the larger family of Americans. If anything, today's growing Latino confidence makes the journey from ethnic Mexican-ness to American-ness much easier. Mexican-Americans are no longer faced with the decision of choosing one identity over the other.

In the era of the booming "Hispanic market," Hispanicity now offers advantages in both the marketplace and politics. As the middle class has grown, the definition of what it means to be "Latino" has broadened. In other words, upwardly mobile Mexican-Americans have begun to define their ethnicity in a way that is compatible with achieving success in America, not just something to cast aside on the road to assimilation. Growing numbers, class diversification and the opening up of American cultural attitudes have all converged to help Mexican-Americans recast their ethnicity as a vehicle, not an impediment to prosperity.

In a small yet significant way, the presence of President George W. Bush's nephew George P. Bush on the 2000 campaign trail spoke volumes about the evolution of Latino identity in America. A generation ago, the child of an Anglo U.S. governor and a Mexican immigrant mother—in this case, Florida Governor Jeb Bush and his wife, Columba—most likely would not have considered himself "Latino." But during the 2000 presidential campaign, in scores of public appearances and thirty-second television spots, the twenty-four-year-old bilingual law student with olive skin and black hair extolled his pride in ethnicity while boasting of his uncle's virtues. After praising his uncle in the television ad, he asked, "His name? The same as mine. George Bush." The melding of the young man's self-declared Latinoness and his patrician pedigree was seamless.

Even as cultural assimilation has become more reciprocal, Mexican civic assimilation is at an all-time high. The anti-immigrant campaigns of the early 1990s boosted the rate of naturalization and political involvement among Mexicans. Traditionally, Mexicans have had among the lowest naturalization rates of any immigrant group. For years, proximity to their homeland allowed migrants to nurture dreams of one day retiring back home. Long-time, well-established immigrants often put off becoming U.S. citizens even after it had become perfectly clear that they could never transplant their American-born children to a village south of the border.

But the campaign in favor of Proposition 187, a 1994 California ballot measure that sought to ban illegal immigrants from receiving public services, forced Mexican immigrants throughout the nation to get off the fence. Although the measure specifically targeted illegal immigrants, legal immigrants, too, felt they had been made guilty by association. This was one of the factors that inspired the greatest rush to naturalization in the history of the United States, with Mexicans taking the lead. In 1996, there was a 212 percent increase in Mexican immigrant naturalizations over the previous year. Mexicans suddenly became the single largest group of new citizens, accounting for 24 percent of the total.

When it comes to language, Mexican-Americans are also successfully joining the mainstream. Low educational levels and the comfort of large immigrant enclaves ensure that first-generation Mexican immigrants acquire English competency at slower rates than do, say, Taiwanese immigrants. But their children show the typical second-generation shift toward English dominance. census data reveal that virtually all children of Latin American immigrants speak English proficiently. By the third generation, fully two-thirds of Latino children speak only English. While Spanish persists as a second language among many Mexican-Americans in heavily Latino regions of the country, it clearly does not slow acquisition of the nation's primary language.

Nor does the continual influx of new immigrants and the proximity of the home country affect the political loyalties of latter generation Mexican-Americans. Indeed, particularly in the Texas border region, the stark contrast between the two nations helps create a strong patriotic streak among Mexican-Americans. Facing such a wide gap in income and standards of living on the two sides of the border, Mexicans in South Texas would understandably be eager to emphasize which side they were born on.

In the fall of 1997, Mexico's Ciudad Juarez hoisted an enormous Mexican flag near the border that was easily visible from most points in El Paso. When asked by the *El Paso Times* whether their city should respond by hoisting an equally large American flag in downtown El Paso, more Latinos said yes than did non-Latinos. "South Texas culture is sometimes a reaction to the border," said Thomas Longoria, a political scientist at the University of Texas at El Paso. "Maybe embracing America became a coping mechanism. We're saying that we're not any less American than anyone else."

In 1992, the Latino National Political Survey, the largest Hispanic opinion poll of its kind, revealed that Mexican-Americans register equally positive attitudes toward the United States as do Anglo-Americans. The same survey found that while they generally look fondly on Mexico as a country, few latter-generation Mexican-Americans follow Mexican political events closely.

As a further sign of Mexican-American political disassociation from the home country, few immigrants have taken advantage of the newly granted option of dual nationality. In April 1998, Mexico began allowing emigrants to retain their Mexican nationality even as they became naturalized American citizens. But in the first five years of the program, only a tiny percentage of an eligible pool of millions bothered to apply.

And even as they celebrate their closeness to Mexico and a unique bicultural lifestyle, most Mexican-Americans along the frontier support strong border enforcement. In El Paso, for instance, a predominantly Mexican-American electorate sent Silvestre Reyes, a former high-ranking INS official to Congress in 1996. Reyes had gained recognition as the architect of Operation Hold the Line, the labor-intensive INS strategy to prevent illegal immigration along the El Paso border. In a 1994 *El Paso Times* poll, 78 percent of local Latino respondents said they were generally in favor of Operation Hold the Line, while 17 percent opposed it.

Paradoxically, the Mexican government's new policy of rapprochement with Mexican-Americans only serves to further strengthen Latino ties to the United States. For decades, Mexico disowned its migrants as renegades who had turned tail on their country and culture. They were "pochos" (watered-down Mexicans) who had cashed in their souls for material possessions. Although Mexico benefited from the escape valve that allowed it to lose large numbers of unemployed and underemployed citizens, the migrants were glaring symbols of the homeland's failures.

Only when Mexican-Americans began advancing politically and economically did Mexico begin to take a sympathetic view of its diaspora. Beginning in the late 1970s, then intensifying under President Carlos Salinas de Gortari in the 1980s, Mexico developed a two-pronged public relations strategy to capitalize on Mexican-American progress. To reach U.S.-born Mexican-Americans, Mexico courted Latino organizations and granted heritage awards to accomplished Mexican-Americans. To appeal to Mexican-born immigrants, Mexican consulates strengthened their community-outreach efforts and encouraged newcomers in the United States to demand their rights. In so doing, Mexico aimed to nurture sympathetic views of the home country among the growing Mexican-American electorate, and to urge migrant families to keep sending money back home.

Responding to the enormous increase in U.S. citizenship applications by immigrants, Mexico sought to preserve these migrants' connections to their homeland by proclaiming that U.S. citizenship would no longer be considered cultural treason. In November 2000, then President-elect Vicente Fox went further than any previous Mexican official in validating not only the dreams but also the political loyalties of U.S.-born and naturalized Mexican-Americans. While saying that he hoped Mexican-Americans would not forget their heritage, Fox acknowledged that Mexican migrants "want to dream the American dream and wake up as citizens." Clearly, the Mexican government recognizes its own interest in Mexican migrant families' becoming productive and loyal citizens of the United States.

This means that when Mexican migrants leave their homeland for the United States, they will no longer be seen as joining the enemy. Narrowing the cultural and political divide between North and South will further facilitate their transition to American life. Certainly, the presence of a growing Mexican-American electorate has provided an extra incentive for the U.S. government to increase economic and political integration with its southern neighbor.

But the critical mass of Mexican-origin Americans has even broader implications for the future of American culture, particularly in race relations. The growing number of Mexican-American mestizos has begun to undermine the traditionally American, binary view of race. On the 2000 census, half of California's Latinos, most of them of Mexican descent, checked "other" as their race. Their response suggests how inadequate the current system of racial categories has become in understanding an increasingly complex America.

In the first half of the twentieth century, Mexican-American advocates fought hard for the privileges that came with being white in America. Since the 1960s, activists have sought to reap the benefits of being nonwhite. Having spent so long trying to fit into one side or the other of the binary system, Mexican-Americans have become numerous and confident enough to simply claim their brownness—their *mestizaje*. By bringing this ancient understanding of racial and cultural synthesis to a nation that is itself rapidly mixing, Mexican-Americans are transforming the melting pot into a more inclusive cauldron that mixes races as well as ethnicities.

11

ASSIMILATION, THE ASIAN WAY

by Min Zhou

L IKE IT OR NOT, assimilation is happening today, as it happened in the past to previous waves of new Americans. And just as in the past, some groups are more successful than others at integrating into mainstream America. They rise more quickly educationally, make faster progress in ascending into the middle class, even feel more at home more quickly in their adopted country. What accounts for these differences?

The Asian-American experience suggests that one of the most important factors may be the strength of the ethnic communities that newly arrived immigrants form here in the United States. Paradoxical as it seems, for Asians, and perhaps for other groups as well, a promising route into the mainstream runs through a period of seeming ethnic separateness. Contrary to the conventional wisdom, assimilation today is not hindered but actually helped by making common cause with one's fellow ethnics and belonging to a strong, tightly knit ethnic community.

THREE VIGNETTES

Today's Asian-Americans are a widely varied group, and they follow many different paths into American society. Some find themselves included, others excluded, and still others straddle two worlds with growing ease. Successful assimilation is a result, not just of the way they are treated, but also of their own values and choices. Consider the following examples:

Sam Leung arrived in New York from Hong Kong in the early 1960s. He was virtually penniless and spoke no English. For more than thirty years, he worked as a cook in Chinatown restaurants. Now retired, he is reaping the benefits of his life of hard work. Each of his five children has received a degree from an Ivy League college. They all have professional jobs. They've purchased homes, married happily and raised children. All contribute cash, on a monthly basis, for Leung's retirement. Leung and his wife live in one of the children's homes in a New Jersey suburb, but he travels daily by train to Chinatown to play mahjong at the Leung Family Association. Though he still cannot speak English well, he knows his way around the New York area. He feels comfortable and settled. America is his home, he says, and his children are his "social security."

Leung is, to all appearances, a "successful" immigrant. But is he assimilated? Arguably not. After several decades in the United States, he still cannot speak English. Though he has retired to a white middle-class suburb, his social life is confined to Chinatown. He has raised his five children to be "quintessential Americans," and for the most part they are just that. Yet they too cling to inherited ways, including the age-old Chinese tradition of supporting their elderly parents.

Drs. Jiangong Li and Meiying Xia arrived in the United States in the mid-1980s to attend graduate school. Now Li is a senior scientist at a federal government research institute, and Xia runs a consulting firm in Washington, D.C. Li and Xia and their two school-aged children live in a beautiful suburban home. They both speak flawless English, albeit with slight accents. In their leisure time, they do what they call the "American thing"—going to the theater, movies and ballgames, bicycling and river-rafting in the summer, skiing in the winter. They vote in local and national elections and volunteer at the school PTA and for neighborhood events. Yet the couple has also helped establish a Chinese-language school in their suburb, which not only offers children instruction in Chinese language and culture but also provides opportunities for other suburban Chinese immigrant parents to socialize. As it draws more and more immigrant Chinese families from surrounding middle-class suburbs, this Chinese language school has become the center of an emerging ethnic community. As Xia described it, "Saturday [when the Chinese school is in session] is the day I very much look forward to. That's when I can speak Chinese, crack some Chinese jokes, and share some nostalgic feelings about the good old days, or bad old days rather. It's sort of like going to church."

Are Li and Xia assimilated? Arguably, yes. But although they have made it by all observable measures—English proficiency, college education, professional occupation, suburban residence, Western lifestyle and civic participation—they find themselves taking the initiative to start a Chinese school and build a new ethnic community far away from inner-city Chinatown.

Congressman David Wu, forty-five, immigrated from Taiwan with his family when he was five. As the first person of Chinese descent ever elected to Congress, he is the embodiment of the American Dream. In May 2001, he was invited by the Asian-American employees of the U.S. Department of Energy to give a speech in celebration of Asian-American Heritage Month. Yet he and his Asian-American staff were not allowed into the department building, even after presenting their congressional IDs. They were repeatedly asked about their citizenship and country of origin. They were told that this was standard procedure for the Department of Energy and that a congressional ID was not a reliable document. But the next day a congressman of Italian descent was allowed to enter the same building by showing his congressional ID, no questions asked.

Is Congressman David Wu assimilated? Yes, by all means. He has made it, like other Americans, by relying on the strength of his family. A quintessential patriot, he has given up a lucrative legal career for public service because he wants to "make a real difference in the real lives of real people." His fellow Americans in Oregon trust him and have elected him twice to be their representative in Congress. Yet despite compelling evidence that Wu is truly American, he still cannot escape the stereotype of his ethnic group as "perpetual foreigners."

✳   ✳   ✳

Assimilation is not a popular concept today, not in the mainstream and not among the activists and scholars who claim to speak for immigrants. Many ethnic spokesmen denounce it as yielding to white oppression and "selling out." At times it seems that the word itself may be disappearing from the language. In fact, however, as these three stories show, assimilation is alive and well. One way or another, sooner or later, new immigrants and their offspring are becoming like average Americans.

Still, these stories also show how hard assimilation is to define, and how many forms it can take. Obviously, it entails some level of objective success in the new country, as well as a subjective sense that one is at home in America. Yet as these vignettes make clear, inner and outer experience can be very different, and they don't necessarily go together. Immigrants who have prospered in America do not necessarily feel the most American, and even those who succeed on both counts aren't always accepted as American by the mainstream. The Asian-American experience suggests that assimilation today is more complex than we ordinarily think, and that the most successful strategies for immigrants are different than they used to be.

THE CHALLENGE

Concern about assimilation runs high these days among scholars and the public alike—and no wonder. The descendants of the last great wave of immigration, in the early twentieth century, have by now dropped their ethnic hyphens; Irish, Italian and Polish immigrants have melted into the white mainstream. But since 1970, a vast wave of new immigrants has been pouring into the country and adding a new set of ethnic identities to the old familiar list. Most of the recent newcomers have non-European national origins: they are Mexican, Salvadoran, Dominican, Chinese, Filipino, Indian, Korean, Vietnamese, Cambodian. Altogether, between 1971 and 2000, the United States admitted approximately 21 million immigrants, far exceeding the number who came during the first three decades of the twentieth century; but this time more than 80 percent of them were Latino or Asian in origin. As a result, America's ethnic makeup is changing drastically. The 2000 census reported that the U.S. population is 69 percent white, 12.6 percent black, 12.5 percent Latino and 4.4 percent Asian.

When asked what they expect of life in America, these new immigrants say they want to be like average Americans. They want to find high-paying jobs, own their own homes, raise children who are more educated and prosperous than themselves and enjoy a secure retirement. Even if they don't use the word "assimilation," their definition of success is the same as every American's: to achieve middle-class status and freely pursue their personal dreams.

But immigrants face a whole different set of obstacles to their pursuit of the American Dream. For native-born Americans, the key to success is usually education. For immigrants, many other factors have to be in place before they can hope to get a good education. Family socioeconomic status is perhaps the most important because it determines where immigrants live and how much access they have to good jobs and schools, as well as to valuable information and social support networks. The state of the broader economy is another factor. Economic restructuring since the late 1970s has destroyed several crucial rungs in the ladder from the bottom of society to the top. Climbing into the middle class is now more difficult than in the past, and it requires more education and more developed skills; it is also easier to fall to the very bottom and be trapped there because of the scarcity of jobs that pay a living wage. Racism is yet another factor. The historical legacy of slavery and racial discrimination lives on in a system of racial stratification, which in turn interacts with class to affect the life chances of many Americans, especially those belonging to racial minorities.

Today's newcomers also face time-honored challenges: they lack English proficiency, transferable education and skills, familiarity with American institutions and social networks that would link them with mainstream society. The poor and unskilled among them have few choices but to take up low-wage jobs and settle in inner-city ghettos, starting their American lives in poverty or on welfare. For such immigrants, catching up to the status of average Americans is like joining a marathon an hour late, and they have little hope of finishing in their lifetimes.

The children of immigrants seem to have it easier. After all, surpassing their parents is no big deal, since their parents are usually stuck at the bottom of the socioeconomic ladder. But the second generation faces a different kind of challenge—equally difficult, if not more so. After all, the foreign-born generation is by definition transitional. First-generation immigrants are likely to regard their disadvantaged status as temporary, and to be optimistic about the future. But the second generation, born in America and raised to be American, expects to be judged by the same standards as other Americans. They hope not only to do better than their parents but to do at least as well as their native-born peers.

This is no easy task, since the children of immigrants often grow up under highly unfavorable circumstances. Many are from families where both parents work hard just to put food on the table. They live in crowded housing in unsafe neighborhoods and attend poorly-performing local schools. Many must deal with urban gangs and the peer pressure to be "cool," which often does not include doing well in school. Nor can they look to their parents as role models. They have little tolerance for the discriminatory treatment their parents regularly put up with, and they know more than their parents about the English-speaking world. No wonder that, at home, they often refuse to defer to their elders: as often as not, they feel that it is they, not their parents, who are leading the household.

Second-generation immigrants who grow up in inner-city ghettos face a still more insidious obstacle: a deeply troubling learned ambivalence about mainstream culture and success. Anthropologist John Ogbu has described it as an "oppositional" outlook, arguing that the most important influence on any immigrant group is the nature of its initial reception by Americans and its way of dealing with that reception. According to Ogbu, many immigrants who are looked down upon manage to turn their distinctive heritage into a kind of ethnic armor. They establish a sense of collective dignity that enables them to cope psychologically, even in the face of exclusion and discrimination, by keeping the host society at arm's length. Others, however, accept and internalize socially imposed inferiority as part of their collective self-definition, and this in turn fosters an oppositional outlook toward mainstream institutions.

For immigrants with an oppositional outlook, symbolic expressions of ethnicity may hinder, rather than facilitate, social mobility. They view assimilation as "acting white," and react to discrimination and other disadvantages by resisting assimilation. For example, research in the past twenty years shows that many inner-city black and Latino youths who desire to do well in school are pulled back by strong ethnic peer pressure, which regards academic success as somehow a betrayal of ethnicity. Such students fear that if they succeed, they will be shunned by their ethnic peers as "sell-outs" or "turnovers." Sociologists call this the "forced choice dilemma," and see it as perpetuating downward assimilation: instead of assimilating to the mainstream, these children of immigrants risk assimilating to the bottom segment of American society, the urban underclass.

THE ASIAN PUZZLE

Asian immigrants face many of these same challenges. A considerable number of them are poor and unskilled, and they often settle in neighborhoods where their children are subject to the undertow of an insidious peer culture. Yet Asian-Americans as a group are doing remarkably well in the United States today. Consider their extraordinary educational achievement. Research on the new second generation repeatedly shows that high school students of Asian origin outperform non-Hispanic white students (who, in turn, outperform black and Hispanic students). Even the Hmong, who come from a preliterate peasant background, outperform native-born American students attending the same school, and so do more recently arrived Cambodians. Compared to whites and other racial minority groups, Asian-Americans show stronger belief in the value of schooling and are more inclined to attribute school success or failure to individual effort; they attend college at a significantly higher rate, and more of their peers do well in school. Asian-Americans are also noticeably overrepresented on the nation's most prestigious campuses—whether the public UC Berkeley and UCLA or private institutions like Harvard, MIT, Stanford and Cal Tech.

But if many of the children of Asian immigrants are making it—arguably better and faster than any immigrant children have ever done before—it is far from clear why. To be sure, some Asians have it a little easier than other immigrants. Many are affluent and highly skilled professionals who achieve occupational status and incomes higher than those of average Americans within just a few years of their arrival. Yet even these more successful Asian-Americans lack accumulated wealth, and few have access to the old-boy associations and other networks that buoy many native-born Americans. As a result, merely sustaining their middle-class status often requires unending hard work. And while class background may explain why the children of foreign-born physicians, engineers and computer specialists show up in elite universities, it is more difficult to understand how

Asian-Americans from more modest circumstances reach the same campuses, and at the same speed.

Often we hear a cultural explanation. Political scientist Francis Fukuyama argues that the values newcomers bring with them from the old country help speed their incorporation into the American mainstream. Asian culture puts a high value on strong families, dutiful children, delayed gratification, education, hard work, discipline, respect for others and moral obligation to the community—virtually all qualities that Americans prize and are now arguably losing. Similarly, economist Thomas Sowell believes that cultural assets—values and attitudes, skills and contacts—play a significant part in the high IQ scores and scholastic achievement of today's most successful immigrant groups.

What is missing from such theories is an explanation of just how cultural values and beliefs adapt to changes in environment, and how they are transmitted from one generation to the next. After all, not everyone from even the most successful culture does well in America. My research on Asian-American communities suggests that Asian-Americans and their children are making it not because of "Asian" values per se but thanks largely to the ethnic community developed since their arrival in the United States. It is this community that sets goals for achievement and standards of behavior and establishes economic and cultural institutions to enforce them.

THE ANSWER: THE ETHNIC COMMUNITY

The role of the ethnic community in immigrant settlement has long been recognized in studies of earlier European-origin groups. But much of the emphasis has been on how the community serves as an interim refuge and a springboard for assimilation. According to this traditional view, new immigrants cluster in ethnic enclaves upon arrival, relying on ethnic networks and institutions to find housing and jobs and help them learn their way around. In the long run, however, the ethnic community and its social structures are thought to obstruct assimilation, trapping immigrants in permanent isolation by discouraging them from learning English and adopting American ways. So, the theory goes, immigrants must eventually move out of the enclave in order to achieve social and economic progress.

For today's immigrants, however, remaining in close contact with the ethnic enclave may actually facilitate rather than hinder assimilation. True, some immigrant neighborhoods have declined or even disappeared as more successful residents become assimilated and move out. But others are thriving—despite the departure of more successful residents—by luring new immigrants from diverse socioeconomic backgrounds and attracting money from overseas. These new ethnic enclaves defy old stereotypes: far from being urban ghettos, they remain a symbolic home base even for successful former residents who have moved to the suburbs.

In such neighborhoods, the enclave economy is no longer the classic immigrant economy of mom-and-pop stores and other small retail businesses. Instead, there is a wide range of economic activities—professional services, manufacturing, retail and wholesale trades—that provides ethnic group members from diverse class backgrounds with employment and entrepreneurial opportunities as well as culture-specific goods and services. This economy is closely linked with various ethnic institutions in the enclave—churches, temples, schools, business and professional associations, nonprofit service agencies—that provide newcomers with networks for self-help and mutual support. The solidarity and trust that come naturally among residents of the same ethnic background is a form of "social capital" that spurs ethnic entrepreneurship and helps reinforce communal norms.

New York City's Chinatown shows how such an ethnic enclave can help immigrants succeed in America without losing their ethnic identities. The enclave economy offers convenient and easy alternatives to mainstream employment. The neighborhood functions as a cultural center, attracting not only tourists but also suburban Chinese for routine activities such as shopping, entertainment, and sending children to ethnic schools. These opportunities tie immigrant Chinese from diverse socioeconomic backgrounds to Chinatown even after they have moved out of the enclave. These ties, in turn, directly or indirectly create a feeling of cohesion that cuts across class lines and strengthens the sense of identity and community.

Nevertheless—and this is very important—nothing about the enclave discourages eventual absorption into mainstream American life. On the contrary, all the values and habits of the ethnic community point toward the communal goal of settlement and integration. In the simple words of one Chinatown worker, "We want to buy a home and move out of here and we want our children to get a job in those office buildings down the street [on Wall Street]."

The experience of Chinatown's working women is revealing. Immigrant Chinese women with little English and few job skills often find working in Chinatown a better option, despite low wages, than taking a similar job outside the enclave. This is because the enclave enables them to more effectively combine their roles as wage earners, wives and mothers. In Chinatown, jobs are easier to find, working hours are more flexible, employers are more tolerant of the presence of children, and the private child-care within walking distance of work is more accessible and affordable. Convenient grocery shopping and the availability of takeout food also make dinner preparation easier.

At work, women are able to socialize with other Chinese immigrant women, some who may not come from similar socioeconomic backgrounds but who nonetheless share the same goals and concerns about family, child rearing and social mobility. Sitting at the sewing machine, the women gossip, brag about their children, complain about insensitive husbands or nagging relatives. They also exchange information and coping strategies and comfort each other in times of hardship. Perhaps most important, they share strategies for succeeding in the mainstream. It is not uncommon to hear non-English-speaking garment workers in Chinatown talking in detail about SAT exam scores and admissions to highly selective magnet schools such as nearby Stuyvesant High School, or even Harvard and MIT.

These Chinatown workers also get valuable information from neighborhood encounters with employers and middle-class Chinese immigrants who have moved out of the enclave but come back to visit. Residents and nonresidents share what they know about assimilation in conversations at Chinese-language schools, cultural centers, churches, temples, restaurants and shops. Extensive Chinese-language media—radio, television and newspapers—also reflect the experience of those who have already made it, and provide valuable information to help newcomers do the same.

Even more important is the role of the ethnic community in aiding the adaptation of immigrant children. Consider how the enclave works to reinforce obedience and respect for elders—one of the core cultural precepts in Chinese families. Relatives and adult family friends often greet children with "Have you been obeying your parents?" or "Have you behaved well?" Parents frequently ask their children "How was that test you took today?" Or they will respond to a straight-A report card with "How come you got an A-minus?" And relatives and friends reinforce the same message. If a youngster is disobedient or disrespectful, he or she is considered without *gui-ju* (discipline) or *jia-jiao* (family principles) or *li-mao* (proper manners), and his or her parents may even be blamed for bad parenting. In an ethnic enclave where behavioral standards are enforced through this sort of everyday interaction, children tend to conform, either willingly or as a way to avoid public disapproval and embarrassment. Obedience, hard work and academic achievement are matter-of-fact expectations for immigrant Chinese children and could not possibly be instilled without the support and reinforcement of the ethnic community.

Involvement in the community not only gives immigrant children the support necessary for academic success. It also helps to ease intergenerational and bicultural conflicts. Second-generation immigrants often perceive their parents as holding onto traditional ways and imposing these old ways upon them, while parents often fear that their children are becoming Americanized too quickly and will be distracted from their goals. In the ethnic enclave, Chinese children do not have to deal with such conflicts on their own, and their shared experience helps them cope more effectively than in situations where they are the only Chinese.

Perhaps even more than Chinese immigrants, Vietnamese refugees in the United States demonstrate the value of clustering in ethnic enclaves. The Versailles Village in New Orleans, for example, is a community of Vietnamese fishermen and peasants who settled in one of the city's most underprivileged black neighborhoods. And here, as in Chinatown, the ethnic community plays a decisive role in determining whether young people move up into the American mainstream or remain permanently trapped at the margins of society.

Most of the Vietnamese children in Versailles Village attend public schools, where many of their American peers feel alienated from the mainstream and discourage academic achievement. Even with parental involvement, many second-generation immigrants would naturally adopt this oppositional outlook in order to be popular with their American peers. In this situation, the Vietnamese community is critical in preventing the younger generation from taking such a downward path, helping young Vietnamese instead to bypass the negative local environment and succeed in mainstream American society. Rather than let their children loose in the dangerous streets of a marginal American neighborhood, the ethnic community binds the children in close relationships with other Vietnamese families and adults through participation in institutions such as the Catholic Church and after-school programs.

Although the ethnic enclave in Versailles Village, as in Chinatown, might seem to encourage isolation and separation from the mainstream, in fact it does exactly the opposite. A supportive and watchful community actually encourages and facilitates integration into mainstream American society. As a Vietnamese teenager from Versailles Village put it, "My parents know pretty well all the [Vietnamese] kids in the neighborhood, because we all go to the same church. Everybody here knows everybody else. It's hard to get away with much."

Among Korean immigrants, too, the ethnic community is vitally important in pushing the second generation to succeed in America. Many Korean immigrants in Los Angeles come from middle-class backgrounds and have settled in suburban communities. But they still maintain ties to Koreatown in the inner city, particularly through involvement in the ethnic economy and churches as well as in an extensive system of social institutions and, most important, a supplementary educational system. In Koreatown, there is an impressive range of private Korean-language schools, after-school tutoring centers and youth-oriented recreational facilities offering sports and music lessons. These ethnic institutions not only benefit Korean working-class families living in the inner city but also attract middle-class suburban Korean children—thus reinforcing the value of education among Korean young people from all kinds of backgrounds.

CONCLUSION

America today is very different from the nation that welcomed European immigrants at the turn of the twentieth century. In those days, the newcomers' children and grandchildren had few options but to assimilate quickly into the white mainstream. And they encountered conditions that were in some ways more propitious to integration. Like the native-born population, they were overwhelmingly of European stock; they entered an expanding manufacturing-based economy with powerful trade unions; and they benefited from a long hiatus in new immigration after the 1920s. Even so, it often took them two or three or more generations to join the mainstream.

In today's arguably more open, inclusive America, new immigrants from diverse backgrounds have more freedom to choose their own destinies and to determine the pace and extent of their assimilation for themselves. Yet many second-generation Asian-Americans, who are considered assimilated, are still subjected to a pernicious system of racial stratification. One second-generation Chinese-American described the discrimination she has faced: "The truth is, no matter how American you think you are or try to be, if you have almond-shaped eyes, straight black hair, and a yellow complexion, you are a foreigner by default."

For this reason too—along with the cultural advantages of clustering in a traditional ethnic enclave—Asian-Americans find it benefi-
cial to maintain a strong ethnic identity. The very fact that they are
often accepted only conditionally prompts them to organize ethnically; and in the end, this greatly facilitates their absorption. Call it
the Asian paradox: in order to fight the negative stereotype that they
are "perpetual foreigners," a seemingly assimilated second generation
falls back on ethnicity for empowerment and becomes actively involved in ethnic politics. Although this strategy for assimilation is
very different from the one their parents used, in practice it serves
them well—and is typically American.

Of course, the Chinese, Vietnamese or Korean way of assimilating
may not work for other Asian-origin groups, much less non-Asian
groups. The circumstances in which immigrants leave their old countries and are received in America vary widely, and every group must
find its own path in the quest for acceptance and socioeconomic advancement. But with any immigrant group, the first requirements for
success are dignity and faith in their own abilities, no matter what ignorance or bigotry they encounter. As America becomes increasingly
multiethnic, and as ethnic Americans become integral to our society,
it becomes more and more evident that there is no contradiction between an ethnic identity and an American identity. The time is approaching when "the ethnic way" will seem like an inevitable part of
"the American way."

12

FOR THE SECOND GENERATION, ONE STEP AT A TIME

by Alejandro Portes

M ARY PATTERSON HAD A DILEMMA. As a black teenager, she was
treated in most places as part of the African-American population. Clerks followed her in stores to prevent her from shoplifting.
Whites added that extra measure of curtness to her transactions. And
all of this despite her family's home in Coral Gables—an affluent section of Miami—and the achievements of her parents, both successful
professionals from Trinidad.

Having attended American schools, Mary spoke American English, to which she deliberately added local black inflections, searching
for acceptance from her black peers in junior high. Mary noticed,
however, that when Patricia, her mother, spoke, she was treated very
differently. Patricia's language is heavily British-accented English,
the English that she learned as a child in Trinidad. And when white
people discovered she was West Indian, their demeanor changed.
"Ah, you are Jamaican, hard-working people. Good English, too,"
they would say. (Never mind that Trinidad and Jamaica are different
countries.)

As Mary approached high school graduation and began seeking a job to help pay for college, she felt that her best defense against standard white racism was for her West Indian identity to get through to employers. Her solution was eminently practical. Mary consciously sought to project her image as a second-generation Trinidadian, or at least West Indian, by her attire and body language, for instance, by carrying a key chain stamped with the name and map of her parents' country. And she began taking lessons from her mother, seeking to regain an island accent. "My mother is so self-assured. She stands tall everywhere . . . at work, when shopping in the stores. I need some of that," Mary said. While she considers herself American, the question of identity is just too important to be left to itself. "Blacks in this country carry a lot of baggage, like the way they dress and speak. I respect them, but I don't have to carry that load. I'm an immigrant." In spite of discrimination, Mary is determined to succeed. She plans to surpass her mother, who is head nurse at a local hospital, by attending medical school.

It is well known by now that immigrants are the fastest growing component of the American population, and that their presence has transformed the culture and politics of several major U.S. cities. There are now over 30 million foreign-born people in the United States; 11.2 million adult immigrants arrived in the 1990s alone, accounting, together with their children, for 70 percent of the growth in the nation's population. Still more important, the flow shows no sign of declining. Driven by the labor demands of a vast economy, and the ever-strengthening social networks between immigrants and their home countries, the influx can be expected to continue indefinitely and to affect every region of the country.

These facts make it necessary to consider the long-term effects that contemporary immigration will have on the fabric of American society and culture. Experts on immigration like to frame the question by comparing the situation today with that at the beginning of the twentieth century. Then as now, the nation was transformed by a human tidal wave that showed few signs of receding. At the peak of that earlier movement, immigrants represented close to 15 percent of the total population, a figure that is being rapidly approached today. Then as now, immigrants went to the areas where demand for their labor was greatest: at that time, this meant the industrial cities of the Northeast, whose demographics and institutions were thoroughly transformed. And then as now, much was made of the foreign tongues, clothes and habits crowding American cities.

In the long term, however, it was not the first generation of immigrants but their children who determined the consequences of the immigrant flow for the nation. First-generation immigrants have always been a restless bunch, many staying in the country only a short time, in order to accumulate the resources for building a life back home. Even those who settled permanently often kept alive their dreams of return. By contrast, their American-born and -reared offspring were U.S. citizens and, overwhelmingly, here to stay.

The story of how these children of immigrants became Americans is part of our national myth, and it still guides our understanding of how the process of assimilation is supposed to work. Children of European immigrants learned English, gradually abandoned their parents' language and culture, and clawed their way through education and entrepreneurship to economic affluence. Fortuitous events, such as World War II and the postwar economic boom, facilitated their economic and social integration. By the third generation, foreign languages were a distant memory and ethnic heritage was a social convenience, displayed on selected occasions but subordinate to a new American identity.

Today, the process of second-generation incorporation is also proceeding apace, with consequences every bit as momentous as those of a century ago. But the traditional model of assimilation, inherited from the European past, is not very useful in describing the current process and its likely outcomes. While Mary Patterson's story may not represent the average experience of immigrants' children today, it offers important lessons. Rapid acculturation to American ways did not pay off for Mary, who was forced to make a U-turn in search of the resources offered by her parents' culture. The same story of the dangers of complete acculturation, and the usefulness of strong family and community bonds, can be told of many different immigrant communities.

The crucial question is not whether assimilation will take place: that is a foregone conclusion. The question, rather, is what kind of assimilation it will be. And often, as in Mary's case, partial or delayed assimilation can help offset the dangers that come with rapid adaptation to American culture in some of its most problematic forms.

THE TRIALS OF GROWING UP AMERICAN

The experience of second-generation immigrants today is fraught with new challenges. Just over a decade ago, my colleague Rubén G. Rumbaut and I began surveying second-generation youths attending the eighth and ninth grades in the metropolitan areas of Miami/Fort Lauderdale and San Diego. In total, 5,262 students from seventy-seven nationalities took part in the survey, known as the Children of Immigrants Longitudinal Study, or CILS, conducted in 1992–1993. The students were interviewed again three years later, when most were in their final year of high school, though approximately 12 percent had dropped out of school or stopped attending. The second CILS survey interviewed both students still in school and dropouts, altogether about 80 percent of the original sample. In addition, a random sample of 50 percent of the parents of the respondents were interviewed in their own languages.

The study reveals two major challenges facing second-generation immigrants today. The first is racial discrimination, which has significant consequences for both assimilation and ethnic identity. Like Mary Patterson, immigrants who are defined as black experience the worst conditions, but by conventional standards the majority of the new second generation is nonwhite, and they have been treated accordingly, often encountering racial hostility. The common effect is to reduce their self-esteem and aspirations, and to trigger a defensive reaction against the dominant white population. Children learn to "racialize" their identities, and simultaneously to build up defenses against the message that such identities are inferior.

As a result, the CILS survey shows, children's self-identification changes dramatically. Many of those who begin adolescence calling themselves Americans or hyphenated Americans (e.g. "Mexican-American" or "Chinese-American") switch to pan-ethnic identifications (Asian, Black, Hispanic, Latino) or embrace their parents' old nationalities (e.g., "Mexican" or "Chinese"). This decline in American self-identification contradicts traditional notions of how acculturation is supposed to proceed, but it can be readily explained once we understand the social context in which the change occurs. Pan-ethnic identities reflect immigrant youths' adoption of the categories in which they are routinely classified by schools and other mainstream institutions. In other words, the abandonment of an "American" identity for a "Hispanic" one is a direct result of acculturation.

Similarly, identification with the parents' nationality without a hyphen reflects the common process by which second-generation youths, rebuffed by what they perceive as external discrimination, re-assert their national origin as a source of pride and as protection against an inferior social status. Predictably, this "return to the roots" is stronger among groups that, like Mexican-Americans, have been targets of widespread prejudice. But the key point is that such reactive identities are not evidence of incomplete acculturation; they are a direct result of the process. These are "made-in-America" labels, and these second-generation "Mexicans" and "Filipinos" have very little to do with their parents' countries of origin.

The same process is still more poignantly reflected in second-generation views of race. Among Latin-origin youths, many have learned to confuse their ethnicity or national origin with their race. Among Cuban parents in the CILS survey, 93 percent defined their race as white, but only 44 percent of their children agreed. Most of the rest racialized their ethnicity, reporting that they belonged to the Hispanic "race." The tendency is still stronger among Mexicans: most adult immigrants defined their race as "mestizo" or multiracial, but a majority of the children (56 percent) reported belonging to the Mexican "race," and another 26 percent saw themselves racially as "Hispanic."

These children have learned that they are nonwhite and have adopted the American racial classification system to the point of believing that they belong to fictitious races. Like pan-ethnic identities, these are "made-in-America" labels that sort out the foreign-origin population into artificial, but socially decisive, categories. In other words, these young people are assimilating American values, but not in a particularly desirable way. Significantly, the CILS survey found that children of immigrants who are cut off from community ties— that is, more "assimilated" to their American environment—are most vulnerable to such messages, and most likely to engage in defensive strategies. Second-generation youths who are part of solid families and close-knit ethnic communities are better protected against racial hostility and the divisive notion of identity it all too often produces.

The second, and still more important, challenge to the successful integration of the new second generation lies in the social and cultural patterns that have emerged at the bottom of American urban society. A set of pathologies, all too well known, has developed in the core areas of major American cities; they are associated with what William J. Wilson calls a "redundant population" increasingly excluded from regular employment. The proliferation of youth gangs and their involvement in the drug trade; high drug-addiction, crime and school dropout rates; teenage pregnancy and single-parent households; early incarceration and high risk of violent assault and death: this is the urban nightmare that a multitude of government and private programs have tried, so far without success, to tackle. And for many new immigrants, it is a dire, unavoidable challenge.

In effect, for immigrants, poverty in urban America has given rise to a set of entrenched outlooks and lifestyles that amount to an alternative model for assimilation. Because of their own poverty, many immigrant families settle in central city areas where their children are relentlessly exposed to such pathologies, in the streets and in schools. Rapid acculturation under these conditions is not, as in the past, a means for upward social and economic mobility, but may lead to precisely the opposite outcome: entrapment in a situation of permanent disadvantage. This path has been called "downward assimilation," and it leads to an unexpected result for the process of acculturation: the possible emergence of a "rainbow underclass." This was never part of the blueprint of those who call for the complete cultural integration of all newcomers.

Immigrant parents are deeply aware of this possibility, and their concern provides the most compelling evidence about the reality and risks of downward assimilation. This is what some immigrant parents interviewed in the CILS survey had to say about the society they encountered in the United States:

> Why? Why? Why should this country, the richest in the world, have such low educational standards and disruptive behavior? It is sad to see this country's children smoking grass or wearing their hair in spikes. How are these youngsters paying back for the opportunities they receive?
>
> —Roger, thirty-eight, Nicaraguan father

> I am concerned about my younger children. I'm afraid they will join with the homeboys. The reason I'm concerned is because I feel I cannot control the peer pressure; when they step out of the house, it's all over them.
>
> —Botum, fifty-one, Cambodian mother

> It was not like this before. He was obedient, well-behaved, went to school every day. Two years ago he joined the Mesa Kings [a local gang] and last year he quit school. He does what he likes. . . . He knows English better than us, thinks that he knows everything. If he continues this way, he'll never finish high school; he'll be killed first.
>
> —Pao Yang, fifty-seven,
> Laotian Hmong father interviewed about his son

Parents from all national backgrounds and all socioeconomic levels see the principal danger to their children's well-being in the alternative role models provided by street culture and an external environment fraught with consumerism and permissiveness. Seventy-eight percent of parents in the CILS sample responded that they were worried about negative influences on their children in school; 66 percent were worried about negative influences from their children's close friends; and a whopping 86 percent acknowledged that their views and goals for their children differed from those of their children's friends.

This overriding preoccupation with downward assimilation explains why more and more immigrant parents do not want their children to be educated the American way. The majority prefers an education based on their country's own customs, or a selective mix of the two. A century ago, many immigrants encouraged their children to forget their native tongues and speak only English as a means of joining the American mainstream. Today, the immigrant family that does so is rare. Retention of parental languages along with English is preferred, not because parents resist their children's integration into American society, but because they have identified a better way to accomplish that goal. Unlike for earlier immigrant generations, full acculturation, or "Americanization," is no longer perceived as a desirable outcome. Instead, it is viewed with suspicion as a process capable of driving a wedge between parents and children, and derailing children from the hard work and academic achievement needed for success.

THE MELTING POT TODAY: SELECTIVE ACCULTURATION

In coping with the threat of downward assimilation, immigrants can draw on two kinds of resources. Clearly, parents with higher levels of education and occupational skills—what economists call "human capital"—are in a better position to support their children's adaptation by providing a home in the suburbs, a private school education and summer trips to the home country to reinforce family ties. The problem is that the average immigrant family generally does not have access to these kinds of resources.

Even less affluent immigrants, however, can benefit from "social capital": the resources available to individuals and families who are part of tightly-knit immigrant communities. Social capital depends less on the economic or occupational success of immigrants than on the ties that bind them to their families and others in their group. After all, it makes little difference whether fellow nationals are highly educated and wealthy if they feel no obligations to one another, or if they are widely dispersed. On the other hand, modest communities with strong internal ties can be a valuable resource. When an immigrant child's relatives and neighbors, and the parents of his peers and friends, are part of the same community, all these adults can support parental efforts to guide the child's behavior and values.

Today, many such communities are encouraging a new kind of assimilation, one that can be called "selective acculturation." Selective acculturation is defined as learning unaccented English and American cultural skills while retaining the parental language and elements of the associated culture. The best empirical indicator of this pattern among second-generation youths is fluent bilingualism. In the CILS sample, this outcome is relatively rare, with less than one-fourth of the students (23.2 percent) categorized as fluent bilingual by age seventeen. More common is English monolingualism, representing 39.4 percent of the sample. While this result will be reassuring to some of today's more ardent mainstream assimilationists, it is not the most desirable adaptation path for the children.

Selective acculturation may be criticized by some as a prescription for cultural fragmentation and national disunity. In this view, it is synonymous with multiculturalism and its alleged pathologies. For nativist groups such as U.S. English, multiculturalism would result in a Babel of languages and the breakdown of the country along ethnic lines. In fact, however, selective acculturation does not lead to multiculturalism but to a more effective integration into the nation's economic and cultural fabric. The goal of selective acculturation is not the perpetuation of the immigrant community but the use of its social capital to improve the opportunities of immigrant children for mainstream educational and career success.

The history of Jewish adaptation to American society provides a good example of the difference between multiculturalism and selective acculturation. This group is commonly regarded as an archetypal example of successful adaptation, though from the point of view of some mainstream assimilationists the early prospects of Jewish immigrants were hardly auspicious. The 2 million Russian Jews who arrived between 1890 and 1917 brought along a non-Christian religion, a strange language and a set of institutions and practices foreign to the country's Anglo-Saxon heritage. Most often the new arrivals did not take jobs in American firms but instead set up on their own as peddlers or small entrepreneurs. What's more, they tended to live in tight ethnic enclaves like the Lower East Side of Manhattan: self-sufficient communities with their own language, religion, economy and cultural institutions.

For American nativists of the time, this was surely evidence of rampant multiculturalism and looming social fragmentation. Indeed, immigrant Jews and Jewish-Americans were repeatedly attacked for their foreignness, their clannishness and the threat they posed to the cultural unity of the nation. As we all know, that threat did not materialize. Instead, second-generation Jews made use of the resources provided by their ethnic enclaves to gain access to higher education, then move into the professions and the corporate world. The economic and social resources they accumulated were eventually turned toward politics: a means to build powerful electoral constituencies and a strong presence at all levels of government.

American Jews are today an integral part of the nation's social and economic mainstream. They lead American institutions, from city and state governments to major universities. They are a force in American intellectual life and are represented in large numbers among social scientists, including those who scrutinize the chances for successful assimilation of today's immigrant groups. Not even the most fervent nativists would question the Jewish-American success story or the contributions made by this group to American society during the last century. When it comes to contemporary immigrants, however, the same pattern of selective acculturation is viewed with suspicion and even attacked as divisive.

LESSONS FOR POLICY

The policy implications of this analysis run counter to what have been, until now, the two dominant approaches to immigration and immigrant adaptation. The first, which may be labeled intransigent nativism, seeks to reduce the flow of immigrants and their presence in American society to a minimum. That goal would be achieved through serious tightening of admittance rules, strong policing of the border and mass deportation of illegal immigrants. The second position may be labeled forceful assimilationism, since it seeks to integrate newcomers as fast as possible into American society and culture. This is to be accomplished through such programs as English immersion and the dispersal of newly arrived refugees across the country in order to speed up their integration. While well-intentioned, such programs may end up retarding or derailing the very integration they seek through the unintended consequences explained in this essay: fragmenting immigrant families, undermining parental authority, compromising children's self-esteem and, most crucially, leaving them bereft of communal guidance at a critical period in their development.

The alternative course is acculturation to English and American values and norms, combined with respect for parental cultures and selective preservation of cultural legacies. Of these, none is more important than language. Children who become fluent in English while preserving fluency in their home language are able to maintain communication with parents, even if the parents never learn English. This enables them to tap into sources of family and community support for sustained academic effort and success. And in fact, the data show that fluent bilingual students not only have higher self-esteem and aspirations but generally do better academically.

Schools are—or should be—the key institutions for implementing this policy of selective acculturation. Unfortunately, most public schools' approaches toward immigrant children have been strongly assimilationist, seeking to "mainstream" them into uniform English-only classes as fast as possible. Even attempts at bilingual education in the school systems of California and other states have hardly lived up to their name, devolving into remedial and second-rate instruction in foreign languages for English-deficient students. As practiced by a handful of dual-language public "magnet" and private schools, true bilingual education begins early and combines vigorous instruction in English for immigrant children with the support of their home language. This approach does not require a 50-50 division of the school day, only one or two hours of daily instruction in the home language. The experiences of these schools, as well as the extensive educational experience of several European countries, show the goal of bilingual fluency is not a dream but an achievable objective.

The ultimate goal, of course, is not multiculturalism leading to isolated and self-perpetuating ethnic communities. Instead, selective acculturation will help immigrants reinforce the positive values of the home and the community, protecting the second generation against both external discrimination and the threat of downward assimilation. The challenge facing America today is to create a new mainstream of diverse and productive citizens who use English to communicate and who are proud both of their common identity as Americans and of the culture inherited from their ancestors. The future of today's second-generation immigrants, and of the cities and regions where they concentrate, hangs in the balance.

13

THE ALLOY OF NEW YORK

by Pete Hamill

LIKE MANY NEW YORKERS, I've never cared much for the metaphor of the melting pot. It has been with us for a long time, of course—since 1908, when Israel Zangwill used it in his play of the same name. But over the years, the melting pot lost its original meaning for those of us who were born in New York, and surely for all those—Americans and foreigners—who came to the city from that mysterious place called Somewhere Else. The metaphor eroded, shifted, changed, with almost nobody noticing. By the time I was young in the 1950s, the melting pot image evoked nothing more than an object resting on a stove tended by amateur chefs consulting the Betty Crocker cookbook, while the heat was provided by the old Brooklyn Union Gas Company. This image did not suggest the extraordinary evolution of the unique New York character. Nor did it explain why so many human beings have found a way—in spite of surface differences, small daily collisions and irritations, occasional outbursts of bigotry and stupidity—to live together in relative harmony.

After the cooling of the melting pot metaphor, there were other attempts to give a name to what had been taking shape in New York for centuries. For a while, during the debates over ethnic identity, some of us embraced the notion of New York as a salad bowl. In a salad, the lettuce, tomatoes, cucumbers, onions and celery retain their individual identities while being transformed into something new by the proportions and the sauce. We might be called the Apple salad, but we also had room for some chili peppers.

But the salad bowl lacked toughness, that essential component of New York character; it was too domestic, too satisfied, too . . . suburban. I've come to believe in another metaphor, knowing full well that any single image is subject to dispute. It's applicable to the oldest New York families and the newest arrivals. It showed itself with extraordinary power after the savage morning of September 11, 2001. It's the result of a process that began in the earliest days of the seventeenth-century Dutch. It evolved without a master plan, or a meeting of committees, or the writing of any manifestos.

For me, New York is an alloy.

✳   ✳   ✳

I use the word "alloy" in the sense of a combination of metals, each with its own qualities, but converted into a new thing: harder and tougher. Zinc combined with copper gives us bronze. Iron merged with carbon gives us steel.

Over nearly four centuries of immigration, New York has developed the toughest and most enduring alloy in the world. That is why talking about New York is not a parochial discussion: what has happened here could be a model for many cities in the contemporary world. European cities, in particular, are today attempting to adjust to the growing influx of human beings from poorer nations or from nations looted by political kleptocrats or ruined by war. Sometimes the new arrivals are called refugees or exiles. But they are all immigrants, most of them young, most driven by the simple human desire to lead better lives. Sometimes they die trying, drowning in the Mediterranean or the Adriatic, victims of cynical rings of people smugglers.

Those who do make the desired shores often must cope with local (and understandable) resistance. New arrivals, without education, job skills or even knowledge of cities, must find their way in the metropolis. New York's history teaches us that this is not an easy process. In Europe, there has been nothing like the new immigrants since the heyday of the Roman Empire, when many thousands of conquered people—slaves, former slaves, internal migrants from the countryside of Italy—flocked to the imperial capital. But in the modern world, people like them have clustered in one crucial place: New York.

They have been in New York from its earliest days. After 1625, when the first houses were erected at the tip of Manhattan Island, the Dutch settlement contained an extraordinary variety of human beings. One reason: the prosperous Netherlands could not muster enough Dutch colonists to populate the place. They were satisfied with life in the country that was becoming one of the greatest mercantile powers in the world. The journey to America was long and dangerous, the destination as remote as an outpost on Mars.

And there was another factor. The place that was soon called New Amsterdam was not an outpost of the Dutch state. It was run under charter by one of the first great multinationals, the Dutch West India Company. The company's basic goal was to make money through trade, and in the earliest days this came from the pelts of animals. But the marvelous harbor and the great river flowing from the north offered visions of a more ambitious future. Clearly, great wealth was possible. But to attain it, the company needed settlers, and it soon offered inducements to people who were not Dutch. Most of those who arrived in the first ships were French-speaking Walloons, but there were volunteers from other countries too, including several Italians. In June 1626, a second Dutch ship, filled with colonists, also brought involuntary settlers: eleven enslaved Africans from Angola.

Power in the tiny colony was in the hands of the West India Company and its Dutch directors. Nobody could vote. No ordinary resident could ask for a say in the governing of the town. But the new arrivals were soon hard at work, establishing shops for their trades, finding wells for water (or drawing upon the enormous sixty-foot-deep Collect Pond, just north of today's Chambers Street), building a fort (with slave labor) and a meeting hall and laying out basic streets on the Dutch model. The Dutch Reformed Church, a branch of Calvinism, also hoped to impose a religious conformity that would bind the various peoples together.

Still, there was cranky toleration of all religions except Roman Catholicism. In 1654, the first twenty-three Sephardic Jews arrived from Recife, Brazil, where Dutch rule had given way to that of the Portuguese, people dedicated to the tender mercies of the Inquisition. Those first Jewish arrivals faced hostility from the authoritarian zealot Peter Stuyvesant, a true believer in religious orthodoxy and an old-fashioned bigot. He was a successful governor from 1645 until the British took the colony at gunpoint in 1664. Stuyvesant wanted the Jews deported, but the Amsterdam directors of the West India Company ordered him to ease his opposition. Although some Jews returned to Amsterdam, a few stayed on in the tiny town at the tip of Manhattan, establishing a private synagogue in rooms on Mill Street, and adding their presence to the alloy.

From the start, communication was a challenge. Even the growing population of African slaves did not share a common language, so they fashioned an argot that would allow them to speak to each other while understanding the commands of their European overseers. In 1643, a visiting French Jesuit named Isaac Jogues (freshly liberated from captivity by the Mohawks) reported that eighteen languages were being spoken among the town's one thousand residents. This didn't please him. "The arrogance of Babel," Jogues wrote, "has done much harm to all men; the confusion of tongues has deprived them of great benefit."

That understandable desire to force a common language on the population would be a recurrent theme across all the years that followed. So would the struggle between the orthodox and the nonconformists, the religious true believers and the ordinary human sinners. Sin always had the edge. In spite of grim Sunday sermons, and Stuyvesant's periodic crackdowns, the colony was essentially a hard-drinking frontier town, which from the beginning established that there would always be a gap between what was said and what was done. The town, and the city that later rose from those first tentative

streets, was, above all, a port drawing to its shores the commerce of
the world, along with the seamen of many nations. Sailors then, as
they would for centuries to come, had an affection for drinking,
wenching and carousing. They were a shifting, transient, sometimes
disorderly presence in the town, but they were essential to its existence. Seeing them, and living with their own neighbors, every resident of the town knew that the world was full of people who were not
like them.

Even then, a template was being cut that would survive to the
present day.

*　　*　　*

The most essential part of that template was the enduring gift of the
Dutch to the city that became New York: tolerance.

This was not the result of wooly-headed Dutch idealism. Their
tolerance came from their intelligence and their clear-eyed common
sense. The age of sail had opened the world to European traders, and
if the Dutch were to succeed, they must treat others with respect.
This process had also begun where it must begin: at home. The
Netherlands in the seventeenth century was the most tolerant country
in Western Europe. It attracted, even welcomed, exiles and refugees
from those countries where creeds and orthodoxy were piling up the
corpses. Among those welcomed were Jews, freed from the enclosing
walls of ghettos and able to go as far as their talents would take them,
which was very far indeed. Unlike the Spaniards and the competing
English, the leaders of the Netherlands did not insist on hypocritical
false conversions to the prevailing religious creed. They had a super-
seding interest: the making of money.

Those values were part of the policy that itself migrated to the
tiny outpost in the northeast of North America. In New Amsterdam,
tolerance was even more important because there were so few people,
and they were so diverse. If the endless bloody religious quarrels of
Europe were exported to New Amsterdam, there would be violence
and chaos—and a failed colony.

As I read the history, it seems clear that the secret of the colony's success was a good healthy dollop of hypocrisy, another element of the Dutch template that has endured to the present day. There was official policy, and then there were private deals. Lip service was paid to sobriety, thrift, responsibility, good citizenship and religious orthodoxy; but over drinks, at tables lit by candles, men could fashion scenarios driven by greed and avarice. I'm reminded of what the Peruvian novelist Mario Vargas Llosa once said about the old authoritarian government of Mexico: it was a perfect dictatorship, humanized by corruption.

The essential Dutch template was refined by the British after they renamed their new colony New York. More and more immigrants arrived, but not all were English. Some were Irish, others Scotch. In the eighteenth century, the British king was himself a German, George I from the House of Hanover, so it was no surprise that thousands of colonists came from Germany. There were also substantial numbers of French Huguenots among the immigrants, in flight from religious persecution on the European continent; the French contribution to building New York is now largely forgotten, but it endures in certain place names, such as Delancey Street, or distant New Rochelle. The British, however, were also practical. They soon realized that Dutch toleration was the only way to keep their new property functioning.

There were, of course, limits. Tight restrictions were placed on the growing African population, particularly after an aborted slave revolt in 1712. The Dutch had evolved a policy of partial manumission, offering a certain consolation to the Africans; the British didn't extend the policy, and even partially revoked it. More and more slaves were brought to the New World by the British, most bound for the Caribbean colonies or the fields of the American South. But many were sold to locals in the slave market at the East River end of Wall Street, to be used as domestic servants, craftsmen, mechanics. They were barred from schools. For a long time, they were even barred from training to become Christians, for, after all, if they were Christians, then they must have souls, and if they had souls, how could they be enslaved? Many learned English anyway, and a few learned to read and write. Their numbers grew. At one point in the 1740s, 25 percent of the population of New York was made up of Africans and their American children. This made many whites nervous, including the British governors.

British toleration did not extend to Catholics either. No Catholic church would be built in New York until after the American Revolution. Most Irish immigrants to New York in the time of the British were Ulster Protestants (many of them Presbyterians, subject to other forms of discrimination). But Irish Catholics came too, in smaller numbers, and often disguised themselves with new identities—with public mask—in the same way that Jews in Europe preserved their lives by becoming *conversos*. They often held secret masses, but at great risk because Catholic priests were subject to execution.

But the mask, the secret identity, also became part of the New York template. It, too, has survived to the present day. For centuries, men and women have arrived in the city to reinvent themselves. A small number were criminals, on the lam from the police of various countries. Others had deserted wives and families and intolerable debts. Some were adventurers, lured by the promise of great fortune, or longing for personal accomplishment that did not depend upon family connections or the private pacts of the old country. In the best sense, they were all involved in an existential project, the fresh invention of themselves. The first thing to be fashioned was the mask.

Still others were political exiles, attracted by the political freedoms of New York. These included men and women who had seen revolutions fail at home, including the Irish rebels (both Catholic and Protestant) of 1798 and many Germans after 1848. But other exiles moved in among us: French in flight from the revolution in Haiti, Mexicans and other Latin Americans, Russians, Hungarians, Greeks opposed to the Ottoman Empire. The most famous were the Italian Giuseppe Garibaldi and the Cuban José Martí. But there were many others, fighting tyranny in the old country from the safe harbor of New York. Most would live and die in New York.

*   *   *

I'm not neutral on this subject. Like so many millions of Americans, I'm a child of immigrants. My father, Billy Hamill, arrived from Belfast, Northern Ireland, in 1923, after the killing of Irish rebel leader Michael Collins seemed to send a signal of doom for the cause of a united Ireland, free from British rule. He had only an eighth-grade education. But in New York, nobody asked him his religion before he was hired to work. In New York, he was free at last of the Irish seventeenth century.

My mother arrived from Belfast in 1929—with perfect Irish timing, on the day of the stock market crash. She too was Catholic. But she had somehow managed to graduate from high school, a rare feat for a Belfast woman, even more rare for a Catholic. Her father had died in Brooklyn in 1916, in an accident on the waterfront (he was an engineer who went to sea). Back in Ireland with her mother and brother, vague images of New York and its gleaming towers appeared in her dreams (as she would tell me later). When her mother died, she came to America, aged nineteen.

They both did what so many millions of others did do after passing through the halls of Ellis Island: they worked. My father found employment for a while at Todd's Shipyards, alongside two of his brothers. He made a few runs to Canada to help transport bootlegged whiskey. He played soccer on weekends in the immigrant leagues, against Spanish, German, Jewish teams (the best was called House of David), and some of his friends would tell me years later that he seemed a man with magical legs. Then, in 1927, he was viciously kicked in a game against a German team. His left leg was broken into several pieces, the bone jutting through skin. The ruined leg was lashed with slats from the fence of the playing field and he was taken to Kings County Hospital. There were few doctors on duty, and no penicillin, and by the next morning gangrene had set in. They amputated his leg above the knee.

My mother did not meet him until years later, at a dance for Irish immigrants in a hall below Union Square. She had worked at first as a domestic for a rich family who had paid her fare from Ireland. They were decent people and fond of her (years later, they sent us the complete works of Mark Twain as a Christmas gift, our personal share in the true wealth of America). She married my father during the Depression, when he was working as a clerk at a now-vanished grocery chain called Roulston's. As the family grew (there would be seven of us, of which I'm the oldest) she returned to part-time work as a nurse's aide in a hospital, a cashier in the movie houses of the RKO chain, later as a clerk at the Metropolitan Life Insurance Company. She loved New York, its splendid variety of races and religions, its tolerance, the way, sooner or later, it kept its promises. The most important promise was a simple one: here everything is possible, if only you work.

But work was not always a splendid enterprise. All my life I've carried with me a summer night in 1948, when I was thirteen. My night dreams then were an innocent amalgam of Jackie Robinson, Bomba the Jungle Boy, the mysteries of girls on the sands of Coney Island. But on that special night, I was woken by the sound of my father weeping in the dark.

He was a room away from me and my bed on the couch of our railroad flat. His voice was a simple *Oooh, ooh, o!* Breathless. Oh. Unwilled. Oooh. I started to get up, but then heard my mother moving in the dark. *It's all right, Billy,* she whispered. *Wait a wee minute. . . .* And I knew what had happened. My father worked across the street in the factory of the Globe Lighting Company, where he helped wire fluorescent lights. He stood all day in all seasons on a poured concrete floor, the stump of his ruined leg jammed into an artificial limb. In the scalding August heat wave that year, there was no air conditioning. And the stump had blistered. Those involuntary sobs were not expressions of self-pity. They were sounds of sheer human pain.

My mother hurried off. I saw the light go on in the kitchen. I heard the refrigerator door open, ice cubes clunking, and then she came back with ice wrapped in cloth, and she began to cool that blistered stump. *It's all right, Billy, don't worry, it's all right.* After a while, his sobs ended. In the morning he got up and went to work.

At thirteen, I could not articulate what I thought, but the image never went away. As I grew older, I knew that somehow I must honor that pain. And because this was America, because it was New York, the only true way to honor it was through work. That year, a giddy postwar optimism was flooding through all of us, including our parents. The Depression and the war were over, and we believed we could become anything. We could play left field for the Dodgers, or train to be doctors or, with any luck at all, find jobs as sports writers. Everything seemed possible. This was America. This was New York. No matter what I would do as a grown-up, I must work hard. And I came to realize that I surely was not the only son of immigrants who heard parents weeping in the dark. It was part of the making of the alloy. Tonight, from Bakersfield to the Bronx, there must be people like my mother and father, people whispering the language of pain and consolation. Becoming Americans—for their American children. Shaped by buried templates.

*   *   *

Today, those templates still exist, the Dutch and English templates, the African, Irish, Jewish, German templates, although the faces and languages are new. They remind me of sights on certain streets in downtown Manhattan where the asphalt wears away after a hard winter and you can see the cobblestones underneath, reminders of the city of horses, the city of Whitman, Poe and Melville, the city of all those immigrants whose names we do not know.

The 2000 census tells us that more than 46 percent of New Yorkers speak a language other than English at home. That other, familial language is usually Spanish (spoken by 53 percent), but as the city adjusts to the greatest wave of immigrants in a century, the other language can also be (among an estimated 160 separate tongues) Russian, Chinese, Korean, Bengali, French Creole, Arabic and various languages from Africa and the Pacific Islands. If he could arrive again in the city, Isaac Jogues would be appalled, but not surprised.

This Babel is, of course, a challenge to the school system, and to the city itself, but it has gone surprisingly well. I'm convinced that the reason for the relative ease of adjustment is the old template. New

Yorkers have been here before. Most of us are products of the tradition. After the British conquest of the Dutch town, Dutch and English stood largely at arm's length. Then the young among them began
to marry each other. The same was true of the Jews, Italians and Irish
of my own childhood. The process has never been without its early violence, its bigotries, its endless stupidities.

But the New York alloy had been formed long ago, and almost all
new arrivals become part of it. There are various ways in which this
process works, or has worked in the past. Humor is essential; the
oversensitive orthodoxies of political correctness have deprived us of
one escape mechanism from the uncertainties of identity. Nobody
likes to be labeled with a stereotype. Labels are often cruel. They are
too often driven by stupidity. But laughter can also help disperse the
stereotype because the racial or ethnic straw figure is almost never
confirmed by the evidence of daily living.

The process of becoming part of the alloy has its own long-famil-
iar patterns. Usually, newcomers establish a presence through food.
They long for the food of the old country, and soon someone opens a
small place to revive it for other newcomers. The food is discovered by
those already here and added to the city's astonishing menu. Today, on
the same New York street, you can find Thai noodles, blini, lasagna
and quesadillas. The alloy.

After food, music. In 1841, Charles Dickens visited a dive in the
Five Points, then the most notorious slum in the United States. There
he saw two young men perform. One was an Irish-American named
John Diamond. The other was an African-American named Master
Juba. The music behind them was a combination of Irish instruments
and African rhythm structures. One would dance, and then be answered by the other. Together they created tap dancing. Together they
invented a form that was uniquely American, but initially possible
only in the mixed society of New York. From them flowed Fred As-
taire and Gregory Hines, and ten thousand others. The alloy.

When I was a young man in the 1950s, I often found my way to a
marvelous place called the Palladium, on Broadway just north of
Times Square. There I would listen to the fabulous bands of Tito

Puente, Machito and Tito Rodriguez, who played extraordinary dance music for an audience that was largely Puerto Rican. The rhythms came from the Caribbean: mambo, cha cha, merengue, charanga. The dancers, male and female, were Saturday night geniuses. But there was something else going on in those years too.

A few blocks down from the Palladium lay Birdland, named for the ingenious bebop musician Charlie Parker, which featured jazz of great invention, complexity and musical surprise. During the breaks between sets at Birdland, the jazz musicians, including the splendid Dizzy Gillespie, began to wander up to the Palladium to listen to the Latin music and try to understand its fresh rhythms. They began to sit in with the foreign musicians. And something new happened: Caribbean rhythms were annealed to American harmonics. That music endures to this day. The alloy.

The process continues. Today, when I descend into the station of the N and R subway trains at Canal Street, there's a middle-aged Chinese musician playing a stringed instrument for all of us who assemble near him. The music is often melancholy, full of longing for places left behind. Almost certainly I hear this music in ways that a Chinese immigrant would not. To me, it's a unique form of the blues. But I am sure that some of those young New Yorkers I see each morning, some carrying musical instruments to their classes at Julliard or elsewhere, are listening too, and absorbing it—and will soon turn it into something new and American.

After food and music, there's language. We still use words given to us by the Dutch: stoop, boss, cruller, cookie. Other words come from the mid-nineteenth-century Irish who spoke only the Irish language (sometimes called Gaelic Irish): saps and suckers, shills and dudes, and dozens of others. When I was a boy, the second language of New York was Yiddish, and we learned such words as klutz and chutzpah, shnorrer and mishegas, and tried to define the difference between a shlemiel and shlemozzel. But one Yiddish word is a permanent part of the language of New York, and one of my favorite examples of it appeared not long ago in a Spanish-language newspaper. A headline read: SERRANO DICE: YO NO SOY UN SCHMUCK.

For centuries, of course, New York's language (and that of the larger United States) has been enriched by African-Americans, and that process continues. And now Spanish is creating its own graftings, in both directions, with Spanish acquiring new words based on English. In this alloy, only fools will insist on purity.

Prophecy is also a habit of fools, but it is clear that nothing seems to be changing the basic nature of the city. Not fifty years of television, not the internet, not the arrivals of new immigrants. The mixture goes on, at once traditional and unpredictable. Almost certainly there will be some conflict, some attempts by demagogues to resist the process itself, to say that today's immigrants are different from the old immigrants. But I suspect there will be few takers. New Yorkers are too tough for such porous arguments, too skeptical and, above all, too busy.

On September 12, 2001, they showed all those qualities by refusing to collapse or retreat or give up. They did what they've always done: they went to work. Or to school. Or to the streets where their friends live, and their children play, and where every sin is forgiven except self-pity. Look: they are working so hard. Listen: a few are weeping in the dark. We must embrace them. We must give them welcome and work.

They are us.

PART FIVE

ECONOMICS AND POLITICS

14

TOWARD A POST-ETHNIC ECONOMY

by Joel Kotkin

B ACK IN 2000, when Dean Bass and his investors were putting together $7 million to launch their Royal Oaks Bank, they felt they
could ride on the back of a booming Houston economy. With former
oilmen about to take over the White House, energy prices high and
firms like Enron on a hiring binge, they looked forward to entering a
strong market with powerful demand for business loans.

Yet Bass and his colleagues—most of them self-described "good
old boys"—soon found that their fortunes lay, not with their old bud-
dies from the oil and gas industry, but with Houston's burgeoning
immigrant business communities. Even when the regional economy
began to weaken, the bank continued to grow, in large part because
immigrant entrepreneurs needed cash to expand their businesses. By
2002, nearly one out of four customers at Royal Oaks came from
Houston's immigrant community, something Bass and his fellow
founders never expected. "The immigrant economy has been a lot less
impacted by the energy downturn," suggested Bass, who has nearly
three decades of experience in banking, both as a regulator and an executive. "When you look at our customers and our growth, much of it
comes from immigrants."

The last time energy prices crashed and devastated much of the Houston economy, in the early 1980s, the city did not have this immigrant-led boom to cushion the blow. But that was a very different Houston than the one in which Dean Bass survived a downturn. During the 1990s, the city experienced a nearly 84 percent increase in foreign-born residents, the third highest among all metropolitan areas in the United States.

In Houston and across the country, immigrants are writing a new chapter in the classic story of how Americans are made by engaging in the culture of capitalism. Today, as in the last great wave of immigration a century ago, newcomers often find their place first in trade and commerce, then later enter the mainstream in a full cultural, political and social sense. But while business continues to be the primary engine of immigrant integration, the way newcomers do business is changing. The traditional model of a separate "immigrant" economy, tethered to small markets in highly congested ethnic enclaves, is increasingly outdated. It is being replaced by a new "post-ethnic" model in which immigrant- and native-owned businesses are closely intertwined.

The phrase "ethnic economies" often conjures up images of sweatshops in anonymous Chinatowns, Latino gardeners or drywallers working out of the barrios of the Southwest, or, further back, Jewish tailors, Greek restaurateurs, Italian grocers and Irish barmen. Each ethnic group occupied its own economic niche and lived in a segregated urban neighborhood. But this notion, although far from extinct, reflects the past, not the future. Increasingly, most immigrants—Latinos, Asians and Middle Easterners— live not in urban ethnic pockets but in sprawling suburban expanses that are polyglot, if not overwhelmingly native-born, in population. The typical mini-mall in Sugarland, Texas, or the San Fernando Valley, California, carries not one ethnic tradition but many: a Thai-Chinese restaurant next to a Vietnamese nail parlor, a Mexican supermarket and a 7-11 run by a newcomer from the Middle East or India.

In Houston, for example, the economy is increasingly driven by entrepreneurs like Niranjan "Nick" Patel, who develops properties mainly for immigrant operators of fast-food restaurants, convenience stores, motels and gas stations. "People come here to get an education, then hope to start a little business, and then make it grow more," the forty-nine-year-old Indian-born Patel explained. "They want to settle down in suburbia and become Americans." In Houston today, they come from a wide range of countries—including India, Pakistan, Vietnam, Palestine and Nigeria—and they operate roughly 60 percent of the businesses in Patel's more than thirty suburban properties. As Houston's example shows, the critical impact of immigration today lies not only in repopulating cities and rebuilding their economies but in creating new patterns of economic diversity—and economic assimilation.

THE CLASSIC MODEL OF ETHNIC INTEGRATION

For two hundred years, immigrants have played a critical economic role in virtually every emerging city economy, from the Northeast to the Far West. But historically, each national group confined its energies to a particular narrowly defined sector of the economy.

In the early nineteenth century, British immigrants helped transplant the Industrial Revolution to America. A British-born Quaker, Samuel Slater, brought with him the technology for the construction of the nation's first textile mill, in Pawtucket, Rhode Island, and ultimately he controlled or held a strong financial interest in ten mills, employing over one thousand people across New England. German mechanics and engineers, arriving mostly in the 1840s and 1850s, played a preeminent role in developing the first foundries and factories across the upper Midwest. Chinese and Japanese farmers, operating in a climate of hostility, were the first to develop the vegetable fields and fruit orchards that would make California the world's leading grower of premium crops.

Similarly, Jews brought with them the skills that would launch the New York garment industry. The sudden rise of Manhattan as a global garment capital was not simply a matter of greater availability of raw materials, or superior port facilities, or the simple luck of being in the right place at the right time. Rather, it was an intersection of immigrant Jewish culture and economic opportunity. Some academics, notes African-American sociologist Thomas Sowell, have written that "the Jews were fortunate to arrive just as the garment industry was about to develop. I could not help but think that Hank Aaron was similarly fortunate—that he often came to bat when a home run was about to be hit."

Other immigrant groups also became associated with specific economic niches. Beer making followed the immigration from Bohemia and Germany. The early merchant banking establishment included a large number of Jews from Germany and France. In retail, the early twentieth century saw the emergence of Italians as greengrocers, Greeks as café operators, Chinese as laundromat owners.

But if first-generation immigrants concentrated in ethnic niches, their children, over the ensuing decades, gradually entered the American mainstream. As early as the 1920s, the children of Jewish *shmatte* entrepreneurs, Italian greengrocers and Irish bartenders tended to move into the professions. By the late 1970s, even top executive positions at Fortune 500 companies, once the preserve of the old WASP elite, were increasingly falling to the descendants of Irish, Jewish, Italian and other immigrants. Eventually, many of the turn-of-the-century immigrant groups not only overcame prejudice but, on average, achieved higher economic and educational status than the mainstream population.

More important, ultimately they *became* the mainstream population, usually losing facility with native languages and customs. Over the past half-century, newspapers in German, Norwegian and Japanese disappeared as the second and third generations became progressively more integrated into mainstream society. At the same time, entire industries that had been ethnic enclaves—garment manufacturing, the movie business, twenty-four-hour diners—are no longer restricted to particular ethnic groups or, in some cases, have seen one ethnic group replaced by another.

THE MESTIZOIZATION OF SUBURBIA

Today, business is still a great force for integration into American society, but the primary scene of action is no longer the urban core. Over the last three decades, newcomers have followed native-born Americans from the inner cities to the suburbs, and for the same reasons: they want to better their lives and those of their families, and because the suburbs are where the most economic opportunity lies.

Between 1970 and 1990, central cities lost 1.3 million two-parent families to the suburbs, and in the process America stopped being a nation of traditional cities with dense urban centers. In 1950, only 23 percent of Americans lived in suburbs; today more than 50 percent do. And today, unlike in the 1950s, the suburbs are hardly lily white. Indeed, nearly 51 percent of Asians, 43 percent of Latinos and 32 percent of African-Americans live in neighborhoods beyond the inner city. The tendency towards greater diversity in the "midopolitan" suburbs—older suburbs, situated in between the urban core and expanding outlying areas—can be seen across the country. The older suburbs immediately around Denver, for example, experienced a 50 percent increase in their Latino population during the 1990s.

The key to the midopolitan melting pot lies in the changing needs of immigrants. In contrast to the early twentieth century, when proximity to inner-city services and infrastructure was critical, many of today's newcomers are integrated into an auto-oriented society. Their journey into the mainstream stops only briefly, if at all, in the inner cities. Their immediate destination after arrival is as likely to be the San Gabriel Valley of Los Angeles as Chinatown or the East L.A. barrios; New Jersey suburb Fort Lee as Manhattan.

Similar changes are taking place in the San Fernando Valley, the northwestern region of Los Angeles. As late as the 1960s, some nine out of ten Valley residents were white. By 1980, however, as much as one-quarter of the population was a racial or ethnic minority. By 1998, according to Los Angeles County estimates, fewer than half of the area's residents were white, while Latinos accounted for 39.1 percent and Asians 9.1 percent of the population. Today the Valley's economy reflects this diversity. Farsi, Hebrew and Hindi signs mingle in the ubiquitous strip-malls.

Even less affluent immigrants, such as those from Mexico and Central America, increasingly settle and start businesses in what have historically been considered suburbs. Enrique Gonzalez, who grew up in rural Santa Isabel, Mexico, started working at age four and quit school when he was seven. In the early 1960s, at the age of fourteen, he immigrated to America. By 1964, he had found a job working in the San Fernando Valley community of Sherman Oaks, a predominantly Anglo, middle-class area. The Valley was booming then, and there were plenty of jobs for unskilled workers like Gonzalez. But soon, the region became heavily Latino. Gonzalez began selling *menudo,* a Mexican tripe soup, to local customers. By the late 1990s, he owned sixteen stores, most of them in the Valley. His biggest challenge now, he noted, is not a lack of customers but other chains— some owned by Latinos or Mexico-based conglomerates—competing for immigrant business.

Similarly dramatic changes have taken place outside California. Many Asian immigrants in the New York area tend to settle in suburbs such as Bridgewater or Palisades Park in New Jersey. This marks a sharp contrast to the immediate postwar era, when New York's suburbs, like their high-tech workforces, remained highly segregated. Between 1950 and 1970, a period of intense development in the New York area, 95 percent of suburbanites were white. "The people you want for neighbors are here," promised one ad for a Long Island development.

Four decades later, that has changed. In established Long Island communities such as Hempstead, the shopping districts trace their lineage to the building boom following World War II. Many such areas suffered major declines in the 1970s and 1980s, victims of competition from new shopping centers, an aging population and the continued push of affluent whites further to the periphery. Yet by the early twenty-first century, Hempstead had found new customers—and entrepreneurs—among the rising population of immigrants, many from Central America. "When we opened ten years ago, we were practically the only one," recalled Robert Rivas at his crowded Main Street restaurant, Antijitos Salvadorenos. "There wasn't much going on. Now people are opening stores around here."

Today, downtown Hempstead, with its Latino record stores, dance clubs, travel agencies and ethnic eateries, may not look like a revival of the glory days of the 1940s and 1950s, when the area was the upscale retail jewel of the burgeoning, and virtually all-white, suburbs of central Nassau County. Yet the Latino-led surge represents a marked improvement over the decline of the 1970s and 1980s. Latinos, Salvadorans in particular, are "very entrepreneurial and opening lots of small businesses," said Glen Spiritus, Commissioner for Community Development for the Village of Hempstead. "The village is changing. We will never be what we were—the shopping center for all Long Island—but we're better." Spiritus credits Latinos, whose numbers in Long Island are estimated at roughly two hundred thousand, and other immigrants for helping reduce the downtown retail vacancy rate from nearly 70 percent in the early 1990s to around 10 percent today.

Suburbanization is even more pronounced among Asians and Middle Easterners. The most heavily Asian counties in the nation are such formerly traditional suburbs as Queens County in New York, Santa Clara and San Mateo Counties in northern California, and Orange County south of Los Angeles. Even traditionally lily white Detroit suburban counties, such as Oakland and Macomb, or the outer suburbs of Baltimore, have experienced rapid growth in immigration, much more so than the traditional inner city.

Today these areas have become as ethnically distinctive as the inner cities themselves. Coral Gables, outside Miami, has become an ethnic and global business center, with the Latin American division headquarters of over fifty multinationals. Immigrants have also taken a leading role in the economy in places such as Orange County, long reviled as the home of ethnocentric, right-wing agitation. By 2001, over a quarter of the county's residents were foreign-born. The county seat, Santa Ana, with its burgeoning working-class shopping district, was one of the nation's most heavily Latino communities, while West-minster, another working-class enclave, was home to "Little Saigon," the nation's largest Vietnamese shopping area. At the same time, other immigrants are making it to the top tier of Orange County soci-ety. Six of its twenty wealthiest people were raised abroad, three in Taiwan and one each in Iran, Croatia and the former Soviet Union.

THE SOUTH GOES MULTIETHNIC

This change in the suburban fabric—and in the geography of immi-gration—is particularly marked in the southern United States. More than 1.3 million immigrants moved to the South between 1990 and 1998. For the first time in modern history, the region has become an incubator of immigrant culture. And in the South, as elsewhere, busi-ness is the cutting edge of integration. As a fast-growing and still evolving economy, the South requires newcomers to develop the kind of expertise that the region has traditionally lacked. In trade, technol-ogy, small business and, increasingly, banking, it is often immigrants who lead the development of the new Southern economy.

Even more than in the rest of the country, immigration to the South has been largely suburban. Over the last two decades, metro-politan areas such as Atlanta have experienced some of the most rapid growth in immigration in the country. But in the absence of existing Asian or Latino enclaves, most new immigrants have clustered in sub-urban areas instead of central cities. In Atlanta, for example, much of the immigrant growth takes place in the midopolitan suburbs of DeKalb County and the newer suburbs of Gwinnet County.

The movement to the South of large populations that are neither black nor white represents an important turning point, not only for the region but for the nation as a whole. These immigrants and their children will surely alter the long-standing cultural norms of the

South. Traditionally the epicenter of biracial social conflict, the region may soon be guiding America towards a new understanding of ethnicity.

North Carolina, long the leader in the modernization of the old Confederacy, is leading this transformation. Drawn by its buoyant economy, new immigrants, largely from Central America and Mexico, have poured into the state, drastically changing its established racial character and adding to its economic vitality. Since the mid-1990s, immigration to North Carolina has risen by 73 percent, the largest increase in the nation. Three of the top four regions in the country for fastest increase in Latino immigration are in the state, and the Charlotte area has seen a 600 percent increase in Hispanic immigration. Overall, the Latino market in North Carolina is now estimated at nearly $3 billion annually.

Of course, in absolute terms—compared to California, Texas, Florida and New York—North Carolina's Hispanic population remains modest. It is barely 5 percent of the total population, according to the 2000 census, while African-Americans account for over 20 percent. Yet the economic, social and political implications of this immigration are profound, and still in their early stages. Over the past decade in North Carolina, Hispanics under the age of eighteen actually grew more in absolute numbers than African-Americans. In some districts, particularly in Charlotte, Latinos now account for over 30 percent of all schoolchildren.

Similar patterns are emerging in many other Southern cities, including Atlanta, Houston and Nashville, to the point that parts of the South are beginning to look more and more like traditional gateway cities, such as Los Angeles. The new immigration patterns have forced some demographers, such as the University of Michigan's William Frey, to reassess their 1990s analysis of America's changing racial profile. Formerly Frey saw America as divided between immigrant "magnets," such as Los Angeles and New York, and areas like Las Vegas and North Carolina that were primarily luring domestic migrants.

But no longer. New immigration to the South and the Rocky Mountain states reflects the labor needs of these growing regional economies. Latinos now dominate the blue-collar workforce of many manufacturing industries as companies recruit Spanish-speaking workers from traditional immigrant hubs in South Texas and Southern California, often using Spanish-language media. Mexican workers now predominate in the carpet-making towns of Georgia, the poultry-processing centers in Arkansas and the textile mills of North Carolina. At the same time, Latino immigrants come to perform service work in areas where there is a growing white middle-class population, allowing these regions to provide the kind of amenities many upwardly mobile workers expect.

Ultimately, these changes will have a profound impact on lifestyle, commerce and politics in the South. On the negative side, some California-style ethnic conflict will surely spread to parts of the country where it has not existed in the past. Yet in the long run, the shift will be good for the South's century-old movement towards parity with the rest of America. The critical question is how the mainstream will react to the immigrant flow. Business success may be the opening wedge for integration, but fuller political, cultural and social integration cannot lag too far behind, or the region could lose its appeal to the immigrant entrepreneur. This will require action on the part of local authorities: English-language instruction, the encouragement of ethnic entrepreneurship, a greater awareness of cultural diversity. With its racial history, the South, in particular, needs to make the newcomers feel comfortable about choosing to move there. "It's not about political correctness for us to welcome these people," says James Johnson, a prominent African-American scholar at the Kenan Institute in Chapel Hill. "It's enlightened self-interest."

THE ETHNICIZATION OF HIGH-TECH

As immigrants move to the suburbs and to booming regions like the South, they are also beginning to move outside traditional ethnic business niches. Nowhere is this more true than in the technology economy. In the San Gabriel Valley, the largest center of Chinese immigrants in the nation, Asian-American entrepreneurs have helped spawn over twelve hundred computer firms, employing over 5,000 people and generating sales well above $3.1 billion. Similar clusters of immigrant-run electronics businesses can be found in midopolitan parts of Dallas and Houston. And Asian immigrants have also played a critical role in the burgeoning technology community around Washington, D.C., particularly in fast-growing counties such as Fairfax and Montgomery, where as many as one out of five migrants come from overseas.

The most important of these high-tech hubs is Silicon Valley itself. Eighty percent white until the 1980s, Santa Clara County is now among the most diverse counties in the nation. Immigrants and their children make up 60 percent of the population, three times the national average, and they are a powerful new element in Silicon Valley's high-tech economy. Most notable has been the contribution of Asian-American entrepreneurs. Asians started roughly 27 percent of all the Valley's new enterprises between 1991 and 1996, twice their share in the 1980s.

This marks a major change from when David Lam first came to Santa Clara in the 1970s, without any capital to invest, but with a doctorate in chemical engineering from MIT and a restless energy natural to someone who had come to the United States by way of China, Vietnam, Hong Kong and Canada. At the time, he recalls, most Asian newcomers to the Valley were seen as little more than high-tech "tools," workers with good attitudes and skills but little entrepreneurial fire. "In those days," recalls the soft-spoken Lam, "even the smartest [venture capitalists] had these stereotypes about what was a good CEO—what looked good on Wall Street—and I didn't have it. They didn't see Asian-Americans as people capable of running a sophisticated business."

Yet increasingly, as Lam suggests, Asians and other immigrants are not content with serving as mere "tools" for those who fit the approved WASP model. By 1996, according to a survey by the Public Policy Institute of California, Indian and Chinese executives ran 1,786 Silicon Valley companies worth $12.5 billion. These include major firms such as Solectron, Sybase and a billion-dollar semiconductor equipment firm with the name of Lam Research.

With these developments, believes David Lam, perceptions about immigrants have changed markedly. "In the 1990s you look at the Silicon Valley, it's become commonly accepted to have immigrants—Asian or not—who might still not fit the traditional stereotypes of a CEO to be seen as leaders and creative people," he suggests. "It's become a natural part of the business environment."

POST-ETHNIC AMERICA

Though economic integration is already taking place, the social integration of new Americans into suburbs and regions like the South will not come easily. Reaction against the newcomers, although somewhat less pronounced than during the early 1990s, remains strong. Roughly 42 percent of North Carolinians, for example, had "negative attitudes" towards Hispanic immigrants in a 1996 poll, and other surveys show similar findings in the San Fernando Valley and Houston. Ambivalence—excitement about immigrants' positive impact on the local culture and economy, but also fear that the newcomers will take jobs and dilute the local culture—runs deep among both white and black native-born residents in all three places.

Yet in the long run, the benefits of economic integration, for immigrants and natives alike, will surely spur social integration. In a capitalist system, money, markets and economic results inevitably trump prejudice. As newcomers move beyond ethnic niches and enclaves, their interaction with the native-born population will intensify. Immigrants will stimulate local demand, increasing profits for mainstream businesses. And when international and mainstream domestic demand is slack, many businesses—from banks and real estate firms to retailers—will find that the immigrant market continues to grow, thanks to a steady stream of energetic newcomers and their higher-than-average birth rates.

Already, immigrant-dominated groups are growing far faster than native-born Americans. In the 1990s, the Latino and Asian consumer market expanded nearly twice as rapidly as the general population, according to a recent University of Georgia study. And as the bankers at Royal Oaks discovered, these communities provide a welcome countercyclical force when local industries are suffering, whether it is high-tech in California, energy in Texas or financial services in New York.

Mainstream financial institutions are particularly well positioned to benefit from the immigrant influx. Naturalized U.S. citizens have a high propensity—above the national average—for home ownership, and in the coming decade they and their children will represent a key growth market. Indeed, during the late 1990s, 1 million Hispanics became homeowners, half of them people born outside the United States. Today, of the ten most common surnames for new home buyers in California, seven are Latino—Garcia, Rodriguez, Hernandez, Lopez, Gonzalez, Martinez and Perez—and two, Kim and Lee, are Asian. "We're not seeing much of a recession in real estate here," notes Brian Paul, a spokesman for the San Fernando Valley Board of Realtors. "The immigrants are fueling growth here that contradicts most of the negative forces."

New immigrants also represent a key market for sellers of business services. By the late 1990s, the number of Asian businesses expanded more than four times the average rate, while new enterprises started at an even more dramatic pace. Increasingly, outreach to such groups will be driven less by social responsibility than by necessity—the imperatives of business growth.

At the same time, as businesses run by newcomers expand, they inevitably come into contact with the wider population. John Levan, whose family came to Houston in the early 1980s from Vietnam and who now runs a large fabric store in the city's multiethnic Midtown section, explains: "To grow, we have to sell to other kinds of people. We used to have only Vietnamese here, but now we have Anglos and Hispanic workers. Every day, we are more and more Americanized. Even at home the discussions are primarily in English. We're becoming educated and we carry a lot of American ideas."

Over time, as these firms spread geographically and expand into more diverse markets, they will create a "post-ethnic" economic environment. This new business culture will not be without ethnic specializations, but it will transcend traditional notions of ethnically determined niches or enclaves. And in the long run, business integration inevitably leads to other kinds of incorporation. Eventually, not only commerce but also neighborhoods and the American mainstream itself will become increasingly mixed.

Latinos, by far the largest immigrant ethnic group, will tend to shape this trend. As they move into increasingly integrated suburbs, they also tend to become more middle-class. In the 1990s, the number of Latino families with incomes from $75,000 to $100,000 grew more than twice as quickly as that segment of the Anglo population, and overwhelmingly they were at least as comfortable in English as in Spanish. Their numbers alone will make Latino cultural influence, already seen in such realms as food and music, more critical to the shaping of the youth culture and market.

But this new Latino-influenced market will be, first and foremost, an American one. Many marketers are already positioning themselves to take advantage of the "crossover" potential created by English-speaking, U.S.-born Latinos, who in the early twenty-first century account for one out of five babies born in the country. Intermarriage alone will mean that many of these new Latinos, perhaps more than one-third, will themselves be part something else. Like earlier waves of immigrants, they too will be subsumed into the larger American society, even as they influence it.

Business represents just the beginning of the process. Latino integration expresses itself in many ways, including high rates of participation in the armed services and, increasingly, politics and government. Culturally, the trend is for younger Latinos to become primarily English-speaking—two-thirds of third-generation Latino youths speak only English—and to consume the vast majority of their media and entertainment in English. This successful post-ethnic future can be seen in the Los Angeles suburb of Walnut, where Latinos, African-Americans, Asians and Anglos cooperate in school and public affairs. In this decidedly middle-class town—the average family income is $64,000 a year—all ethnic groups seem committed to building a truly interracial community.

A new America is being formed in suburbs like Walnut, where ethnicity plays a role but is not seen as exclusive or limiting. Older suburban neighborhoods and shopping streets, now transformed by the immigrant influence, provide focal points for entertainment, retail businesses and ethnic marketing, as well as for the development of new arts and design communities. Architect Ernie Vasquez, who is helping design a new arts-centered district in Santa Ana, observes: "People create stereotypes about these areas that they are heavy-duty Latino, but they are also areas that have broad appeal to younger people and artists. You have the opportunity in Santa Ana to create a place for all the people in Orange County, particularly the kids. The kids do not see white, black or brown on their own, and they need places where they can experience each other."

As this integration proceeds, individual immigrants will increasingly emerge as business and community leaders. This is already taking place in Houston and Southern California. In 2000, for example, both the chairman of the Los Angeles Chamber of Commerce, toy distributor Charles Woo, and the chairman of the fund-raising campaign for the United Way, banker Dominic Ng, were Hong Kong-born entrepreneurs who first rose to prominence in the aftermath of Southern California's early-1990s economic meltdown. "We are feeling comfortable about being leaders," declares Ng, the president of East West Bank, the third largest bank based in the Los Angeles area.

As such new leaders emerge, old stereotypes about ethnic businesses and immigrant communities will fall away. Following the time-honored pattern, immigrants are first integrating economically. Yet this is only a first step; today, as in the past, a more profound integration is sure to follow. By the middle of the twenty-first century, the American marketplace will be made up of many colors, but they will be increasingly blended. Culturally diverse and essentially post-ethnic, this new milieu will reflect a uniquely American way of doing business.

15

ECONOMIC ASSIMILATION: TROUBLE AHEAD

by George J. Borjas

O NE OF THE MOST IMPORTANT ASPECTS of assimilation is economic: the narrowing of what might be called the "opportunity gap" between immigrants and natives. Immigrants typically enter the United States with substantially lower skills than the native population and therefore face a significant disadvantage in economic opportunities. In the late 1990s, for example, a newly arrived worker earned about 34 percent less than the typical American-born worker. Over time, however, newcomers acquire skills, such as English language proficiency, that are valued by American employers and that allow them to approach parity with native-born workers. This is assimilation, but it isn't clear whether it is good for the country as a whole or whether our immigration laws should be designed to encourage it.

Most participants in the immigration debate assume that it is—that economic assimilation benefits both immigrants, who are clearly better off as their economic situation improves, and the native-born population. As a result, such thinkers argue, the United States should promote the assimilation process. But other scholars argue that in fact the opposite is true, questioning whether, from an economic perspective, the well-being of natives improves when immigrants assimilate rapidly.

In this more skeptical view, the economic gains from immigration arise from the complementarities that exist between immigrants and natives—in other words, society benefits precisely because the two kinds of workers have different skills and are productive at different kinds of work. It is often argued, for example, that the current immigration of large numbers of low-skill workers benefits the native population because immigrants take jobs that natives do not want. And, in fact, less-skilled immigrants make up large parts of the low-paid service, manufacturing and agricultural industries. In this view, as the skills of immigrants become more like those of natives, it becomes less and less likely that immigrants will want those undesirable jobs. Hence the presumed economic gains to the host country from immigration will eventually vanish. Only a continuous replenishment of the low-skill immigrant population can halt the decline of native economic well-being. In short, the sooner immigrants become like American workers—in other words, the faster the rate of economic assimilation—the sooner the gains accruing to native workers disappear.

I myself do not believe this argument is correct. The economic gains from complementarities between immigrant and native workers are quite small to begin with, probably less than $10 billion annually. On the other side of the equation, economic assimilation helps narrow the gap in opportunities between less skilled immigrants and natives, thus reducing the immigrants' drain on social services. The rapid assimilation of disadvantaged immigrants would also reduce the chances that this population, clustered in poor ethnic ghettoes, could become a new underclass, the potential source of a great deal of social conflict. A simple cost-benefit calculation suggests, therefore, that the United States enjoys a net gain when immigrants undergo economic assimilation. It follows that the country should encourage the immigrants to acquire the "human capital"— the job skills and cultural fluency—that increases their marketability in their newly adopted country.

What's more, there is an important link between economic assimilation and the cultural issues that are traditionally emphasized in the immigration debate. In order to experience economic assimilation, an immigrant must acquire skills that are valuable in the American labor market. The immigrant has to learn the English language, adopt the norms of the American workplace and eventually move to economically vibrant areas outside of ethnic enclaves. Each of these acts helps weaken the link between the immigrant's foreign past and his or her American future.

For many immigrants, this is a difficult trade-off. In order to achieve economic progress, they have to discard the habits and attitudes that reduce their chances for success in the American economy and adopt a lifestyle that increases those chances. In other words, economic assimilation and cultural assimilation go together: there will be more assimilation of one type when there is more of the other. And the important question facing the country is not whether we should encourage economic assimilation—obviously we should—but whether current social, political and economic conditions, some of them beyond our control, will help or hinder the assimilation of the huge influx of mostly non-European immigrants who have arrived in recent decades.

ECONOMIC ASSIMILATION WITHIN A GENERATION

The most important economic feature of immigration since 1965 has been a significant decline in the performance of successive immigrant waves. From one decade to the next, each new group of immigrants is less skilled than the one before. What's unknown is whether this economic disadvantage is permanent or will disappear as assimilation takes place.

Economists often measure the rate of economic assimilation by calculating how the wage gap between natives and immigrants narrows over time (see Figure 1). Consider the young men who arrived

Figure 1. Economic assimilation
(Immigrants arrived when they were 25–34 years old)

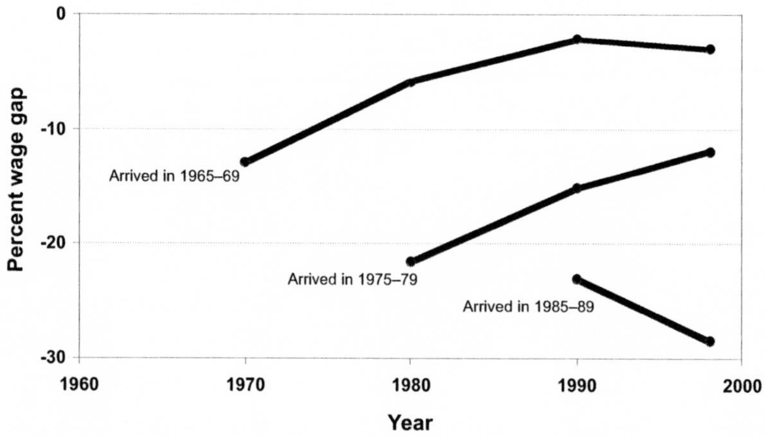

in the late 1960s, and were from twenty-five to thirty-four years old in 1970. At the time of entry, they earned 13 percent less than native workers of the same age. But this wage gap had narrowed to about 3 percentage points by 1998, when the immigrants were from fifty-three to sixty-two years old. Over a thirty-year period, the process of economic assimilation had significantly reduced their disadvantage, allowing them to almost "catch up" with the earnings of natives.

But the young immigrants who arrived after 1970 face a bleaker future, primarily because they started out at a greater disadvantage. Consider those who arrived in the late 1970s: by the late 1990s, twenty years after arrival, they were still earning 12 percent less than natives. The situation is even gloomier for those who arrived in the late 1980s. They started out with a 23 percent wage disadvantage, and their gap actually grew, rather than narrowed, during the 1990s. Based on historical trends, these newer immigrants should eventually narrow the gap by about 10 percentage points; but even so, they will still earn much less than natives throughout their working lives.

A great deal of evidence indicates that immigrants earn substantially more if they understand and speak English. Hispanic immigrants who speak English earn 17 percent more than those who do not, even after adjusting for differences in education and other socioeconomic characteristics between the two groups. Indeed, as much as half of the narrowing of the wage gap between immigrants and natives in the first twenty years after arrival can be attributed to gains from learning the English language.

The rate of economic assimilation also depends on whether immigrants reside in an ethnic enclave. Immigrants tend to cluster in a small number of areas. Thus in 1990 a third of the immigrant population lived in only three metropolitan regions (Los Angeles, New York and Miami), a geographic clustering that gave rise to the large ethnic communities that are a distinctive feature of many American cities. And while it is reasonable to suspect that this clustering influences the economic performance of immigrants, it is not clear how this influence works.

Some observers, particularly sociologists, argue that geographic clustering and the "warm embrace" of the enclave help immigrants escape the discrimination they would otherwise encounter in the labor market. But there is also a more pessimistic view. It is possible that the ethnic enclave creates incentives for immigrants *not* to leave and *not* to acquire the skills that might be useful in the larger national market, thus obstructing their move to better-paying jobs. The existing evidence suggests that immigrants who live in ethnic enclaves are less prosperous than those who move into the economic mainstream. Consider, for example, the typical newly arrived Mexican immigrant living in Los Angeles, where 11 percent of the population is of Mexican origin. If he had moved to New York instead, where only 0.1 percent of the population is Mexican, the wage gap between his earnings and those of a typical native worker would have narrowed by an additional 4 percentage points during his first ten years in the United States.

In sum, it seems that immigrants who choose to enter the economic mainstream—by becoming proficient in the English language and avoiding the warm embrace of the ethnic enclave—are likely to assimilate more rapidly and successfully to American economic life.

ETHNIC DIFFERENCES ACROSS GENERATIONS

This is not the only non-economic factor that affects economic assimilation. Among first-generation immigrants—those who actually made the trip from the old country to the new—different ethnic groups vary significantly in economic status. In 1998, for instance, immigrants from India earned 22 percent more than the typical native worker in the United States, while immigrants from Colombia earned 24 percent less. How much of these ethnic differences persist into the second and third generations?

To answer this crucial question, one can track the economic performance of the children and grandchildren of the European immigrants who arrived in the United States a century ago, a wave known as the First Great Migration. Nearly 24 million people entered the country between 1880 and 1924, and, not surprisingly, there were sizable ethnic differences in economic achievement among the ethnic groups that made up that migration. In 1910, for example, English immigrants earned 13 percent more than the typical American worker, but Portuguese immigrants earned 13 percent less and Mexican immigrants 23 percent less.

What happened over time? It turns out that about 60 percent of this wage differential persisted into the second generation, and a quarter of the difference remained even with the immigrants' grandchildren. In rough terms, the relative wage gaps between ethnic groups have a half-life of one generation, so that half of the "wage distance" between any two groups disappears between the first and second generations, and half of what remains in the second generation disappears between the second and the third.

This persistence of ethnic difference has important implications for the long-term consequences of today's immigrant influx, often called the Second Great Migration. In 1990, for instance, British immigrants earned 40 percent more than the typical native worker, while Mexican immigrants earned 40 percent less. If the historical pattern holds, a century from now the third-generation descendants of today's British immigrants will earn about 10 percent more than the typical native worker, the descendants of today's Mexican immigrants about 10 percent less.

The lesson from history is straightforward: ethnicity matters in economic life, and it seems to matter for a very long time. The metaphor of the melting pot does not apply to economic assimilation; a better metaphor would be the "simmering pot," where ethnic differences dissolve slowly—sometimes painfully so.

DO CURRENT CONDITIONS PROMOTE ECONOMIC ASSIMILATION?

The post-1965 resurgence of immigration has introduced many new ethnic groups into the American mosaic, with substantial differences in skills and economic outcomes. But it seems unlikely that these groups will achieve even the slow rate of assimilation of their predecessors a century ago. The assimilation of immigrant groups during the past century was influenced by unique historical events, and by social and economic circumstances, that cannot be replicated today.

First, the immigrants who entered the United States at the beginning of the twentieth century faced dramatically different economic conditions. That large influx of less-skilled workers coincided exactly with the emergence of the American manufacturing sector. Three-quarters of the workers at the Ford Motor Company in 1914 were foreign-born, and over half came from the less-developed areas of Southern and Eastern Europe. These manufacturing jobs provided stable and well-paying economic opportunities for many immigrants and their descendants.

But the American manufacturing sector has been in decline for many years now, and as a result the post-1965 immigrants, many of whom are again relatively unskilled, have far fewer well-paid job opportunities. During the 1980s and 1990s, the wages of low-skill workers fell to a historic low relative to high-skill workers, indicating that the demand for low-skill labor has declined dramatically in recent decades. This makes it unlikely that today's less-skilled immigrants will find the same opportunities for economic assimilation that their counterparts enjoyed a century ago.

Second, the expansion of the welfare state has radically altered the economic incentives facing disadvantaged groups and will likely slow the rate of economic assimilation. In 1998, immigrant households were much more likely than native households to receive public assistance in the form of cash payments, food stamps or Medicaid: twenty-two percent of immigrant households received benefits of some type, compared to 15 percent of native households. Welfare programs in the United States, though not generous by Western European standards, stack up pretty well when compared to the standard of living in many less-developed countries. In 1997, for example, the typical two-child welfare household in California received around $12,600 worth of assistance, while per-capita income in China and the Philippines was around $3,500.

These welfare opportunities may attract immigrants who otherwise would not have migrated to the United States; and the safety net may discourage immigrants who fail here from returning to their home countries. In short, the welfare state may change the immigrant population in ways that are not economically desirable. Little is known about the persistence of welfare dependency from one generation to the next. But the income provided by welfare removes an important incentive for immigrants to acquire job skills and cultural fluency, and could thus affect the rate of economic assimilation of the second generation and beyond.

Third, and contrary to popular perception, there is significantly less ethnic diversity among post-1965 immigrants than there was among early twentieth-century immigrants. In 1990, for example, Mexicans made up almost 30 percent of the immigrant population. In contrast, Germans and Russians—the two largest groups of the First Great Migration—accounted for only 15 and 12 percent of the influx. The relative lack of ethnic diversity in post-1965 immigration may greatly reduce the incentives for assimilation by allowing the largest ethnic groups to develop separate enclave economies with few links to the economic mainstream.

Fourth, the socioeconomic climate is much less encouraging of assimilation today than it was in the past. Reaction to the dislocations caused by the First Great Migration was relatively swift and severe. By 1924, the United States had adopted strict limitations on the number and type of foreigners who could enter the country. This policy shift, combined with the poor economic opportunities available during the Great Depression, effectively imposed a moratorium on immigration. In the 1920s, 4.1 million people entered the United States; in the 1930s, only half a million did. This provided a "breathing period" that may have fueled the assimilation process by cutting off the supply of new workers to ethnic enclaves and reducing the economic and social contacts between immigrants and their countries of origin.

Fifth, there is an important sense in which some of the large immigrant groups that arrived in the United States before 1924 were forcibly assimilated by the changes in social attitudes that occurred as a result of the two world wars. After all, many immigrants came from countries such as Germany and Italy, which were America's enemies in these wars. During World War I, Americans cracked down hard on the German language and culture in immigrant enclaves: by the summer of 1918, about half the states had restricted or eliminated German-language instruction in the schools. The total number of German-language publications declined from 554 in 1910 to 234 in 1920. The dominant American attitude towards these groups was expressed in General George Patton's colorful exhortation to his troops on the eve of the American invasion of Sicily on July 9, 1943: "When we land, we will meet German and Italian soldiers whom it is our honor and privilege to attack and destroy. Many of you have in your veins German and Italian blood, but remember that these ancestors of yours so loved freedom that they gave up home and country to cross the ocean in search of liberty. The ancestors of the people we shall kill lacked the courage to make such a sacrifice and continued as slaves." Surely such attitudes hastened the assimilation of Germans and Italians in the United States.

Finally, the ideological climate that encouraged assimilation and acculturation through much of the twentieth century has all but disappeared. The consensus summarized by the motto on the United States seal, *e pluribus unum,* no longer exists; it has been replaced by such multicultural sound bites as "Death by English." The effect of this shift in attitudes is compounded by government policies that encourage some immigrants to retain their ethnic and racial identities in order to qualify for public benefits. Affirmative action programs effectively require that a Cuban entrepreneur who wishes to apply for minority set-asides in government contracts refrain from joining the economic mainstream. Not only are these grievances not the issues that the original framers of affirmative action programs wished to redress but such programs may also exact a toll on immigrants themselves by slowing down their economic assimilation.

In sum, given all the ways in which the country has changed, the experience of the immigrants who arrived a century ago may not be a good predictor of the prospects of current immigrants. It is still too early to determine whether these changes will prove decisive in slowing the economic assimilation of post-1965 immigrants, most of whose children have yet to enter the labor market. Nevertheless, the dramatic shifts in the social and economic climate suggest that ethnic differences will remain significant far longer than in the past.

POLICY IMPLICATIONS

Concerns over the assimilation of new immigrants have dominated the policy debate since colonial days. In 1753, Benjamin Franklin, doubting the wisdom of German immigration, called the new arrivals "the most stupid of their own nation" and warned that "through their indiscretion, or ours, or both, great disorders may one day arise among us." Still, Franklin appreciated the benefits of assimilation and even made specific recommendations about how to speed up the process: "All that seems necessary is, to distribute them more equally, mix them with the English, establish English schools where they are now too thick settled."

Over the course of the twentieth century, the United States developed a highly nuanced immigration policy, resulting in immigration statutes almost as long and complicated as the federal tax code. Current policy awards most entry visas to people who have relatives already residing in the United States; generally, those with closer family connections—a parent, spouse or child who is a U.S. citizen—are granted speedier entry. Incredibly, however, our immigration law has nothing to say about assimilation. Not only are a potential immigrant's assimilation prospects ignored when awarding him an entry visa, but there are no regulations to encourage his economic assimilation once he arrives. The reach of immigration policy largely ends once the immigrant enters the country.

This omission makes the United States unique among immigrant-receiving nations, most of which build incentives directly into the system that awards entry visas. In the late 1990s, New Zealand required that the "principal" immigrant in the household be proficient in the English language; a family member who could not pass the "English standard" at the time of entry had to post a bond of $11,000. If this family member passed an English test within three months of arrival, the entire bond was refunded. If he or she failed the test at the three-month point but passed it within a year of arrival, the government refunded 80 percent of the bond. If he or she failed to meet the standard within a year, the family forfeited the entire bond.

Because the social and economic conditions facing immigrants are not as favorable today as they were a century ago, it would be prudent for the United States to reform its entry standards to give preference to those immigrants who are most likely to assimilate successfully. One such measure would be to discard the family preference system used to award entry visas and instead adopt a point system, similar to that used by Australia and Canada, that filters the applicant pool on the basis of socioeconomic characteristics. A point system would "grade" the economic potential of visa applicants, using such variables as age, educational attainment, occupation and English language proficiency, and award entry visas to applicants who most closely match the country's economic needs. A system that favored the entry of skilled workers would boost the immigrant population's chances for successful economic assimilation.

It would also be valuable to extend the reach of immigration policy to promote the assimilation of immigrants already residing in the United States. We could toughen the civics and English-language examinations that immigrants must take to become citizens; provide financial incentives for particular immigrant groups to resettle in nonimmigrant areas; and overhaul the defective system of bilingual education, which physically and culturally isolates the children of immigrant families. The problem, of course, is that any such changes would be highly contentious, particularly in a political climate that values multiculturalism and doubts whether assimilation is a goal worth pursuing. As a result, it seems that the best chance for accelerating economic assimilation lies in reforming entry criteria to favor immigrants who are most likely to be successful in the long run.

The United States has a clear stake in ensuring that the immigrants who make up the Second Great Migration join the economic mainstream—and the country will benefit more if this occurs sooner rather than later. It took a century to erase the differences in economic opportunities among the ethnic groups that made up the First Great Migration. But the assimilation of those immigrants occurred under highly favorable conditions that are unlikely to be replicated in the next century; and even so, it was a long and arduous process. There is reason to be concerned that, unless we take deliberate action, the process will be even more difficult for today's immigrants.

16

ASSIMILATION
TO THE AMERICAN CREED

by Amitai Etzioni

M UCH HAS BEEN MADE of the fact that the 2000 census showed a substantial increase in the proportion of the U.S. population defined as
"minorities." The percentage of Asian-Americans and Pacific Islanders
has increased nearly ninefold since 1960, from 0.5 percent to 4.5 percent. African-Americans, about 11 percent of the population in 1960,
have increased to about 13 percent. Native Americans make up 1.5 percent of the population today, up from 0.3 percent in 1960. Hispanics increased from about 5 percent of the total population in 1970 to about 13
percent in 2000. And, along with minorities, the proportion of immigrants has also grown: more than 10 percent of U.S. residents are foreign-born today, almost double the percentage in 1960. By mid-century,
all over the United States, European-Americans (or "non-Hispanic
whites") are expected to become a minority.

What are the implications of these demographic projections? Do
they spell the end of what some characterize as "white" values, long
shared by most Americans? Do they point to the rise of a new American creed based on African, Asian and Latino values? Will the great

American experiment continue along the same lines laid down by the Founding Fathers? Is there, in fact, any correlation between pigmentation—and other such skin-deep ethnic and racial features—and the beliefs and dreams of Americans? Few questions could be more pivotal for the future of American society, culture and politics.

IS THE AMERICAN CREED "WHITE"?

Many critics take for granted that the values expressed in our Constitution, embedded in our political system and taught in our public schools—values that stem from the Judeo-Christian tradition, the teachings of the Ancient Greeks and the powerful ideas of John Locke and Alexis de Tocqueville—are essentially "Western," European, or white. If this assumption is correct, it is only to be expected that new Americans from non-European backgrounds will seek to replace these values with their own. Like a new family moving into an old house, they would not only replace the furnishings, but would also redesign the structure.

But this expectation—whether it is viewed with hope on the left or with trepidation on the right—stems from a profound error. In fact, values are either compelling and justifiable in their own right or they are not valid at all, no matter when or where they were formulated. We either find commands such as "Thou shalt not kill," "Thou shalt not steal" and "Honor thy father and mother" to be self-evident and justifiable, or else we consider them empty and outmoded. Either way, their validity is not determined by whether we found them in Europe, Africa or Asia. Similarly, our respect for democracy, liberty and individual rights would not be diminished if we found out that the ancient Greeks got these ideas from the Egyptians. Indeed, Americans cherish many values without knowing exactly where they came from. Maybe we don't care because it doesn't matter. Belief, not geography, is what gives moral precepts their power.

Still more important, the American creed has never been a rigid dogma, immune to changing times. Within it there is considerable (though not endless) room for difference and debate. Our understanding of the "self-evident truths" articulated by the Founding Fathers, and their implications for our lives, have been modified through the centuries. Moreover, the American creed specifies large areas of belief and conduct, such as religion, that are decided by the individual. There is ample opportunity and precedent for new Americans to interpret the national creed instead of breaking with it.

BELIEFS AND VALUES

In fact, there is ample evidence that Americans of all racial and ethnic backgrounds hold their most important beliefs in common. Far from resulting in profound political or social disagreement, the increased diversity of the U.S. population goes along with widespread commitment to basic American values. By looking at detailed data from numerous public opinion polls and surveys, we can see that the danger of fragmentation along ethnic lines is largely a fiction.

A poll of New York state residents, conducted by New York State United Teachers in the early 1990s, shows that the vast majority of respondents consider teaching "the common heritage and values that we share as Americans" to be "very important." One might expect this statement to be particularly embraced by white Americans. In fact, minorities endorse it more strongly than whites: eighty-eight percent of Hispanics and 89 percent of blacks agree, compared with 70 percent of whites. When asked whether "to graduate from high school, students should be required to understand the common history and ideas that tie all Americans together," approximately 85 percent of all parents agree—including 83 percent of African-American parents, 89 percent of Hispanic parents and 88 percent of foreign-born parents.

Conventional wisdom has it that African-Americans are the minority group most alienated from the mainstream. However, if one considers attitudes towards the fundamental American beliefs, the overwhelming majority of blacks endorses them. A 1998 Public

Perspective poll finds that when asked whether "in the United States today, anyone who works hard enough can make it economically," 54 percent of blacks agree, compared with 66 percent of whites. Similarly, 77 percent of blacks say they prefer equality of opportunity to equality of results (compared to 89 percent of whites). When asked "Do you see yourself as traditional or old-fashioned on things such as sex, morality, family life and religion?" the difference between blacks and whites is only 5 percentage points. And when asked whether values in America are seriously declining, the difference is only 1 point.

A 1998 NBC News/*Wall Street Journal* poll finds that similar percentages of whites (46 percent), blacks (42 percent) and Hispanics (51 percent) think the words "hard-working and diligent" describe America extremely or fairly well. Sixty-nine percent of whites, 58 percent of blacks and 69 percent of Hispanics think the words "believe in competition and the free market" describe America extremely or fairly well. And 59 percent of whites, 62 percent of blacks and 70 percent of Hispanics think the words "ambitious, always looking for ways to get ahead in life" describe America extremely or fairly well. On the other hand, concerns about America are also shared across racial lines. Only 24 percent of whites, 31 percent of blacks and 21 percent of Hispanics think the words "religious" and "moral" describe America extremely or fairly well. In a 1998 Gallup/CNN/*USA Today* poll, 77 percent of whites and blacks and 86 percent of Hispanics think excessive materialism is a very serious or somewhat serious problem for children where they live.

Still, one might object, minorities can share the American Dream while doubting whether they have a chance to achieve it. Actually, this is not at all the case. For instance, 70 percent of blacks and 60 percent of whites agree that "the way things are in America, people like me and my family have a good chance of improving our standard of living," according to the National Opinion Research Center's (NORC) 1994 General Social Survey. Likewise, 81 percent of blacks and 79 percent of whites report that "the quality of life is better in America than in most other advanced industrial countries." In a 2001 Gallup poll, 49 percent of whites, 40 percent of blacks and 44 percent of Hispanics pronounce themselves very satisfied with the opportunities they've had to succeed in life.

People's dreams and hopes may be similar, but what about their views on particular political issues? Americans of all social backgrounds do hold widely ranging opinions on matters of social policy. But the main dividing lines are not racial. For instance, according to the Justice Department, in a 1996 survey, whites, African-Americans, Latinos and Asian-Americans all concur that education is "the most important issue facing [their] community today." Similarly, more than 80 percent of blacks, Latinos and whites share the belief that "it is 'extremely important' to spend tax dollars on 'educational opportunities for children.'" In a 1994 *Wall Street Journal*/NBC News poll, 54 percent of blacks and 61 percent of whites rank "increased economic opportunity" as the most important goal for blacks. And 97 percent of blacks and 92 percent of whites rate violent crime a "very serious or most serious problem."

On other social problems too, surveys highlight the agreement among different racial and ethnic groups. "Between 80 percent and 90 percent of black, white and 'other' Americans agree that it is 'extremely important' to spend tax dollars on 'reducing crime' and 'reducing illegal drug use' among youth," according to the Justice Department. Among whites, African-Americans, Latinos and Asian-Americans surveyed by a *Washington Post*/Kaiser Foundation/Harvard Survey project in 1995, between 30 percent and 41 percent, depending on the group, believe that Congress should legislate limited tax breaks for business; between 46 percent and 55 percent believe that Congress should cut personal income taxes; between 53 percent and 58 percent agree that Congress should reform Medicare. Similarly, 67 percent of all parents, 68 percent of African-American parents, 66 percent of Hispanic parents and 75 percent of foreign-born parents agree that the most important thing for public schools to do for new immigrant children is "to teach them English as quickly as possible, even if this means they fall behind in other subjects," according to Public Agenda.

Admittedly, other surveys show larger differences among ethnic groups. It is because the divisions are so often played up, while the areas of agreement are ignored, that I have deliberately drawn attention to studies showing that there is no great divide between America's majority and its minorities. Differences along color lines do exist, but they must be seen against this background of important shared understandings on basic values, attitudes and policies.

RACE RELATIONS

When survey questions zero in directly on issues related to race, the differences among racial and ethnic groups are naturally larger. But even in this area, Americans are much less divided than is often assumed. When asked about the state of American race relations, 32 percent of blacks, 37 percent of Hispanics and 40 percent of whites feel that they are holding steady; 46 percent of blacks, 53 percent of Hispanics and 44 percent of whites feel they have declined (the rest feel that they have improved), according to a 1996 report by James Davison Hunter and Carl Bowman. Similarly, in a 1998 Roper survey, 81 percent of blacks, like 71 percent of all Americans, think that blacks and whites "generally get along fairly well." When asked in a 1995 Louis Harris survey, "When today's/your children reach your age, do you expect that race relations will have improved, will have worsened, or will be about the same as today?" a nearly identical 48 percent of blacks and 51 percent of whites concur that relations will be better. A 1998 Gallup survey finds that a majority of both whites (60 percent) and blacks (54 percent) agree that only a few white people dislike blacks. Only 5 percent of blacks and 2 percent of whites say that "almost all white people dislike blacks."

Even in response to a deliberately loaded question, a 1997 *Time*/CNN poll shows that similarities between the races are much larger than the differences. When asked, "Will race relations in this country ever get better?" 43 percent of blacks and 60 percent of whites reply in the affirmative. And significantly, nearly half of both blacks and whites want to set racial questions aside as much as possible. A 1995 *Newsweek* survey finds that 48 percent of blacks and 47 percent of whites agree that the census Bureau should stop collecting information on race and ethnicity "in an effort to move toward a more color-blind society—even if it becomes more difficult to measure progress on civil rights and poverty programs."

Still, there are also pronounced differences on questions about race. For example, in a 2001 *Washington Post*/Kaiser Family Foundation/Harvard University poll, 52 percent of whites think too much attention is being paid to racial issues, while only 17 percent of African-Americans, 31 percent of Hispanics and 28 percent of Asians think the same. Another poll, this one a 1998 NBC News/*Washington Post* survey, found that while 100 percent of Asians surveyed approved of marriage between whites and nonwhites, only 85 percent of Hispanics, 79 percent of blacks and 64 percent of whites felt the same way—quite a spread. Again, 65 percent of whites favor a smaller federal government with fewer services, while only 38 percent of blacks and 28 percent of Latinos do, according to a 1999 *Washington Post*/Kaiser Family Foundation/Harvard University poll.

DIFFERENCES AMONG MINORITY GROUPS

Many on the left dream that a "rainbow coalition" of racial minorities, allied with labor unions and feminists, could grab the reins of power from the white majority and radically change America. But the very notion of a "majority of minorities" as a social and political force ignores the fact that the dreams and ambitions of minority groups are often similar to those of whites. Indeed, the differences between particular minority groups on many issues are as big as, or bigger than, the differences between the minority group and Anglo-Americans. (This reality came to light in the Los Angeles mayoral election of 2001, when a white candidate was elected, largely thanks to support from blacks and Hispanics, over a Hispanic rival.)

When asked, in a 1998 Gallup survey, "Do you think the Republican Party or the Democratic Party would do a better job of dealing with . . . moral issues?" 46 percent of Hispanics chose the

Republicans, compared with only 20 percent of blacks. Differences also appear on religious questions; when asked how important religion is in your every day life in a 2001 *Washington Post*/Kaiser Family Foundation/Harvard University poll, 37 percent of African-Americans replied that religion is the most important thing in their life, compared to 19 percent of Hispanics. And while 52 percent of African-Americans described themselves as "born again" or evangelical Christians, only 16 percent of Hispanics and 17 percent of Asians describe themselves that way. In the presidential elections of 2000, 88 percent of African-Americans voted for the Democratic candidate compared with 58 percent of Hispanics and 42 percent of Asians.

DIFFERENCES WITHIN MINORITY GROUPS

We can see that there is no such thing as a set of "minority" beliefs, opinions or political positions. Still more important, even minority groups we think of as monolithic—"Hispanics," "Asians"—do not share a single, uniform set of beliefs. There are significant differences within these groups, and also, to a lesser extent, among African-Americans, whose growing middle class is differentiating from other blacks.

Among Hispanics, there is considerable variation based on country of origin. For example, 74 percent of Mexican-Americans and 73 percent of Cuban-Americans have made contributions to charitable organizations, compared with only 35 percent of Puerto Ricans. Again, 69 percent of Cuban-Americans identify themselves as Republicans, while 67 percent of Mexican-Americans and 71 percent of Puerto Ricans call themselves Democrats, according to the 1989 Latino National Political Survey.

Likewise, Americans of Asian origin are far from a unified group. First-generation Vietnamese-Americans tend to be strong anti-Communists and favor the Republican Party, while older Japanese and Chinese-Americans more often lean toward the Democrats, and Filipino-Americans are more or less equally divided between the parties.

To put it even more strongly: the very notion that "Hispanic-Americans" or "Asian-Americans" (or even African-Americans) constitute a single group, in any meaningful sense, is a phantom created by the way statistics are kept. Such pan-ethnic identities are promoted by some community and political leaders, but they are not shared by most members of these groups. Indeed, most so-called "Hispanics" prefer to be identified by their country of origin. The Latino National Political Survey found that 75 percent of respondents choose to be labeled as Mexican-American, Puerto Rican, or Cuban-American, as opposed to "Hispanic" or "Latino."

The most accurate and useful way of looking at American minorities is not to classify them into different "races" or pan-ethnic groups. Rather, we should see them as immigrants or descendants of immigrants from many different countries of origin. Just as in the past, children of immigrants will surely shed their hyphenated identities as they become Americanized and move up the social ladder. Indeed, American history teaches that the very notion of race is a malleable social construct; people with Jewish, Slavic, Irish or Polish ancestry were considered distinct "races" a hundred years ago. There is at least as much reason to expect that, a hundred years from now, ethnic minorities now defined racially will come to be seen simply as the American descendants of various immigrant groups.

DIVERSITY WITHIN UNITY

All these findings point to the conclusion that America's diversity does not undermine our common values. America's success in this area stands out if one examines numerous other free societies, many of which experience great difficulty in dealing with new immigrants and with long established minorities. The American way is based on the idea that diversity does not threaten national identity and culture but, on the contrary, invigorates and enriches us all. At the same time, this entails a commitment by all Americans to a strong framework of shared values and institutions, which themselves evolve over time.

Today, Americans are not expected to melt into one homogeneous mass, stripped of the heritages of their countries of origin, denying their differences. To adapt to America, immigrants and members of minorities need only embrace the civic principles we all share. These include a commitment to the Constitution, the Bill of Rights and the democratic form of government; general respect for the law; English as the shared language (even if unofficially); mutual respect for people who are different; and at least some shared notion of morality. Last but not least, the American design of diversity within unity entails that, in cases of conflict, loyalty to the United States must take precedence over loyalty to one's country of origin.

In numerous other matters—religion, pride in one's country of origin, cultural preferences—being different is not un-American. On the contrary, diversity within unity is the source of America's success. Though our principles and institutions will certainly change, along with changing times and a changing population, these will be evolutionary, not revolutionary differences. Today, as throughout history, Americans have come to these shores in different ships, but now sail in the same boat and fly the same colors.

17

"THIS WAS OUR RIOT, TOO": THE POLITICAL ASSIMILATION OF TODAY'S IMMIGRANTS

by Peter Skerry

A BOUT A MONTH AFTER THE RIOTS that traumatized Los Angeles in the spring of 1992, I found myself at a reception attended by the city's Latino political elite. I was there with a Mexican-American woman who had befriended me a few years earlier when I interviewed her about what was then called "Chicano politics." I knew her and her husband well, having enjoyed many a meal at their suburban home. A former activist who was now part of the political establishment, she had two teenagers headed soon for college.

So I was surprised when, in response to my questions about the riots, my friend pulled me aside and urged me to communicate to my fellow Anglos that "This was our riot, too." When I pressed her to explain, she said that Latinos were concerned that the 1990s would be a repeat of the 1960s, when riots brought attention and resources to blacks, not to Latinos. Hence the need to inform the public that Latinos were among those participating in one of the worst civil disturbances in the nation's history.

With a rueful smile I asked her whether this was really the image of Latinos that she and her colleagues wanted to convey. She grimaced to acknowledge the point, but then insisted that they had no choice. A few weeks later, she was vindicated—sort of—when it was revealed that more than half of those arrested during the riots were Latino.

This vignette is not meant to suggest that Latino leaders in Los Angeles wanted civil disorder. Far from it. Mexican-American leaders were at pains to point out that the established Mexican barrio, East L.A., had remained calm, and that the epicenter of the rioting had been the heavily Central American Pico-Union district. The Latino leaders present at that reception were just as troubled and anxious as anyone else. But as political professionals, they understood that they not only had to make sense of those tragic events but also had to make use of them.

What the vignette does suggest is how thoroughly Latinos—and, by extension, other immigrant groups—have assimilated to the political system that now exists in America. The current regime grew out of the black civil rights movement of the 1960s, whose legacy includes affirmative action and the Voting Rights Act. Such institutions do not—as many Americans believe—prevent immigrants from assimilating; but they do result in a different and more problematic form of assimilation.

So when Americans complain that immigrants today are not assimilating as their predecessors did, they are half right. When Latinos demand affirmative action benefits, they are not assimilating as European immigrants before them. Still, Latinos are assimilating. However controversial or objectionable their demands may be, they demonstrate that immigrants are adapting to contemporary political institutions.

✳   ✳   ✳

Most Americans like to think assimilation means that migrants work hard, blend in and ponder how lucky they are to be here. American society is so absorptive and tolerant, we believe, that assimilation leads automatically to consensus and social harmony. In fact, history shows that the assimilation of immigrants has never been smooth or painless. On the contrary, it has been full of tension and conflict, for individual immigrants as well as for immigrant communities and society as a whole.

On the personal level, assimilation has always entailed immigrant parents losing control and authority over their Americanized children. This generational divide is as difficult today, when a Chinese-American youngster must translate for his mother at the gynecologist's office, as it was a hundred years ago, when Jane Addams, founder of the settlement house movement, tried to deal with it by encouraging immigrant children to appreciate the culture of their elders.

On the broader societal level, there is the equally classic example of ethnic groups competing for neighborhood turf or recognition by local politicians. Or the example of immigrants learning to exercise their political rights as Americans by arguing over the direction of U.S. foreign policy—whether between Muslims and Jews over the Middle East today, or between German and British immigrants over our entry into World War I. Or the native-born children of European immigrants battling their way into the mainstream of American life by organizing militant industrial unions during the 1930s.

What's more, assimilation has never been a simple process. It unfolds in at least three different dimensions: the social, the economic and the political. And different immigrant groups have pursued different paths to assimilation. The Irish who came here at the end of the nineteenth century gained political power before fully entering the social and economic mainstream, while the Eastern European Jews who arrived a few decades later focused more on economic and educational success than on politics.

Of these three dimensions, the one that is least talked about, but in many ways most crucial, is the political. America's social and economic institutions have changed a great deal since the last great wave of immigration. But our political institutions have changed just as drastically, and the immigrants of today encounter a political system that is in certain key respects the opposite of what their predecessors encountered.

The older system, based on big-city political machines, certainly had its problems. But in many significant ways, machine politics was actually better at assimilating politically inexperienced newcomers than today's institutions. This is ironic, because current programs like affirmative action and the Voting Rights Act were intended to empower disadvantaged minorities.

When European immigrants arrived in Eastern cities like New York and Boston a century ago, machine politicians literally reached out to them as they stepped off the steamship, sometimes flouting the law by making them citizens and bringing them to the polls to vote within days of their arrival. Then as now, the overwhelming majority of immigrants came to America for economic reasons, not political ones, but the machines were successful in large part because they established a link between the two. They taught immigrants and their children the valuable lesson of reciprocity: political support for the machine would earn them direct economic benefits.

This quid pro quo cut against the grain of middle-class reformers, who took a more high-minded view of politics. What they demanded from immigrants was something quite beyond their ken: disinterested civic-mindedness—voting for an individual not because he had done you a favor but because he was the best qualified candidate who would act with the public good in mind. The machines were more realistic. They met struggling newcomers halfway, and they spoke directly to their self-interest. Alarming as it was to those on the lookout for corruption, the machine approach nevertheless succeeded in taking large numbers of uneducated peasant newcomers and drawing them, by degrees, into participation in a modern democracy.

In doing so, the machines did not rely exclusively, or even primarily, on ethnic loyalties. It mattered less that a person was Irish or Polish than that he or she voted as the machine instructed. And the rewards for doing so—jobs, housing, tax abatements and the like— were handed out not to groups defined by ethnicity or race but to individuals and families. The precinct captains called those rewards "favors," a term that underscored the personal and private nature of those relationships.

Nor is that the only difference between then and now. Today's minority political leaders cater to constituent needs by passing legislation explicitly directed at specific neighborhoods or groups—a practice that requires them to explain themselves publicly using the language of minority rights. For example, politicians seek laws against dumping toxic waste in minority communities, then justify this by arguing that racial discrimination has been occurring. But the old machine politicians worked differently, implementing existing laws to benefit specific clients and supporters discretely. This helps explain why machine politicians, the legendary Mayor Richard Daley of Chicago being one notable example, were usually inept public speakers, and why they rarely made public declarations of specific policy goals. That wasn't their style.

Today the machines are gone, for good and ill. However tainted or flawed, the ties between immigrants and machine politicians were considerably more concrete than anything in evidence today. Where the precinct captain once stood, giving politics in immigrant neighborhoods a physical presence and a human face, there is now a vacuum. Indeed, to spend time in contemporary immigrant communities is to mark the almost total absence of organized political life.

During the 1993 mayoral campaign in Los Angeles, for instance, I accompanied a film producer looking for ways to document grassroots politics in action. After considerable effort to find examples of community-based politics worth filming, she abandoned the project. There simply were not enough rallies and meetings to bother with. Even at the local level, politics in many cities has been reduced to sidewalk press conferences and other staged media events.

Without the kind of patronage that local politicians used to control, it is extremely difficult to organize or mobilize immigrant communities. Yet today's immigrants have real interests and needs, which sooner or later seek political expression. Immigrant leaders continue to pursue recognition and power. Even more to the point, the political upheavals of the 1960s have left a legacy of heightened expectations about the representation of disadvantaged groups in the political process.

So what are immigrant leaders to do? They have little choice but to adapt to our post–civil rights regime, which responds best to immigrants' needs when they define themselves as "people of color" and victims of racial discrimination. This strategy has been particularly evident among Latino organizations such as the Mexican American Legal Defense and Educational Fund (MALDEF), established by the Ford Foundation in 1968 with the explicit goal of doing for Mexican-Americans what the NAACP Legal Defense and Educational Fund had done for African-Americans.

To be sure, not all immigrant groups have followed this path of political assimilation. Many Asians have either avoided politics altogether or pursued much more traditional immigrant political goals. But in today's political system, this latter approach is very difficult to sustain, so even some Asians define their interests in racial minority terms.

But claiming racial minority status risks stigmatizing the group, as both Asians and Latinos, today's largest immigrant group and the one most heavily committed to racial minority politics, understand. In 1998, for example, MALDEF sponsored a million-dollar television ad campaign designed to persuade whites in Southern California that "we worry about the same things, and fight the same battles"—which if true, of course, would undercut MALDEF's very reason for existence. But let there be no mistake. Despite such invocations of classic immigrant themes, the dominant thrust for immigrant politicians today is to present themselves as an aggrieved racial minority.

Not surprisingly, this approach to gaining political power has come in for much criticism, especially from conservatives. Many such critics insist that, if not for their misguided leaders, Latinos would pursue traditional immigrant political goals. Yet today's minority politics is not simply the result of willful perversity on the part of individual leaders. Nor does it mean that they have been seduced by the left. Rather it reflects rational adaptation—assimilation—to the game of politics as currently played in America.

Beyond such criticisms of group rights and benefits, many now condemn any assertion of group identity or interests as a failure to

assimilate. As former Colorado governor Richard Lamm has complained:

> Increasingly, the political power of more than fifteen million His-
> panics is being used not to support assimilation but to advance
> "ethnic pride" in belonging to a different culture. The multiplica-
> tion of outsiders is not a model for a viable society. . . . If immi-
> grants do not feel that they are fully part of this society, as
> American as everyone else, then we are failing.

Such pronouncements echo Theodore Roosevelt's fulminations, a
hundred years ago, against "hyphenated Americans." Roosevelt's
booming voice can also be heard in today's condemnations of ethnic
enclaves "where not a word of English is spoken" and immigrants "socialize only with themselves." Now as then, some native-born Americans call for immediate conformity to some ideal Anglo culture,
which neither reckons with the realities of America's ethnic past nor
affords immigrants any time to adapt.

What such critics forget is that, throughout our nation's history,
immigrants have typically adopted American values and learned how
to participate in American institutions, not as individuals but precisely as members of ethnic groups. Ethnic pride, along with ethnic
identity, has long been integral to the assimilation process. The classic example is the thousands of peasants who came to the United
States thinking of themselves as Sicilians, Calabrese and the like, only
to gradually come to see themselves as they were seen by other Americans—as "Italians." Later on, these immigrants, or more likely their
offspring, came to call themselves "Italian-Americans." And just the
same thing is taking place today. Villagers from Mexico, Guatemala,
Colombia and other Spanish-speaking countries do not come to the
United States thinking of themselves as "Hispanics" or "Latinos."
That is an identity they acquire on these shores.

The point, paradoxical as it sounds, is that the politics of group-
based entitlements, as practiced by Latino and other immigrants
today, is evidence that these groups are assimilating. Do Mexicans in

Mexico agitate for the Voting Rights Act? Of course not. Only those who have settled in America, where there is a Voting Rights Act, make such demands. And they are encouraged to do so by our post–civil rights political institutions. Regardless of whether one approves or disapproves of such political strategies, it is important to understand that they are an indication of immigrants' successful adaptation to the current American system.

*   *   *

This does not mean that everything is hunky-dory. Group-based entitlements are especially controversial today, in part because they are seen to represent a substantive departure from earlier efforts to benefit the disadvantaged. Some critics argue that affirmative action and other racially defined group benefits were designed to address the unique situation of African-Americans and are ill suited to the problems of immigrants. As a result, immigrants today are being afforded entitlements that earlier immigrants neither needed nor received.

For other critics, group-based entitlements violate the deeply embedded American principle of individual merit. Again, the comparison to machine politics is illuminating. During the machine era, the emphasis was on "favors" discreetly provided to individuals who, because of their willingness to cooperate, were deemed deserving. Today, the emphasis is on benefits publicly accorded to groups who, because of a history of racial discrimination, are deemed entitled to those benefits as a matter of right.

This emphasis on rights is part of a larger shift in American political culture. Over the past century we have created for ourselves—through the courts and the legislatures—a panoply of new rights that are now taken as the norm. These include civil rights, of course. But they also include entitlements to various social programs, as well as procedural rights when dealing with government, especially the criminal justice system. And not surprisingly, this new emphasis on rights has become part of what immigrants learn about when they assimilate.

This approach is evident in Aurora, Illinois, an old industrial community about forty miles west of downtown Chicago, where the Latino population has more than doubled over the past decade. I recently paid a visit to the Centro Cristo Rey, an agency supported by the Catholic Church that provides an array of social services to Latinos. One of the staff explained to me that the agency offers not only classes in ESL (English as a second language) and citizenship but also legal services. Indeed, the staffer noted proudly that one of the lessons she teaches has to do with the Bill of Rights, especially the Fourth Amendment's protections against unreasonable search and seizure. An immigrant herself, she takes particular pains to explain these protections to male laborers, who are routinely stopped by the local police. I do not know what this person's views on assimilation are. She might well be a devoted multiculturalist who discourages her students from assimilating on the grounds that American culture is offensive and hostile to Latinos. But intentionally or not, she and her colleagues at the Cristo Rey Center are bringing immigrants into the rights-oriented political culture of twenty-first-century America.

I have suggested that assimilation has always been contentious. Indeed, one is tempted to ask how it could be otherwise, as immigrants learn to maneuver in this intensely competitive society. One evident pattern is that once a group achieves some economic progress, enough to start moving up the social status ladder, it meets resistance. This was certainly true of Jews during the late nineteenth century, when their economic progress led to increased social contacts and hence new occasions for rejection by non-Jews. In a similar pattern today, Latinos experiencing assimilation report both declining levels of economic discrimination and increasing levels of social discrimination. For example, in the working- and lower-middle-class suburbs of Chicago, Latino families buying their first homes meet resistance from Anglo neighbors.

Once again, this aspect of assimilation is not what most Americans want to hear about. They expect immigrants to blend into the woodwork and not to rock the boat. When faced with the spectacle of immigrants behaving . . . well, like Americans and elbowing their way to the table, the conventional response is to invoke the nation's highest ideals and to call upon immigrants to adhere to them. Scolding pundits ask, for example, whether today's immigrants take sufficient pride in their American identity, and, in particular, in America's liberal democratic and egalitarian principles.

But, one might reasonably ask, which principles—liberal democratic *or* egalitarian? After all, these core American values are in tension, if not outright conflict. Latino leaders demanding the protection of the Voting Rights Act and affirmative action are asserting their fervent belief in equality, just as their critics are asserting their faith in liberty. The point is that such demands are not disloyal or "un-American." I remember very vividly when the Los Angeles County Board of Supervisors was compelled by Voting Rights Act litigation to create a Latino supervisorial district. It was on that day that a Mexican-American community leader expressed to me his profound pride in being an American.

*   *   *

The political philosopher Bernard Crick reminds us that time is how politics reconciles the inevitable tensions between ideals and realities. Yet this process calls for patience, which is precisely what America's post–civil rights regime lacks.

Compare the situation of Italians early in the twentieth century with that of Latinos today. Like Italian immigrants, Latinos have had difficulties in making educational advances. This can in part be explained by both groups' strong family values, which contribute to concerns that high-achieving, socially mobile children will grow distant from their kin. By now, of course, Italian-Americans are part of the educational mainstream; but the process stretched out over several generations. Estimating that it took ninety years, journalist Michael Barone draws the parallel with today and confidently predicts that for Latinos, "with luck, it will take less than ninety years."

But will Latinos be that patient? I don't believe so—but not because they are failing to assimilate. On the contrary, it is because they have assimilated to our post–civil rights political institutions that Latinos and other immigrants today are so impatient.

Consider the demand for higher education in California. It is now widely taken for granted that because Latinos (including large numbers of recently arrived immigrants) constitute one-third of the state's population, they ought to represent one-third of the student body at the University of California. But how can this be? How can we expect uneducated newcomers, many from rural, agricultural backgrounds—or even their children raised here—to gain access to one of the world's great university systems so rapidly? To be sure, such high expectations undoubtedly inspire extraordinary individual and societal efforts. But because they are ultimately unrealistic, such expectations also set us up—all of us—for frustration and disappointment. We seem unable to wait for today's immigrants to settle in and get used to their new home before declaring them victims of a society that refuses to include them. Such is the force of the institutionalized impatience that characterizes our post–civil rights regime.

Where does this impatience come from? In no small part, it derives from the struggles of African-Americans. By the 1950s and 1960s, generations of black Americans had been told to be patient, to slow down, to wait for justice—which is why the civil rights movement called for "Freedom Now." In that context, impatience was understandable, even laudable. But shaped by this struggle, today's post–civil rights institutions foster a generalized impatience with the obstacles faced by disadvantaged groups.

So, unlike previous generations, we now measure the social and economic progress of immigrants by the standards we have come to use for African-Americans. Relying on a policy framework developed in response to the black civil rights movement, we interpret statistical disparities in income, education, residential settlement and other outcomes between immigrants and nonimmigrants through the lens of racial discrimination.

This is unfortunate, for two important reasons. First, this preoccupation with racial discrimination leads us to underestimate many of

the other barriers to immigrant advancement: lack of economic resources, lousy schools, limited English skills, a high proportion of
nonvoting-age youth and a high incidence of noncitizenship, including illegal status. Second, it blinds us to our own history, which
teaches us that the immigrant struggle for full participation in American life has been long and difficult—but ultimately successful.

So we do have a problem with immigrant assimilation—just not
the one we think we have. More to the point, this problem is deeply
entrenched in our political institutions and cannot be explained away
by attributing it to the misguided efforts of immigrant leaders. The
fact is that we Americans today have essentially one way of talking
about social and economic disadvantage—in terms of race, specifically
in terms of the African-American experience. Immigrants figure this
out quickly and define their interests accordingly. If we are troubled
by the results, we should consider either changing our immigration
policy or reforming our post–civil rights political institutions. But
we should stop accusing immigrants of failing to assimilate.

PART SIX

RACE:
THE EXCEPTION OR THE RULE?

18

THE MELTING POT
AND THE COLOR LINE

by Stephen Steinberg

"EVERY NATION, UPON EXAMINATION, turns out to have been a
more or less successful melting pot." So wrote Robert Park, the
founder of the famed Chicago School of Sociology, in 1930. It is a tes-
tament to Park's prescience that he was able to imagine the melting
pot at a time when the United States was ethnically more diverse, and
more fragmented, than ever before. During the previous half-century,
the nation had absorbed some 24 million immigrants, mostly from
Eastern and Southern Europe. These "new immigrants"—Italians,
Poles, Russian Jews, Ukrainians, Hungarians and others, far removed
geographically and culturally from the people who settled the United
States during its first century—were widely believed to be "unassimilable." In Chicago, for example, 70 percent of the population
consisted of immigrants and the children of immigrants, and the city
was divided into a patchwork of ethnic neighborhoods. In 1921 and
1924, Congress responded with legislation that cut the volume of immigration and instituted national quotas biased against further immigration from Southern and Eastern Europe.

Against this background, Park's dictum provided reassurance that the intermingling of peoples was a universal process and that America's ethnic discord would resolve itself over time. This optimism was shared by Chicago sociologists W. Lloyd Warner and Leo Srole, who conducted field studies of immigrant communities in the 1940s. Warner and Srole argued that appearances were deceptive, that the ethnic enclave, though it seemed to nurture isolation and separatism, actually functioned as a decompression chamber, helping immigrants adjust to their new surroundings and preparing the next generation to venture into the mainstream. Whatever its original raison d'etre, the ethnic community actually functioned as an instrument of assimilation.

But if early sociologists were confident about assimilation, a later generation rejected the idea of the melting pot. Ironically, many of these scholars were themselves children of immigrants who have risen to the top of the academic ladder. Their revisionist view of the melting pot can be seen as part of a broader trend among second-generation immigrants: assimilation breeds nostalgia. First-generation immigrants, who are most authentically steeped in ethnic culture, tend to throw it away, often with both hands, as they pursue the opportunities that led them to come to America in the first place. Decades later, their largely assimilated children engage in desperate, but usually futile, efforts to recover the very culture that their parents relinquished. As the children of immigrants entered the ranks of social science, they brought this same nostalgia to their analysis of ethnic trends.

The turning point came with the publication of *Beyond the Melting Pot* in 1970. Scholars Nathan Glazer and Daniel Patrick Moynihan, who had each ascended from immigrant poverty to the ivory tower, concluded from their study of New York City that "the most important thing about the melting pot was that it did not happen." The syntax of this much-quoted passage warrants a moment's reflection. To say that the melting pot "did not happen" is not the same as saying that it was not happening. After all, Park and other theorists of assimilation never claimed that the melting pot was a fait accompli;

nor did they project a deadline for the completion of this evolutionary process. Nevertheless, the book's title and argument found a receptive audience. Aside from selling over half a million copies, *Beyond the Melting Pot* marked the beginning of a paradigm shift in the study of ethnicity.

Other books soon appeared that trumpeted the survival of ethnicity over the sinister forces of assimilation. Their titles celebrated *The Decline of the WASP* (1971) and *The Rise of the Unmeltable Ethnics* (1971). A year later, an article in the *New York Times Magazine* proclaimed, "America Is NOT a Melting Pot." Indeed, these writers contended that the United States was undergoing an "ethnic revival" that would resuscitate immigrant cultures. Again, there is a striking historical irony. When ethnic groups were intact and cultural differences pronounced, leading sociologists held that assimilation was inevitable. Several decades later, when these groups had undergone profound transformation, forsaking major elements of their ancestral cultures and assuming comfortable identities as Americans, the prevailing view was that the melting pot had "never happened."

But such attempts to turn back the clock of assimilation would prove difficult. With the exception of Native Americans, ethnic groups in America are transplanted peoples, far removed in time and space from their original homelands. The necessity of adapting to life in America made assimilation, in Park's words, "progressive and irreversible." By the late 1970s, a number of scholars, myself among them, had begun to argue that the so-called ethnic revival was in fact a symptom of decline, a dying gasp of ethnic consciousness. In fact, all the long-term trends suggested that the melting pot was working as predicted: during the twentieth century, immigrants largely lost their original language and culture, ethnic enclaves dispersed as economic and occupational mobility increased, and the rate of ethnic and religious intermarriage accelerated.

It may be that some observers deny the evident fact of assimilation simply because of the ambiguous terminology that we use to describe it. "Melting pot" conjures up an image of a bubbling cauldron into which immigrants descend—whether they jump or are pushed is another matter—and are quickly dissolved into oblivion. Though rhetorically effective, this imagery obscures the evolutionary nature of assimilation. Correctly understood, it is a process that occurs incrementally across generations. To argue that ethnicity is still an active force in American life—as Glazer and Moynihan did in 1970 and other scholars have repeated ever since—is to beg the crucial question. Just because assimilation isn't complete doesn't mean that it isn't taking place.

How we view assimilation also depends on our conception of culture. Revisionists argue that the melting pot theory is based on a static view, in which the original culture of an immigrant's homeland is simply replaced by American culture. Such critics concede that Italian-Americans, for example, bear little resemblance to Italians in Italy, but they argue that Italian-Americans are nevertheless a distinct community, forged on American soil, complete with its own identity and subculture.

Yet melting pot theorists also realize that immigrant cultures evolve and take new forms as newcomers adapt to life in America. The crucial issue is not whether change occurs, but rather the direction and the end result of that change. The key question is this: will the ethnicity of formerly hyphenated Americans endure, or is it merely a transitional stage in a long-term assimilation? My position has long been that, even if we assume a greater tolerance for diversity than actually exists in American society, the conditions were never promising for a genuine and lasting pluralism.

✱　　✱　　✱

Today there is an emerging consensus that the descendants of the great waves of European immigration have reached an advanced stage of assimilation. The most striking evidence is provided by the soaring rates of intermarriage across ethnic lines. According to a 1990 study by sociologist Richard Alba, the percentage of white ethnics aged twenty-five to thirty-four who married outside their own groups was as follows: Germans, 52 percent; Irish, 65 percent; English, 62 percent; Italians, 73 percent; French, 78 percent; Scots, 82 percent; Poles, 84 percent. Even in the case of Jews, for whom intermarriage was historically low, the figure is now thought to approach 50 percent. The conclusion seems inescapable that the melting pot, in the most literal sense, is a reality for groups of European ancestry.

Indeed, sociologists now lump these groups together under the rubric of "Euro-American," thus resolving with a single word the assimilation question that was debated for half a century. It is now conceded that the various nationalities of European descent have become simply "white." As a result, ethnic pluralists and opponents of the melting pot have retreated to a new position: the melting pot does exist, but it is "for whites only." On this view, the common "whiteness" of the Irish, Italians, Poles, Jews and other groups destined them to "melt," even though they were once regarded as distinct races whose cultural and genetic differences rendered them unassimilable. A new genre of "whiteness studies" has documented the process through which these erstwhile pariahs were incorporated into the white majority. The core argument is encapsulated in the titles of several recent books, including *How the Irish Became White, How Jews Became White Folks* and *Whiteness of a Different Color.*

But this argument goes on to hold that the current wave of immigrants, composed mainly of "people of color" from Asia, Latin America and the Caribbean, will not be able to follow in the footsteps of the white ethnics. The fault line dividing ethnic groups in America is no longer nationality or religion, but race. Indeed, a number of scholars have declared that "assimilation theory is dead," since its Eurocentric bias renders it useless for understanding the condition and destiny of people of color.

Aside from racism, the new ethnic pluralists cite several positive factors that, they argue, will spare the new immigrants from the dreaded melting pot. Today's immigrants enter a society that is far more tolerant of ethnic diversity. The ideology of multiculturalism extols ethnic difference and provides institutional mechanisms, such as bilingual education, for the preservation of immigrants' language and culture. As a result, the Asians, Latinos and Caribbeans who make up the new immigration have formed cohesive ethnic communities with flourishing economies and foreign-language media, including cable television, that provide institutional anchorage for language and culture. Furthermore, compared to earlier immigrants, the new immigrants have easy access to their homelands, thanks to telecommunications and cheap airfare. And finally, many new immigrants arrive with education and skills, and often capital as well, and therefore are not forced to compromise their ethnic identities for the sake of economic survival. Indeed, in today's global economy, it is not a handicap but an asset to be multilingual and multicultural.

These are all valid points. The question is whether they add up to the conclusion that assimilation is dead, and that the new immigrants will not "melt" as did their predecessors from Europe. It must be conceded that this is a possible scenario, given what we know about racism as a divisive force in American history. One cannot immediately discount the argument that the melting pot is "for whites only," and that today's immigrants will be prevented from assimilating.

In fact, however, this proposition receives little empirical support from the large body of research on today's immigrants. Indeed, the most compelling evidence leads to the conclusion that, notwithstanding their racial difference, the new immigrants are not only assimilating but are doing so at an even faster rate than did earlier immigrants from Europe.

In retrospect, an early indicator of the eventual assimilation of European immigrants was the rapidity with which they lost their native languages. A pattern emerges with stubborn consistency. Immigrants, of course, retained their native tongues; their children typically were bilingual; and by the third generation, the vast majority were monolingual in English. The virtual eradication of languages in only two generations shows just how fragile culture is, at least once it loses its "survival value" and is severed from the institutions that nourish it. Needless to say, immigrants and their bilingual children were not indifferent to the snuffing out of their native language. But the lesson of history is that sentiment—even passionate loyalty—is not enough to withstand the powerful forces of assimilation.

This process is being reenacted—if anything, at an accelerated pace—among the new immigrants. In a study of Los Angeles based on 1990 census data, David Lopez found that, among Asians, the shift to English monolingualism was nearly universal by the third generation. Consider what this means for family relations. Unless the immigrant grandparents acquire a basic fluency in English, which often is not the case, then grandchildren cannot converse with their grandparents except through the mediation of their bilingual parents.

The picture is somewhat more complex among Latinos, though the overall pattern is still one of rapid language loss. If retention of Spanish were to occur anywhere in the United States, it would be in Los Angeles. Not only do most L.A. Latinos live in predominantly Latino neighborhoods, but the city also has a thriving ethnic press and electronic media. Furthermore, Los Angeles has had an official policy of promoting multiculturalism, including bilingual education and bilingual ballots. Yet Lopez found that 57 percent of third-generation Latinos spoke only English at home. Closer examination of the data revealed that Spanish was retained mainly in households where a foreign-born person—presumably that all-important immigrant grandparent—was present. In the case of Mexican-American youth living in households with no immigrants, only 20 percent spoke Spanish at home.

A study of Cubans in South Florida also found that most young people preferred to speak English at home, even when they were bilingual. Nor was this true only of the middle classes. Among second-generation youth who classified themselves as working class or poor, three-quarters preferred to speak English. Clearly, even though today's society is nominally more conducive to language retention, the new immigrants are moving very rapidly to English monolingualism.

If loss of a native language marks the beginning of the assimilation process, marriage across ethnic lines represents the last (or next to last) stage. Here again, the data do not support either the assumptions or the hopes of the new ethnic pluralists. A study based on the 1990 census found that 40 percent of Asians born in the United States married non-Asians—and these are mostly the children, not even the grandchildren, of immigrants. The figures ranged from 22 percent among Vietnamese to 31 percent among Japanese, 38 percent among Asian Indians, 46 percent among Chinese, 65 percent among Filipinos and 72 percent among Koreans. These figures are so high that they call into question the very category of race in describing Asian-Americans. Indeed, the level of marriage between Asians of different nationalities is strikingly low, suggesting that they do not see themselves as members of a pan-ethnic Asian "race." Rather, most Asians who intermarry do so with whites, giving rise to speculation that Asians are in the process of "becoming white."

Rates of intermarriage for Latinos are lower than for Asians, but they are high nevertheless. Almost one-third of U.S.-born Hispanics between the ages of twenty-five and thirty-four are married to non-Hispanic whites. Indeed, marriage across racial lines has become so commonplace that some commentators have raised the possibility of a "mestizo America"—a racial mixture that blurs the boundaries among ethnic groups. On this view, it is not a question of minorities being absorbed into the white majority, but rather of a fusing of these diverse peoples into a new amalgam. This is the literal meaning of a "melting pot," and a fulfillment of Robert Park's prescient observation that every nation is a "more or less successful melting pot." Like it or not, and the dissent of the ethnic pluralists is clear, assimilation does appear to be progressive and irreversible, the inexorable byproduct of forces put into motion by the very act of immigrating.

*　　*　　*

Admittedly, this sweeping conclusion, while it captures the main thrust of American ethnic history, does not tell the whole story: in particular, it does not account for the African-American experience. Here we speak of a group that came to America in slave ships, not immigrant steamers. While successive waves of immigrants flowed into the country, first to settle the land and later to provide labor for burgeoning industries, blacks were trapped in the South in a system of feudal agriculture. Even in the North, a rigid color line excluded them from the manufacturing sector. In short, the Industrial Revolution was "for whites only," depriving blacks of the jobs and opportunities that delivered Europe's huddled masses from poverty.

This was the historic wrong that was supposed to be remedied by landmark civil rights legislation in the 1960s. But by the time most blacks arrived in Northern cities, the manufacturing sector was undergoing a permanent decline, reflecting the impact of labor-saving technology and the export of jobs to low-wage countries. Not only did blacks encounter far less favorable opportunities than did immigrants, not only did they suffer from the economic consequences of past discrimination, and not only did they encounter pervasive racism in the world of work, but they also experienced intense labor competition from yet another huge wave of immigrants, which began in the 1960s and continues to this day.

Though these new immigrants are conspicuous for their "racial" difference, they are not subjected to the all-encompassing system of racial discrimination that was the legacy of slavery. Furthermore, many of these immigrants arrived with education and skills—and sometimes capital as well—that accelerated their mobility and social integration. As noted earlier, Asians and Latinos already display a far greater degree of "residential assimilation" than blacks. And at a time when marriage across racial lines is soaring for Asians and Latinos, it has inched up only slightly for blacks, again indicating that a fundamentally different dynamic is at work. The conclusion is unavoidable: America's melting pot has been inclusive of everybody but blacks.

This is not to deny the obvious fact that there has been enormous progress over the past half-century. Jim Crow is a thing of the past, thanks largely to the black protest movement. The emergence of a large black middle class is another encouraging development, though in my view this does not reflect the deracialization of labor markets so much as the favorable impact of affirmative action policy over several decades. Finally, there has been an unmistakable shift in America's fundamental attitudes toward race. The prominence of blacks among the nation's elites, as well as its pantheon of folk heroes, is stark proof that skin color is no longer a badge of inferiority.

Nevertheless, ours is still a society riven by race. Claims of "progress" invariably depend on comparing the situation today to a retrograde past. The problem here, as James Baldwin observed, is that the crimes of the past are used to gloss over the crimes of the present. When comparisons are made between blacks and whites today, a far less sanguine picture emerges. For example, blacks today earn only three-fifths as much as whites. Furthermore, although the income gap between blacks and whites closed somewhat in the 1960s, there has been little or no progress since the mid-1970s. So long as nearly a quarter of blacks, and half of black youth, live below the poverty line, these class factors will continue to engender and reinforce racial division.

Even more germane to the question of whether America is a melting pot, black and white Americans are as residentially segregated as ever. Nor is this true only of inner-city blacks. Middle-class blacks also encounter pervasive discrimination in housing, and their arrival into white suburbs usually triggers white flight, resulting in resegregation. It is a mark of the melting pot's failure that African-Americans, whose roots go back to the founding of the nation, are more segregated than even recent immigrants from Asia and Latin America.

In short, despite "progress," ghettoization is still a fact of life. And here we confront a great historical paradox—for these ghettos, the enforced "home" of the nation's racial pariahs, also nourished a vibrant African-American subculture. As sociologist Bob Blauner has observed, while immigrant ghettos "functioned as way stations on the road to acculturation and assimilation," the black ghetto has been permanent, "a continuing crucible for ethnic development and building." And unlike immigrants, who clung to vestiges of cultures ripped from their moorings in distant places, black culture evolved out of the lived experience of black people in America. Instead of isolated fragments selected precisely because they did not interfere with mainstream American culture, black culture is an integral part of the everyday lives of black people. As a result, black culture displays a vitality and dynamism that is generally lacking among the ossifying cultures of the nation's immigrant groups.

Ironically, generations of sociologists have taken precisely the opposite position, on the one hand celebrating the cultures of the nation's immigrant groups and, on the other, holding that blacks were merely "white Americans in black skin," lacking a culture of their own. In the same book where they declared that the melting pot "never happened," Glazer and Moynihan wrote that "it is not possible for Negroes to view themselves as other ethnic groups viewed themselves because—and this is the key to much in the Negro world—the Negro is only an American and nothing else. He has no values and culture to guard and protect." Under a barrage of criticism, Glazer subsequently explained that he meant blacks had no *foreign* culture to guard or protect. However, this only compounds the error, since these foreign cultures—and precisely because they were foreign—were destined to a gradual but inexorable decline. On the other hand, as an indigenous product of the American experience, black culture continues not only to thrive in segregated black communities but also to exert a powerful influence on mainstream American culture.

* * *

Throughout this essay, I have emphasized that the melting pot is still at work and that, like past immigrants, today's immigrants from outside the Western Hemisphere will also be fully assimilated at some indeterminate point in the future. The problem, of course, is that we live in the present. It may be our national destiny to become a melting pot, but today the United States is a remarkably polyglot society in which ethnicity flourishes. Despite an overriding trend toward assimilation, ethnic loyalties and attachments remain strong even among segments of older immigrant groups. New immigrants, freshly arrived on American soil, are only at the early stages of the assimilation process. To turn a blind eye to these realities by focusing on long-term trends runs the risk of blotting out the lives and sensibilities of entire communities.

Nor does this warning apply only to ideologues on the political right who, in the name of the melting pot, have waged a relentless crusade against bilingualism, multicultural education and affirmative action. In recent years, a left discourse has emerged that looks "beyond race" and "beyond ethnicity," imagining a post-ethnic future where people are not defined by genes or ancestry. This vision promotes intermarriage across racial and ethnic lines as a way of eliminating, once and for all, the dissonances and conflicts attending racial and ethnic diversity.

For example, historian Gary Nash, a pioneer of multicultural education, has published an essay titled "The Hidden History of Mestizo America," in which he argues that we "need new ways of transcending America's Achilles' heel of race, now that a certain amount of progress has been achieved in living up to our own credo." Like Nash, sociologist Orlando Patterson advocates miscegenation as the ultimate solution to America's intractable race problem. Never mind that African-Americans—not to speak of other ethnic groups—may not wish to miscegenate themselves out of existence. Never mind that it would take generations, if not centuries, to produce the hybrid nation that they envision. Instead of confronting the urgent problems of race in America and addressing the challenges of a multicultural society, these visionaries are throwing in the towel. They use a utopian vision of the melting pot as a façade for moral capitulation.

Let me be clear. There is compelling evidence that the United States will one day become a melting pot, and that this day is approaching faster than ethnic pluralists are willing to acknowledge. From a moral standpoint, however, it is imperative that this melting pot evolve through the operation of historical forces rather than through public policy interventions. It is wrong—to continue the metaphor—to turn up the temperature under the melting pot, or to nudge, cajole or push people into the bubbling cauldron. Any use of state power to undermine ethnicity or to force assimilation is incompatible with democratic principles and violates the rights of ethnic minorities to hold onto their languages and cultures.

The irony of the matter is that, like earlier waves of immigrants, today's newcomers will find their way to the melting pot in due course. So, presumably, will African-Americans, but not until the structures of American apartheid are thoroughly dismantled and the persistent inequalities are resolved. These groups will pursue the personal and social integration that is the promise of the melting pot. But they must do so of their own accord, and not on somebody else's timetable. Here we can take another lesson from history: the carrot, not the stick, has always been the more effective instrument of assimilation.

19

GETTING OVER IDENTITY

by John McWhorter

For African-Americans, the traditional rhetoric of assimilation often strikes a sour note. To our ears, the melting pot smacks of co-optation and even extinction—of a battle being lost. Since black American culture is the result of centuries of survival under hideous conditions, it is only natural to feel that its dilution or disappearance would constitute the white man's last laugh. And for recent immigrant groups, too, the melting pot has become a suspect metaphor. Far more popular today is the image of the "salad bowl," where ethnic groups retain their distinctiveness in a larger mix.

In fact, this new metaphor is a direct development of the race ideology that permeated America in the wake of the civil rights revolution. Fresh from the horrors of segregation, and taking their cue from the countercultural movement of the 1960s, a new African-American leadership rejected the classic integrationist paradigm for a new, separatist ideal. By the early 1970s, the belief that America needed to adjust to "the Other," rather than vice versa, was conventional wisdom not only among spokesmen and intellectuals but also on the street. With the ghetto established as subculture rather than pathology, and with mainstream America classified as aberration rather than "normalcy," the stage was set for many new immigrants to claim that they were not joining the party but busting the house wide open.

As a result, the understanding of immigration preached today—from the ivory tower, the media, the literary world and the social services industry—treats any dilution of native ways as a cause for indignation. Our Zeitgeist teaches newcomers to America to seek the perpetuation of their inherited cultures to an extent that would have seemed alien to earlier immigrants, who usually embraced becoming American in a much less ambivalent fashion.

Surely there is wisdom in a conception of America that allows room for contributions from elsewhere. But in the long view, any immigrant group that adopts the black post–civil rights ideology strays into what history will judge as a detour. Velveeta America has always been more susceptible to hybridization than it appeared to be. But, more important, a subculture can resist assimilation only by perpetuating the very sense of alienation that the salad bowl ideology is designed to combat.

Of course, one needn't be an angry black nationalist to share the feeling that there is something worth preserving in being black. Many blacks, including educated members of the middle class, are no strangers to the gut sense that for us to integrate completely would somehow mean to lose "ourselves." I worry that, when I have children, they may not inherit much of what my race means to me. They will inhabit an America even more integrated than the one I grew up in and will attend fine schools in university towns where there is little identifiably "black" culture. As a result, they may well lose the deeply ingrained sense, which I had as a child, that the black world is their "home base."

This will affect, among many other things, their ear for music. If I, like increasing numbers of black people of my generation and younger, marry a white woman, then half my children's family will be white and unable to pass on black musicality. This is a sensibility that includes but goes beyond rhythm. Soul music of the 1970s like Earth, Wind and Fire can still rivet me to my seat; the blue notes and gospel tinges of *Porgy and Bess* make the hairs on my neck stand on end; the sound of a gospel choir makes me feel like I'm home, even though I'm an atheist who wasn't even brought up in the church.

Will my children be able to hear why the "Clara" sequence in *Porgy and Bess* is such a sublime evocation of black folk music? Will they be able spontaneously to hum comfy old bass lines to black gospel or soul music, the way my grandfather could and my father could—and the way my sister and I can? If my kids are going to get even further beyond race than I have, then maybe not.

But all too often in black America, these heartfelt concerns lead to a sense that differences must be preserved at all costs, so that the essence of authentic blackness becomes alienation from the white mainstream. Most blacks feel black first and American second; but I would venture that, today, this is more because blacks work at maintaining such a self-conception than because whites force it on us. African-Americans have a tacit sense that we deserve a pass on the usual calls to join the melting pot. Integration is nice in the formal sense of access to schools and employment, but take it too far and we fear the death of black culture.

This fear is rarely spelled out explicitly, but it shows itself at work in various aspects of modern black consciousness. One of the most important can be seen in the documentary *American Tongues,* a survey of dialects of English in America, when a black father displays his discomfort with the fact that his kids sound like "The Man." A great many black kids get teased for "sounding white" when they talk; the sense that true blackness entails defining oneself against whites is especially vivid here because to talk is to express one's soul. In black America, "folk festival"-style accoutrements like clothing and food are not considered nearly as essential to authenticity as the cadences and vowels of black speech.

For similar reasons, many young black Americans of all social classes deeply cherish hip hop music. It is not uncommon to see affluent young black executives slide into their BMWs, then hear the confrontational cadences of from-the-streets rap rise out of their speakers. Educated, successful blacks have clearly embraced mainstream values in the way they live their lives. Yet the street theater of Tupac Shakur and Jay-Z still "speaks to them" in some way. (I once noticed a distinct hush in a room full of educated young blacks when I mentioned Tupac Shakur's name, such an icon has he become even far beyond the poor.) The place of hip hop in black America's heart signals a quest to keep at least a symbolic flame of opposition burning inside—in spite of the surface trappings of success and assimilation that we also desire deeply.

For many African-Americans, an ideal future would look roughly like this: Black Americans would inhabit their own distinct communities containing a range of social classes, with the higher mentoring the lower and serving as role models, much as in the grand old black districts of American cities a century ago. Blacks would own all or most of the property in these communities. Most blacks would marry within the race, and black American cultural traditions would be passed down the generations, safe from dilution or "co-optation" by whites. Many African-Americans might not object if some blacks opt not to live in these communities, but would still hope that a representative number would choose to do so—and in the black world, the choice would remain a sensitive, oft-discussed issue. The discomfort many blacks in New York feel when whites buy property in Harlem suggests the thinking at work: even if blacks spend their working hours in white environments, we will have our own communities to come home to, where we can be "comfortable" and "ourselves."

This is a beautiful, even stirring picture. But it would also be a tragedy. For in any human society, when groups live separately and do not intermarry, the reason is either that one group has its foot on the other's neck or that they are kept apart by morally indefensible caste barriers. The rare exceptions to this rule are tiny, intensely inwardly focused subcommunities, such as the Amish or the Hasidim, whose small numbers allow them to keep their traditional folkways.

If there are no such barriers, and people from different groups see one another as simply human, then people will fall in love across group lines and produce hybrid children. These children's cultural allegiance will be split between two groups, and the children they produce will have an even more hybridized self-conception. Eventually, the original communities cease to exist, and the society is inhabited by a new, mongrel people, for whom the initial "salad bowl" echoes for a while as a rote, folkloristic memory, and then is finally lost to living awareness.

The legacy of the slave trade leaves us today at an intermediate stage in this eternal story of cultural contact. There are no indications that our advances in technology somehow lend us the ability to halt cultural hybridization—if anything, modern communications only accelerate the process. Nor do any intellectual developments appear likely to interfere with a mixture that takes place on an everyday level—especially among people who do not attend to the musings of academics and literary writers.

And it is not clear that black Americans should want it otherwise. After all, we are already a highly hybridized people. The separatist sentiment of the 1960s teaches us to seek the roots of our identities in Africa, but for all its spiritual comforts, these origins will always be largely a matter of decoration. Black Americans speak English; black singers like Mahalia Jackson, Mos Def and Missy Elliott all perform in a language that emerged among whites in the mists of Northern Europe two thousand years ago. Black Americans are a fervently Christian people who feel to the depths of their being a religious impulse born among Caucasians in Mesopotamia about three thousand years ago. The blues, ragtime, jazz, R&B and even hip hop are rooted as deeply in white Western music as in African music; Africans today adopt black American music as a foreign form.

And this marvelous miscegenation continues apace. True enough, children whose parents come from different cultures can, for a time at least, be pressured into choosing one side over the other. This has certainly been the case for "mulatto" children in the United States: when I was growing up, the "mixed" kid was considered definitionally "black." If she did not incorporate this view of herself by her teen years, then black observers were likely to surmise that she was denying "who she really was," and maybe just didn't like black people very much. At the same time, most whites would make clear to such a person that she was not exactly considered one of them. This was doubly dismaying. The parochialism of the whites revealed them at their worst, while the blacks were enforcing a "one-drop" rule as vigilantly as any white bigot.

But times are changing. Today, there is a growing contingent of people who classify themselves as "biracial" rather than black or white, who simply say "my mother was white and my father was black" and leave it there. In other words, they are replacing the meaning of "mixed" that I grew up with, still redolent of the plantation, with the way an American of Irish or Italian or Japanese parentage understands being "mixed"—less loaded, more individual and, ultimately, less significant.

This change has been hastened by the fact that the number of Latinos in the United States now surpasses the number of blacks, resulting in an increase in black-Latino unions. The Latino influx is to a considerable extent the product of the Immigration Act of 1965, which, in also bringing waves of voluntary African and Caribbean immigrants to our shores, has only further nuanced the choices available to biracial people. Today, many Americans are the progeny of black Africans or Caribbeans and white Americans, making African-American culture only one of many "identities" they might choose.

There persists a powerful strain in modern black identity that reads a biracial person's insistence that they are "just who they are" as evidence of not liking black people. But in the end, to endorse this resentment is to give in to the remnant of self-hatred in the African-American soul. It's not hard to understand this visceral impulse to read a black person's stepping "outside of the race" as an insult—and I myself am not exempt. As frustrating as I find black women's assumption that a black man who dates a white woman must think of black women as lesser, there is yet a part of me that feels a tinge of the corresponding feeling when I see a black woman with a white man. But I consider this an irrational tic, to which I give no quarter in my conscious reasoning. It stems from a sense, lingering in the corners of our minds, that our race just might not be good enough. If we didn't have that sense, we wouldn't need slogans about Black Power and Black Pride.

Our job is to get past all that, not sing plangently of it as a way of reminding whites that they are still on the hook. There is already an almost absurd dissonance between blacks' new rendition of the one-drop rule and the mundane realities of physiognomy. In a recent conversation on this subject with a Russian speaker, my knowledge of Russian didn't allow me to enter into the subtle explanations I usually present as to why I "identify" as black. The best I could do was to say, "Here in America, there is no choice. Either you are white or black. There is no in between." And really, the absurdity of that statement is an accurate reflection of an absurd situation.

Outsiders often see a continuum of "blackness" in America, analogous to more fluid conceptions of race in the Caribbean and Latin America. And the ranks in the middle range of that continuum are only increasing, in both the genetic and cultural senses. In the realm of popular culture, Mariah Carey (black Venezuelan father, white mother) and Tiger Woods (black, white and Native American father, half Thai and half Chinese mother) are both ambivalent about designating themselves "African-American," despite the African component of their ancestry. But their multinational heritages make it incoherent to insist that they are spiritually deficient in not feeling that they share the same "ethnicity" as, for example, Louis Armstrong. People like Carey and Woods are only the most public examples of a deep-seated shift in the meaning of race in modern America.

The most logical conclusion is that America is gradually getting past race. Many have assumed that this would mean whites miraculously shedding all vestiges of racial bias. But this would take much too long to wait for, given the resilience of racial and ethnic bias in every society throughout history. Instead, we are getting past race the way humans always have: through races melding together.

Of course, this does not mean that we should forget the history of blacks in America. Africans were brought here in chains; they did not come voluntarily like most immigrant groups. This profound difference makes it tempting to assert that blacks should be exempt from the forces that affect all other immigrants and should fight to preserve a separate group identity. But in the long run, this would only mean fighting a rising tide and becoming curiosities in the history books.

The unavoidable reality is that the classic assimilation model does, and must, apply to black America, just as it does to everyone else.

But that classic model also tells us that assimilation is not a one-way street. There can be no doubt that blacks have had a profound cultural effect on whites, just as whites have had on blacks. Here again, it is useful to look at American entertainment, which despite its rampant commercialization remains very much a keystone of our culture. Blacks' victory over our oppressors begins with the emergence of blues and jazz and continues through rock and roll: none of this music would exist if African slaves had not been brought to these shores. And that is only the most obvious example of mutual influence.

These days, the hybridization runs even deeper and takes more baroque forms. For example, in 1997, *The Wonderful World of Disney* produced a version of Rodgers and Hammerstein's 1957 television musical *Cinderella*—starring black singer Brandy, with Whitney Houston as the fairy godmother, Whoopi Goldberg as an evil stepsister and a Filipino as Prince Charming—the score slightly adapted to contemporary R&B sensibilities. The contrast with the lily white original of the Eisenhower era, starring Julie Andrews, is jarring, heartening and significant—this 1997 *Cinderella* would have been an ill-fated gamble just twenty years before.

But more to the point, whites no longer watch black music only from afar. Today, any white pop singer who wants to succeed sings and moves in a way that white Americans at the turn of the twentieth century would have perceived to be oddly "Negro-ish." In the early 1990s, Britney Spears, still in high school, was doing a dead-on imitation of Billie Holiday, and today she dances in a way that can be traced directly back to black dance styles. Crucially, Spears gives no evidence that she is consciously imitating black people. Earlier white performers like Sophie Tucker, Mae West and Elvis Presley openly borrowed from the black closet and became famous for their singularity in a basically Wonder Bread pop scene. But Spears, who never even knew the 1970s, is just a creature of her time, when black performance style has become, to a large extent, mainstream. Nor is this new hybrid performance style limited to celebrities. Working with undergraduate theater productions in my college and graduate student years, I often had to teach white singers to hit notes dead-on, rather than sliding into them. This is great in Billie Holiday but isn't appropriate singing Stephen Sondheim—it is a musical style that goes back directly to Africa, where the division of the scale into thirteen discrete notes was unknown.

There remains a contingent who insist this is not blending, but rather a case of black culture being "co-opted" by the oppressor. Thus some activists grouse that Eminem "takes our music and sells it back to us." One faction even insists that when whites do what we do, they are seeking to "negate" us by taking over our folkways. But most of us can recognize this as staged, professional indignation, having little to do with the sheer human joy of people coming together and sharing ways they have found to express passion in this vale of tears called life. It is as silly as if a Native American were to grouse that invaders from Europe had "co-opted" corn from their people and were now selling it back to them. Eating popcorn at a movie theatre, we cannot help enjoying our food and thinking, "Get over it."

And in the end, that is just what most of us do. The horror of how black Americans were brought to these shores cannot change the fact that we have no choice but to take a deep breath and get over it. This is perhaps the most difficult task before us. But there is no other logical choice we can make. We're here now, we've been here for a very long time, and there is nowhere else most of us are going, or would even want to go. We long ago drifted irreversibly beyond being "Africans" in any meaningful sense. In the same fashion, over time, we not only will but must drift—with understandable regret—beyond being "African-American."

Our emotional burden is made easier to bear by the fact that whites are getting "black" just as we are getting "white." Yes, black people are going blonde, but then white people are wearing dreadlocks. Yes, black people are listening to country music, but for whatever it's worth, most of rap's purchasers are white. Yes, increasing numbers of blacks will "sound white" in their speech, but then white people have now so internalized the salutation "Man" that they no longer even realize they got it from us. (Whites in the 1950s did not call each other "man.") Yes, blacks are marrying whites, but then it's not as if the whites had no say in the matter. Black nationalist dreams will live on, but in real life, the die is cast. And that's the way it should be. It's the only way it possibly could be in an America where being black is considered less and less of a problem—by whites or by blacks themselves.

We descendants of African slaves did not choose our fate here in America. But the irony, both bitter and portentous, is that the only salvation we can seek is to brace ourselves for the eclipse of "black identity." In this, we will take our place as immigrants to America. For a good while now, new arrivals' adoption of the black protest model has yielded far more heat than light. The time has come when black America ought to take a page from other immigrants, borrowing the coping strategies that have worked so well in a nation that, with all its imperfections, provides the richest opportunities in the world. Besides, these strategies may work even better for us. After four centuries, it can't be denied that, in many ways, we *are* this nation.

PART SEVEN

WHAT IT MEANS TO BE AMERICAN

20

NEW AMERICANS
AFTER SEPTEMBER 11

by Michael Barone

W ARS HAVE ALWAYS BEEN UNIFYING events for new Americans, occasions for them to show their allegiance to this country. This
has been true ever since the American Revolution, when important
roles were played by immigrants like Thomas Paine and Alexander
Hamilton, and by foreign soldiers like the Marquis de Lafayette and
Baron von Steuben. Not all of them remained Americans after the
Revolutionary War, but all were honored for their contributions, and
those who did stay were considered as American as any Virginia- or
Massachusetts-born patriot.

As the United States increasingly became a nation of immigrants,
thanks to heavy immigration between 1840 and 1924, the question
of immigrants' loyalty to their new country arose each time the nation
was at war. The Civil War came after fifteen years of very heavy immigration, and the response of immigrant groups varied. The Irish,
heavily Democratic in politics and with a strong dislike of blacks,
were in many cases opposed to the conduct of the war; they were the
chief participants in the New York draft riots of 1863. The Germans,

more sympathetic to the new Republican party, tended to favor the war. Even in Confederate Texas, the German population was pro-Union.

In the twentieth century, the loyalty of immigrants was especially questioned when they came from enemy countries. German- and Scandinavian-Americans formed the major political constituency which opposed World War I. In response, the Wilson administration and its propagandists conducted a campaign against German culture, renaming sauerkraut "liberty cabbage," suppressing German-language schools and newspapers, prosecuting political opponents of the war. Nonetheless, the American commander in Europe, John Pershing, was a German-American, and the roster of World War II military leaders is full of the German names of men who served as junior officers in World War I: Eisenhower, Nimitz, Spaatz.

By the time of World War II, German ethnicity was no longer a vibrant force, and the rallies of the German American Bund were regarded, correctly, as the expression of just a few voices on the fringe; the loyalty of the great masses of German-Americans was largely unquestioned. Questions were raised about the loyalty of Italian- and Japanese-Americans, whose immigrant heritage was more recent than that of the Germans. But the sympathy expressed by some Italian-Americans for Mussolini and his regime essentially vanished by the time America entered the war in 1941; and although there was a brief internment of some Italians, it was quickly ended. Not so with Japanese-Americans. In an episode well remembered, and lamented, today, Japanese nationals and Japanese-Americans in the three West Coast states were placed in internment camps between 1942 and 1945. (But not in Hawaii, where they were too numerous, or east of the West Coast states, where they were too few.) This was prompted by the fear, shared vigorously by President Franklin Roosevelt himself, that there were many saboteurs in their ranks.

The response of these groups was to prove their loyalty as American citizens by serving in the military. Japanese-Americans had to overcome great obstacles to be allowed to volunteer and serve in the European theater, notably in the 442d Regimental Combat Team, later famous as the most decorated unit in the United States Army. Italian-Americans did not have to overcome such obstacles, but attention was drawn to their contribution by the service of sports and entertainment celebrities like Frank Sinatra and Joe DiMaggio. Service in World War II qualified many Italian- and Japanese-Americans, as well as the sons of other immigrants, for the G.I. Bill of Rights, which enabled men who would otherwise never have done so to get college degrees. Military service was thus a spur to socioeconomic upward mobility; but more important, it was part of an annealing, unifying process, making clear that these new Americans were a loyal and valuable part of their country.

This process was successful because, in two important respects, the United States was unique among all countries in the world in its attitude towards immigration. First, it was, at least until the 1921 and 1924 immigration acts, more welcoming of immigrants than almost any other country—not just allowing immigrants to arrive, but giving them a chance to weave themselves into the national fabric. To be sure, there were many examples of bigotry (as well as vivid ethnic humor, much of it distasteful by today's standards) and acts of restriction, such as the anti-Jewish quotas in elite colleges and universities; but the barriers were much less forbidding than in almost any other country.

The second way in which the United States was unique was its promotion of assimilation or, as elite Americans like Theodore Roosevelt called it, Americanization. Until the 1920s, immigrants and their children were not barred; William Howard Taft and Woodrow Wilson both vetoed immigration restriction bills. But immigrants were expected to learn to speak, read and write the English language, and to become familiar with and participate in American civic culture. Theodore Roosevelt could sound quite fierce when he demanded that "hyphenated Americans" must give up allegiance to their former countries. But this vision was also a welcoming one. Roosevelt and others like him believed that millions of Italian *contadini,* Jewish *shtetl* dwellers, Polish peasants—millions of people from the backward corners of Europe, places as backward then as the villages of Latin America and the peasant fields of Asia are today—all could become Americans, as the Irish and German immigrants had before them.

✳　　✳　　✳

The response of today's immigrants to the events of September 11, 2001, was very much like the response of earlier immigrants to Pearl Harbor. In fact, it was very much like the response of all Americans to September 11: We have been attacked, and we will respond. It was lost on no one that the victims at the World Trade Center and the Pentagon included immigrants, both new citizens and foreign nationals, in large numbers.

And who can forget the scene when George W. Bush came to Ground Zero on Friday, September 14? Someone yelled that he couldn't hear him. Bush responded, unscripted, "I can hear you. The whole world can hear you. And the people who knocked down these buildings will hear from all of us soon." Immediately the crowd of rescue workers began chanting, "U.S.A.! U.S.A.! U.S.A.!" As the camera panned in on them, the viewer could see that under the yellow hats were faces of all kinds of Americans, of all complexions and races and ethnic origins. And their message was: We are all Americans.

Ever since, it has been plain that support for the war against terrorism among new Americans is as high as it is among Americans generally. Poll results show no difference between Latinos or Asians and other Americans on war-related issues. American flags were seen in the same profusion in Latino neighborhoods as in the rural Midwest and South (indeed, rapidly growing numbers of Latinos live in the rural Midwest and South). Cab drivers from Pakistan and Ethiopia proudly displayed American flags. Applications for citizenship soared in the months following 9/11: over 60 percent more immigrants applied in that period than in the same period the year before. In south Florida, immigrants from many Latin American countries watching the World Cup games referred to the U.S. team as the team of *todos los nosotros*—the team of all of us. America is our country, they seem to be saying, loudly and proudly, and as strongly as any American whose ancestors have been here for many generations.

The war against terrorism does not present as many opportunities for military service as did World War II; we no longer have a draft, and the size of U.S. armed forces does not seem likely to be substantially increased. But Latinos already serve in large numbers in the military: in September 2001, there were over a hundred thousand Hispanic enlisted men and women, representing about 9.5 percent of active-duty military personnel. Their participation is especially great in the Marine Corps, where nearly 14 percent of enlisted personnel are Hispanic—possibly because the Marines have resisted the feminist-inspired move toward a less macho culture that has affected the other services. (Citizenship is not required for military service, and many noncitizen Latinos served in Iraq. Two were killed and were posthumously granted U.S. citizenship; George W. Bush stood by in a room at Bethesda Naval Hospital as a wounded serviceman was sworn in as a U.S. citizen.) Asians already work in large numbers in the high-tech industries that are so important to the creation of the precision-guided weapons and sophisticated electronic communications systems used by our high-tech military force.

The one identifiable group that seems not to have joined wholeheartedly in the war against terrorism is Muslim Arabs. Official Islamic organizations have made only perfunctory denunciations of the September 11 attacks, and have given only perfunctory support to the war against terrorism. Their spokesmen have been much more vociferous in opposing measures taken in the war effort and in asserting claims that civil liberties have been violated (though civil liberties are for the most part nonexistent in every Muslim Arab nation).

These actions are evidently prompted by fear of a xenophobic reaction against Muslims and Arabs. But there have been only a few such acts of violence in a nation of 285 million people. Much more frequent have been spontaneous acts of friendliness and reassurance directed at people of Muslim and Arab origin by Americans of all descriptions. Public officials, starting with then Mayor Rudolph

Giuliani and President George W. Bush, have spoken out vigorously and often against any negative reaction to Muslims and Arabs generally. Bush has often said that America is fighting not Islam but terrorism. Indeed, public officials have been reluctant to label even obvious acts of terrorism as such—notably the July 4, 2002 attack by an Egyptian on the El Al counter in Los Angeles International Airport. This is a country bending over backwards not to engage in acts like the persecution of German-Americans in World War I and the internment of Japanese-Americans in World War II.

In the early twentieth century, the United States was unique among nations in its response to immigrants and new citizens: we were more welcoming to newcomers, and we insisted more strongly on assimilation. The United States that was attacked on September 11 had changed somewhat. We are now, if anything, still more welcoming to newcomers than we were a century ago. Overt bigotry has greatly diminished, even as the heritage of the immigrant experience in this country is still vividly recalled. But at the same time, we are less insistent on assimilation than we used to be; today, the word "Americanization" sounds harsh and even bigoted to many ears.

My prediction is that September 11 and the response to it will change this trend. America will still welcome immigrants, despite fears that our borders may be vulnerable to terrorists. But we will no longer embrace the notion that it is somehow oppressive to encourage assimilation and Americanization.

America's welcoming attitude towards immigrants will not change because it is deeply rooted in the hearts and histories of the American people. John F. Kennedy, the first president of post-1840 immigrant stock, memorably said that the United States is "a nation of immigrants." And in fact most Americans today—thanks to the volume of immigration and to the intermarriage of people who were once thought to be of different "races"—are descended at least partly from immigrants who came here after 1840. If it is a tendency of Europeans to identify with the most ennobled of their forebears, it is the habit of Americans to identify with the humblest.

This habit was strengthened by the ceremonies commemorating the one hundredth anniversary of the Statue of Liberty in 1986; it is witnessed by the popularity of the Ellis Island website; it is evident in the happy profusion of ethnic cuisines of immigrants new and old. Americans are inclined to tell pollsters that immigration should be reduced somewhat from current levels. But there is no political strength behind the idea, advanced by Patrick Buchanan and others, to cut off immigration altogether. Nor has there been great political strength behind proposals to reduce immigration sharply for fear of terrorist infiltration. Americans looking at immigrants today realize that their own ancestors once lived in similar situations.

This helps to explain the benign response of the great mass of Americans to Arabs and Muslims in their midst. Some unknown number of Muslims living in this country cheered the September 11 attacks, and believe that in a battle, as they see it, between Islam and the United States, they will support Islam. But this fact is largely ignored; most non-Muslim Americans assume hopefully that such people are few in number. There seems to be no great appetite for cracking down on the Saudi-financed Wahhabi-run mosques and *madrassas* and Islamic organizations that, in the United States as well as other places, preach terror and hatred of Americans and Jews. The government's refusal to single out young Arab or Muslim males for special scrutiny at airport checkpoints elicits little loud opposition. It is more important, evidently, to avoid "racial profiling" and ethnic discrimination. Proposals to change immigration law have gotten no serious hearing. Americans today, even after an attack on our nation, are more welcoming than ever.

By contrast, our aversion to assimilation or Americanization will be weakened by the response to September 11. This is because that aversion, far from being deeply rooted in the American people, is felt and promoted primarily by elites—the university, media and corporate elites that dominate the mainstream media and have disproportionate influence on policymakers.

The elite's aversion to Americanization has its roots, like so much else in this country, in the 1960s and the civil rights movement. In that era, immigration and the treatment of new Americans was seen, not through the prism of earlier immigrants' experience, but through the prism of the civil rights experience. Indeed, the Kerner Report on civil disorders in 1968 devoted a chapter to the argument that the immigrant experience was no longer relevant to poor Americans because the American economy could no longer generate large numbers of low-wage entry-level jobs—a prediction that proved as wrong as could be. In the wake of the Kerner Report, Latinos and Asians were added to the list of groups protected against discrimination and favored with racial quotas and preferences. The unspoken assumption was, evidently, that benighted white Americans were itching to treat Latinos and Asians as badly as Southern whites had been treating Southern blacks before the 1960s; therefore these new "people of color" needed protection against discrimination and government preferences if they were to have any chance to get ahead. This assumption turned out to be largely untrue: no one in America is treated as badly as Southern blacks were before the 1960s. But the policies based on that assumption are still in place.

So also is the idea that it is somehow wrong for the larger society to insist that disadvantaged people assimilate to the norms and mores of the majority. The experiences of the 1960s—the civil rights movement, the Vietnam War, urban riots—prompted a large part of the American elite to take an adversarial view of their own country, a country they nevertheless still felt entitled to lead. Ordinary Americans were seen through the TV camera lens that showed the police dogs and fire hoses directed at peaceful demonstrators in Birmingham, or through the newspaper reports of the massacre at My Lai. Americanization was seen by such elites as the wrongful imposition of a rather nasty culture upon other cultures that were presumed to be morally superior. While a Theodore Roosevelt could robustly advocate Americanization, to his social equivalents in the late twentieth century university, media and corporate elites, Americanization sounded like a form of oppression and bigotry.

Instead, the view is that we should encourage groups of new Americans to hold on to their old cultures, and do nothing to encourage them to assimilate or to think of themselves as part of a larger America. This view has had some bad policy consequences, notably in the so-called bilingual education programs, which too often have kept Spanish-language students from mastering the English language, as they must to move upward in our society. Fortunately, it has been unavailing in other respects. The emergence of a large Latino middle class, the spectacular rise of many Asians through our universities into careers in science, engineering, medicine and other disciplines, the high rates of intermarriage of people of different "races"—these are all evidence that new Americans are assimilating and becoming Americanized despite the moral qualms of the elites.

September 11 and the response to it should accelerate these trends. September 11 gave great strength to the idea that, for all our cultural differences, we are one nation, united in support of great principles, ready to work together to preserve the decent society in which we live. It has undermined the assumption of the elites, a hangover from the 1960s, that America is an indecent or unworthy society, its people so vicious that they must be tamed by the constant social engineering of an enlightened elite to keep them from oppressing others. The new Americans' solid support for the American war against terrorism show that they share the majority's vision of America as a decent society. And their contributions to the war effort show that they are doing their share to make sure our common values prevail.

The war against terrorism will prove to be a unifying event for new Americans, just as wars have been for earlier generations of immigrants. But, perhaps as important, it also seems likely to be a unifying event for the American elites, who for four decades have doubted the decency of their country and tried to retard the process of assimilation. Americanization has worked in the past, and it will work once again to weave new Americans into the national fabric— one that will be stronger and richer and more vivid for their presence.

21

GOOSE-LOOSE BLUES
FOR THE MELTING POT

by Stanley Crouch

W E WOULD DO OURSELVES A FAVOR by backing away from the rhetorical hostility that attends the issue of assimilation. Assimilation is not the destruction of one's true identity. It is not, as advocates of separatism would teach us, a matter of domination and subordination, nor the conquest of one culture by another. On the contrary, it's about the great intermingling of cultural influences that comprises the American condition: the fresh ideas brought forward in our folklore, our entertainment, our humor, our athletic contests, our workplaces, even our celebrity trials and political scandals. Only the rhetorical violence left over from the 1960s prevents us from understanding what assimilation really means and how it actually happens in America.

This isn't to pretend that we as a nation have shed all bigotry based on skin tone, or sex, or religion, or nationality, or class. But if we still have troubles, and plenty of them, that doesn't mean we haven't advanced remarkably when it comes to race and ethnicity (and it doesn't mean we aren't capable of going even further). If we examine things as they actually are, we can see that what it means to be American has never been fixed or static or impervious to outsiders; we are continually creating and re-creating our traditions. In fact, American society is now so demonstrably open to variety, and so successful at gathering in those who would join it, that it is the international model of a free and progressively integrated nation.

✳   ✳   ✳

When the civil rights movement began, its enemy was racism, not white people per se. But as the irrational elements of Black Power congealed, the boldly nonviolent movement began to descend to a politics based in ethnic identity, sexual identity and sexual preference. The hysteria, sentimentality, bigotry and fantasies of Black Power extremists were taken up by other (so-called) ethnic minorities, by women and by homosexuals. And over time, this politics of identity corroded into a politics of hostility, to the point that many Americans confused the real enemy—hateful visions like racism, sexism and homophobia—with the white race.

Among the effects of this shift from understanding to misunderstanding was the creation of "alienation studies" programs on campuses from one end of this nation to the other. Purportedly oppressed groups were taught that their only hope was "within their own." This separatism was often joined to a naïve internationalism rooted in the paradigm of Marxist liberation. Black Americans were supposed to see themselves as part of a Third World struggle. People of color were supposed to reassert their "true" cultures, which had allegedly been ground to dust under the heels of the whites.

Not surprisingly, in this upside-down world, assimilation was seen as the destruction of true identity. Why should one want to disappear into an unvaried mass when one could be part of something more vital, more "authentic"? Under no circumstances was a black American to forget that, as Malcolm X had said, "You are not an American, you are a victim of *Americanism.*" One had to get back to one's true roots (which were in Africa), one's true religion (which was

Islam) and one's true interests (which could never coincide with the
interests of the United States). Variants of these Black Power ideas
have been adopted by other ostensibly oppressed groups: Latinos,
Asians, women and homosexuals have each invented versions of the
"Oreo" motif (black on the outside, white on the inside), regarding
assimilation as a form of "selling out." Authenticity, according to this
outlook, has become an absolute—and it is an impossible condition
to achieve in a melting pot.

But the separatist alienation-studies crowd couldn't be more wrong
about assimilation. For most Americans, identity has never been static.
It never could be, especially in an experimental society that has forever
had to create its own traditions. Indeed, even against our will, we
Americans have a difficult time being provincial. The different groups
that make up the nation need and attract and influence each other—
even those brainwashed by alienation studies partake of the nation's
shifting common culture. The notion that any group could remain separate and untouched is nothing more than a mad joke.

*　　*　　*

Decades ago, the great Constance Rourke, author of the classics *American Humor* and *The Roots of American Culture,* proposed that there are
four mythic figures at the core of American culture: the Indian, the
Yankee, the Frontiersman and the Negro. Director John Ford picked
up the idea from her, or at least made use of it, at the conclusion of his
1939 film *Drums Along the Mohawk,* which is set during the Revolutionary War. The Indian, the Yankee, the Frontiersman and the
Negro all watch as an American flag is raised over an upstate New
York fort, and they realize that its flapping colors and stars symbolize
a human connection, one finalized through the death and tragedy of a
war fought to make a new nation. From those four archetypes come
our sense of the land, our folklore, our vision of adventure, our humor,
our dance, our music and our acknowledgment—as Ralph Ellison
would add—of the importance of improvisation, of learning to absorb
and invent on the spot.

Improvisation is essential to understanding these United States. It was especially necessary for a nation always faced with the unknown, forever at a frontier of some sort. The unknown was often the natural environment, as the frontier moved at first gingerly and then brutally west. The unknown frontier could also be the big city, drawing people from the countryside and teaching them breathtaking, illuminating and destructive lessons. These encounters with the new quite often demanded invention-on-the-spot. Bringing mother wit to emergency situations is surely our national ideal, so much so that in Hollywood films the villain or the monster is often dispatched by an improvised turn, an unexpected solution, a jerry-built contraption that does the job.

As the nation expanded through immigration and other means, it became equally necessary to improvise the idea of what it means to be American. The result is that cultural improvisation has become second nature as Rourke's four archetypes have been expanded. Mexican, Asian, Irish, Italian and Eastern European strains have become part of the national identity, affecting our cowboy culture, our cuisine, our dance, our music, our slang, our Broadway shows, our films, our popular music and our spiritual practices. American identity is never fixed or final; we are always working towards a better and deeper recognition of how to make one out of the many. The diffuse nature of our democracy leaves us with no choice. Consequently, out of this perpetual negotiation comes a collective identity that has to be, finally, as loose as the proverbial goose.

This goose-loose identity also involved some ongoing and usually constructive conflict—the struggle of the most high-minded Americans against the worst elements of our social past. Even when our sense of ourselves was profoundly bigoted—as far back as the three-fifths rule agreed upon by our Founding Fathers, which made black slaves less human than white men—we always had a sense of a collective American reality. And even bigotry never stopped people from making use of any part of any culture that they found enjoyable or functional. Already in 1930, when psychoanalyst Carl Jung visited the United States, he observed that white Americans walked, talked and laughed like Negroes, something we would hardly expect if we were to look at the stereotypical ways in which black people were depicted at the time in American writing, theater, film, cartoons and advertisements.

This cross-cultural borrowing and influence works the other way as well. As more than a few Negro Americans have found out when they went back to "the motherland," Africans look upon them—unless they are trying to hustle them for money—not as their brothers or sisters but as white people with black skins. In other words, Jung could see how much black Americans had influenced white Americans, and Africans can see how much white Americans have influenced black Americans. In the same way, European immigrants to America soon discovered that their kids were influenced by what they picked up while playing in the streets and by what was being sung and laughed about in popular entertainment. This is not the result of any melting pot that destroys distinctions; it is the expression of the mutations of choice and style that occur through our living close to each other.

Again, Ralph Ellison is important to our understanding of this messy, mixed-up way of being. Ellison knew that improvisation is essential to what we make of ourselves as Americans. He recognized that we are constantly integrating the things that we find attractive in others, whether the integration is conscious or unconscious. We all know that the American wears a top hat with an Indian feather sticking out of it, carries a banjo and a harmonica, knows how to summon the voice of the blues by applying a bathroom plunger to the bell of a trumpet or a trombone, will argue about the best Chinese restaurants, eat sushi with you one on one, turn the corner and explain the differences between the dishes on the menu at an Indian restaurant, drink plenty of tequila, get down with the martial arts, sip some vodka, recite favorite passages from the Koran, have some scotch on the rocks, show you the yarmulke worn at a friend's wedding, savor some French and Italian wine made from grapes grown in the Napa Valley, charm a snake, roll some ham and cheese up in a heated flour tortilla, tell what it was like learning to square dance or ballroom or get the pelvic

But, look, isn't the to cherry-pick the products + symbols of many cultures to be an à la carte consumer — detaches these elements from most of the deep meaning that birthed them. Is there no loss in that? Is that really a "culture" in the end?

twists of rhythm and blues right or how it felt in one of those sweltering Latin dance halls when the mambo got as hot as gumbo on a high boil. That's how *American* assimilation works. It's a quintessential part of our national adventure. *Our* society maintains its essential identity while new layers and nuances give greater vitality to the mix.

*   *   *

Perhaps the best way to understand where we are now, and what we have made of ourselves as Americans, is to look at the Kennedy era that began in 1960 when a handsome young Irishman became the first of his ethnic group to take the Oval Office. Back then, newspapers, magazines, television and presidential conventions told us that just about anything of true importance was thought about, argued about and accomplished by white men. They ran the country, the states, the cities, the towns, the villages, the networks, the stock market, the athletic teams, the entertainment world, the universities—and they were not shy about letting you know it. It was not so much that they were arrogant; they were simply the only ones around. You did not see black people, or any other people who were not white—or any women—in the highest governmental positions in Washington, D.C., or in individual state or city government. Such people were, of course, human, but they just didn't make the cut. America walked through a blizzard of white men.

Only a lunatic would cling to the idea that the America of today is that same America of 1960. That world is as long gone as the Los Angeles through which saber-toothed tigers once strode and roared. When one turns on the television today, one sees people of every color and both sexes anchoring the local news, giving their analysis of the stock market, international politics, the entertainment industry and whatever else might be of human concern, whether important or trivial or somewhere between those extremes. Ours is now a far more integrated society, and the aspirations of children from every group are far different now that there are flesh-and-blood human beings upon whom they can base their dreams.

I began to see how deeply things had changed when my daughter, born in 1977, was around six years old and I asked her what she intended to be when she grew up. She answered that she might be an astronaut, a Supreme Court justice, a police officer, a fireman, a doctor or maybe a pilot. I was rather startled, to be honest, because, having been born in 1945, I had heard six-year-old girls say "a mother, a teacher or a nurse." In the early 1950s, no rational young girl—or woman—would have thought she could become a Supreme Court justice. But when I considered what my daughter had said, I realized that the feminists had won the battle for the minds and aspirations of her generation. A black girl living in Compton, California, had absorbed, through all those vastly different television images, a sense of life and possibility that included imagining women in every significant career. Life seemed an open sky.

More than a decade and a half later, the influences that inspired my daughter to express such a broad range of career options have only intensified. Over and over, throughout the day and night, our advertisements project an integrated America. What's more, they tell us that no group of Americans is defined by the worst among them. Above all, we see that whites, Negroes, Hispanics and Asians— whether men or women—work in every capacity, from the world of the blue collar all the way up to the business suites. We also see that every group, across all classes, has families—wives, husbands, children—and what sociologist Todd Gitlin has called "common dreams." This is profoundly important, no matter its commercial motivations. In attempting to sell products by making all Americans feel free to spend money, the brain trust of the advertising world takes every opportunity to tell us that, no matter what we look like, we are all human and have as much access to what is good as the next person. Come on in. Feel welcome. Sit down. Pull out your credit card.

Toward that end, our advertising culture is based on the assumption that normal, everyday life is integrated. We are shown that people need not be ill at ease when talking with others superficially different from themselves. Nor should they assume that any kind of human problem is color-bound. In the civil rights era of the mid-1960s, it used to be joked (playing off the stereotype that dark people smelled worse than white people) that blacks would have made it all the way into American society once a Negro could be shown in a deodorant commercial. That problem has surely gone by the boards in an era when anybody can advertise anything.

Skill, intelligence and advice cross all racial lines. In one commercial, a white man who promises his kids that he will build a tree house for them finds himself in the lumber store getting perfect advice from a black man. In another, a black woman who wants to repaint the inside of her house buys paint from a white woman who tells her that she can't be afraid of yellow, advice she repeats both to her husband and to an Asian woman and a white man who come over to see what she has done. Insurance meant to appeal to older Americans has crosscuts of various ethnic faces. Advertisements for vans show smiling families that may or may not be white. It is not surprising to see an integrated group of women laughing and joking together or extolling the supposed virtues of brands of lipstick and facial powders and lingerie and sanitary napkins. A supervisor and his or her employees can cross the spectrum. And when children are depicted at schools or playing together or Christmas shopping, the gang's all there, providing our young people with early recognition of their common connections.

By the time they are teenagers, most Americans are completely converted to this notion, above all by music television. No matter what we might think of the songs they promote or the obnoxious attitudes they celebrate, in these shows integration is a given. It does not surprise the audience to see an Asian girl compete with a black one in learning dance routines from a rap group—and win! Using the inarticulate language of adolescent self-promotion, the Asian girl assumes she is as much of a fan as the black girl, and has such confidence in her ability to dance that she laughs off the idea that *anyone* else could learn faster or move with more finesse. An All-American girl of our moment.

Talk shows also convince us of our common humanity—and of everyone's capacity for every human quality, from heroic compassion to unflappable crassness. The popularity of Oprah Winfrey and Montell Williams obviates all color lines as they address human problems of almost every sort. We see black and white men and women and young people, as well as members of every other ethnic group, discussing their troubles in their romances, in their marriages, with their children, with their addictions, in their careers and elsewhere. We see every kind of emotion expressed by white, black, red and yellow people. We see women and men of every hue break down in tears, overwhelmed by their humanity and reiterating what deep feeling can do to all of us.

On those talk shows, we also see a wide range of knuckleheads, male and female, from troubled children to repulsive adults. Jerry Springer has surely proved to those who might have doubted it that neither ethnicity nor religion is automatic protection from ignorance or stupidity or trivial obsessions or abysmally crude thoughts or even more abysmal behavior. In that sense, regardless of his obvious appeal to the very lowest common denominator, he has provided us with a public service.

Nor is democratic recognition of our humanity limited to the worlds of advertising and television. In every team sport we see integration at work. In our streets, we see men and women of every ethnic group employed as public servants. Our armed forces are distinguished by male and female professionals of every hue and religious background. It is no longer odd to see a black person or a woman at the top of city government. We even saw a Negro, Doug Wilder, elected governor of Robert E. Lee's home state: Virginia, that pearl of the Confederacy. Venus and Serena Williams dominate tennis. Tiger Woods, his father black and his mother Asian, is the miracle man of a game that once lay under a snowdrift of white men that seemed beyond melting. When someone is reporting on television from Washington, D.C., that person could be of any color or either sex.

This recognition even extends beyond color and class and religion to include those with physical disabilities. We are beginning to understand what Victor Hugo was after with his famous character Quasimodo: to see the nobility beneath a grotesque surface, the spirit of the prince within the frog. Yes, just as we have learned that skin tone and genitalia do not obviate humanity, we have been battling our way toward embracing the humanity of the blind, the lame, the disfig-ured, the obese, the person who might have to struggle through cere-bral palsy to have his or her heart and soul and mind recognized. Here—in our classrooms, in our workplaces, in our popular media—is the melancholic grandeur and compassion of democracy. Here, in slow and accumulating human detail, is how we play out that very demanding American game, working ever harder to see ourselves in others and others in ourselves.

*   *   *

Of course, if you are in the wrong place at the wrong time, none of this matters—and it can often seem that the American Dream does not apply if you are black or brown. Racial hatred can seem to run deep, the police and the courts can be grimly disappointing. Take the example of New York City, where race relations could not have been more bitter or raw in recent years. Surely, many say, this makes a mockery of what we as a nation seem to have achieved since the 1960s. Maybe it does, maybe it doesn't. For some of the worst racial conflicts of the last decade turn out to be more complex than we usu-ally think, and even offer some potentially encouraging lessons.

True enough, there was a terrible race riot in New York in 1991, in the mixed black and Jewish neighborhood of Crown Heights. The motorcade of a powerful Orthodox rabbi drove through a red light and swerved onto the sidewalk, killing a seven-year-old black child, Gavin Cato. A black mob gathered, grumbling—even though the city was then governed by a black mayor—that Jews were running the city and black life had no value in New York. Soon they were yelling "Get the Jew," and a few hours later a rabbinical student from Australia was fatally stabbed. As he died, Yankel Rosenbaum identi-fied a young black man, Lemrick Nelson, as his assailant. When Nel-son was brought to trial, his black lawyer implied that the black police officers testifying for the prosecution were no more than slaves following the orders of their masters. Nelson was ultimately found innocent by a predominantly black jury.

Six years later, in the summer of 1997, Haitian immigrant Abner Louima was arrested, beaten, taken to a precinct house in Brooklyn and sodomized with a broken broom handle. He nearly died from the wounds he received in his rectum. From his hospital bed, he charged that the cops who assaulted him had jeered: "It's Giuliani time!" To some, this seemed proof enough that New York policemen using excessive force were acting on racist orders from the white mayor, Rudolph Giuliani.

Nor was the Louima case the end of the story. As Giuliani's mayoralty continued, the cops were often accused of turning New York City into a police state. An aggressive plainclothes division, working in the crime-ridden streets of Harlem and the Bronx, could claim as the official motto of their unit: "We own the night." On February 4, 1999, four white members of that division fired forty-one shots at Amadou Diallo, an unarmed immigrant from Africa, hitting and killing him with nineteen bullets. Surely, it was said, there is something racially rancid at the center of the American Dream. Had Diallo been white, even in a high-crime Bronx neighborhood of the sort in which he lived, he would not have been shot in such a hysterically clumsy, deadly display.

The Diallo case was tried not in New York City but upstate, in Albany. The jury consisted of eight whites and four blacks. The prosecution demonstrated that Diallo had been shot repeatedly even after going down. The defense countered that the four policemen had been looking for a criminal; when they approached, Diallo didn't answer questions and appeared to have drawn a gun. One of the cops wept on the stand. When the jury foreman, a black woman, read the verdict, the cops were exonerated of all charges. Black New Yorkers seethed with anger, and the Reverend Al Sharpton, not always known for acting responsibly, admonished them not to besmirch the slaughtered man's memory with the kind of violence that had brought him down. There were no incidents. Yet race relations seemed at a dismal low.

Then, over the next few years, tempers began to cool, and the truth about the city's decade-long racial nightmare began to come out. In Crown Heights, reporters discovered that the racial antipathy behind the riots had been brought in from outside the community by rabble-rousers quite unknown to the black kids who lived there. In fact, it turned out, the black and Jewish people in the neighborhood got along rather well. In 1997, Lemrick Nelson was brought to justice again, found guilty and sentenced to nearly twenty years for violating Yankel Rosenbaum's civil rights. That decision was later overturned on appeal due to the judge's heavy-handed attempt to fight racism with more racism by insisting that the jury be racially balanced. Still, in June 2003, after three trials, Nelson was convicted of stabbing Rosenbaum to death, though not of depriving him of his civil rights. (His defense was that he had nothing against Jews; he was just drunk, got excited and went along with the flow of the mob.)

In the Louima case, the sodomizing cop, Justin Volpe, was identified by fellow officers, tried and sentenced to thirty years in prison. What's more, however monstrous his actions, it turned out that Volpe may not be a racist in any way that we can ascertain: he was never accused of being a bigot by his coworkers, and he even had a black fiancée. In fact, she was often harassed by black cops for going out with him—and it's possible that this is what lit a fuse in him. Without forgiving Volpe for the unforgivable, it's worth considering: if the NYPD had offered a program to address such harassment of interracial couples, perhaps Louima would have been spared his assault.

Louima, meanwhile, admitted to having lied when he claimed his assailants yelled, "It's Giuliani time": he said he had been advised to say so to bring attention to his case. When his civil case got to court, he was awarded millions by the city, something that would never have happened in his native Haiti. And in the wake of the Diallo tragedy, the New York Police Academy has instituted an elaborate set of training procedures designed to prevent anything of the sort from happening again.

Those high-profile cases did not all come out perfectly, to say the least. Yet in no case was the truth as stark as it seemed at first. In almost every instance, both blacks and whites participated in bringing the city back from the brink—and again and again justice transcended race. Our deeply American humanity triumphed over even the most divisive kinds of violence and xenophobic murder.

*   *   *

These lessons from New York's recent history are even more important in the wake of the terrorist attacks of September 11, 2001. Since then, we have learned the deeper reason why the twin towers were called the World Trade Center: the three thousand people who worked and died there were of every color and both sexes, they believed in all of the major religions and they worked in every capacity from cleaning floors to trading stocks. What we saw on September 11 was integrated America under attack—and our hearts collectively broke as the buildings went down and the clouds of dust spread. Black and white and red and yellow people helped and supported one another. Americans and immigrants on their way to becoming Americans, in their work clothes and their business suits, their police uniforms and their fire department gear—all moved together through the streets and across the Brooklyn Bridge. And at that tragic moment, in their collectivity and their willingness to suffer with and for each other, they symbolized the ability of the species to stand up to disaster as human beings. The one thing that has always been true about the nation became even more true on that unforgettable morning: our surface differences are far less important than what we have in common and what we will ourselves to be, as men and women and Americans.

22

THE NEW TWO-WAY STREET

by Gary Shteyngart

IN 1999, UPON RETURNING from a trip to St. Petersburg, Russia, the city where I was born, I ran into a logjam at the immigration checkpoint at JFK. Apparently too many planes bearing too many foreigners had landed at once, and several INS workers had been dispatched to separate the incoming passengers into two lines—American citizens and foreigners (or "visitors," as the official sign would have it; strange how passing immigration so handily turns you from a *foreigner* into a *visitor*). Although we had arrived on a FinnAir plane from Helsinki, Finland, the majority of passengers seemed to be Russians and Americans, with just a smattering of Finns. The INS set to work on us, gently pushing us in the right direction and chanting the mantra "This line for U.S. citizens *only!*" Before I had fished my U.S. passport out of my carry-on—I have been an American citizen for approximately half of my life—I instinctively joined the citizens' line, while most of my former Russian co-nationals, many of them wearing thuggish-looking leather jackets and toting matching leather man-purses (an unfortunate Russian peculiarity), were shunted into the other line.

I dress in a style I like to call Immigrant Chic. Essentially it's the lexicon of the downtown hipster, which in the winter means a retro

1970s coat with an outrageous fake fur collar. My Russian friends say it makes me look like a bookkeeper from the provinces, which fits right into the belabored irony of Immigrant Chic. At JFK on that day, however, they weren't having it. As soon as one of the INS workers spotted a hairy young man in a fake-fur-collared coat stepping into the American citizens' line, a line peopled almost exclusively by clean-cut young men and women in Gortex, she ran toward me screaming, "No! No! No!"

I instinctively put my hands up in the air, in both protest and surrender. The middle-aged woman, dressed in some kind of maroon INS get-up, pointed to me and said, "You." Then, waving an index finger, "No, no, no." Then, pointing to the floor, "American citizen *only.*" Then, pointing at me, once more, "You." Then, finally pointing toward the line of beleaguered Russians, "Go! There!"

When at last I produced my blue American passport, embossed with our fine golden eagle, the INS woman said, simply, "Oh." She looked me over once more, as if naturalizing me with her steely official gaze, and repeated to herself: "Oh." She went off in search of more people to classify, other transnational oddities to put in their proper place.

*   *   *

This little incident left an impression on me. Since the tragic events of September 11, 2001, I have rarely boarded a plane without having my shoes (and my person) thoroughly searched, as if I were walking through the metal detector wearing a "God is Great" T-shirt and chanting, "Down, down USA! Down, down Bush!" Truth be told, I hold no grudges against airport personnel, and I feel no particular animosity toward the INS woman who tried single-handedly to change my nationality at JFK in 1999. After all, how could she have known? Everything is topsy-turvy these days. I know an Ohio native who has lived in Moscow long enough to speak English with a kind of improvised Russian accent (it sounds like he's working on an Irish brogue); and I know a Kenyan national who has lived in New York most of her life, speaks English with an upper-class Middle-Atlantic inflection and dresses in downtown black.

America's tradition of tolerance beckons newcomers with a simple promise: if you learn a minimum of English and adopt the most basic of our values, you will find yourself a berth in our country. But while the implied social contract between the newcomer and her adopted land remains unchanged, the traditional roles taken up by immigrants and the native-born are in flux. The melting pot has given way to a complicated fusion cuisine, one that may leave a strange taste on the traditional American palate.

The reason for the confusion, I believe, is simple: mobility. Whereas immigrants once boarded stifling American-bound steamships and waved good-bye forever to Sicilian ports and Scandinavian fjords, the modern immigrant is a nonstop flight away from the land she has left. When my parents emigrated from the Soviet Union in 1979, they were bidding farewell to the gray cement buildings, the hammer and sickle, the flora and fauna of their youth—not to mention, heartbreakingly, many of their loved ones—with a finality verging on madness. Today, Russia is just nine hours away on Delta Airlines. You wake up after a long cognac-fueled nap, look out the window, and the crumbling, sepia-toned landscape you left behind gathers itself up before you, broken facades crowned with ads for Sprite ("Don't let yourself go dry—drink Sprite!") and Samsung electronics ("The White Nights—brought to you by Samsung"). But the question remains: are we, the new Sprite drinkers—Russian-born and American-bred—ultimately Russians or Americans? Or Russian-Americans? Or something entirely different? What's going on here?

*   *   *

When I came to the United States in 1980, assimilation seemed a clear-cut proposition. Where you came from was wrong and America would set you straight: Assimilate and live! The immigrant was pressed to the bosom of his new society, given a crash course in Americanism. I was wearing my very fine Russian fur coat, made out of a bear or an elk or some other fierce woodland animal, when my first grade teacher took me aside and said, "You can't wear that anymore. We don't dress like that here." The dear secretaries at the Hebrew school I attended started a little clothing drive for me, a gathering of the Batman and Green Lantern T-shirts their sons had outgrown, so that I could look half-way normal on the playground.

It was a sweet idea and it got me thinking. I bit into this country as if it were a cold slice of melon. Whereas I once read Chekhov and listened to Tchaikovsky and Rimski-Korsakoff on the record player (Soviet children from good families were expected to ripen at an early age), I soon discovered the endless pleasures of the television show *Dallas.* Over a supper of farmer's cheese and tea—we weren't *entirely* assimilated yet—my mother and I cheered on the machinations of the ever-evil villain J.R. as he screwed over everyone in sight and raised Texas dust behind his sleek Mercedes convertible. Every penny I earned doing chores was spent decorating my room to resemble J.R.'s office. Luckily, my bedroom already came with the requisite wood paneling, and to further the look I installed a little computer, a luxurious chair and a fancy-looking telephone with an LCD display. All I needed was a model golden oil derrick to make the look complete. But even without the derrick I would purposefully stride into my "office," grab the phone, and say, with what I thought was a Texan accent, "They're sellin' Gold Barrel Oil? I'm a-gonna kill those SOBs! You just hang tight, darlin'. I'll be right there." I was maybe twelve, a small immigrant boy with asthma just learning to twist his mouth around the English language. But I knew what I wanted. America was going to make me rich.

Money. To this day, immigrants come to America because the elites of their native countries are committed to keeping the middle class small and stunted, since banana republic-style crony capitalism can exist only in a country with a vast, impoverished labor pool. From Ecuador to Bangladesh to present-day Russia, this quasi-feudal system makes immigration the only option for millions. After Hebrew school and my early J.R.-worship, I attended Stuyvesant High School, an elite math and science high school in Manhattan, where the student body was composed overwhelmingly of ambitious immigrant children whose parents had left their homelands primarily for economic reasons.

Work hard, please your parents, make a killing—these were the three unspoken principles of Stuyvesant High School. And there was a fourth, sometimes conflicting tenet: Become an American. We chided each other for our perceived un-Americanisms: the wrong shirt (tucked too tightly into the wrong pants), the wrong accent (too outer-borough or too Chinatown), the wrong lunch (homemade squid-and-noodles instead of a pizza burger at the local diner). The most vicious insult, one that circulated mainly among the Asian kids but haunted the rest of us immigrants as well, was FOTB, or Fresh Off The Boat. I tried to avoid the FOTB label by wearing a sweatshirt featuring teenage surfers alongside, for some reason, a kangaroo and the Australian flag. I ate only pizza burgers and hardly said a word to anyone, often hiding out in the bathroom during my lunch break while some rebellious Chinese kids smoked cigarettes.

This anxiety didn't disappear until I gave up on outright assimilation. Instead, I joined the so-called hippie clique at Stuyvesant, most of whom seemed to be not only from a different country but from a different planet (actually, they were mostly native-born losers from the Upper West Side). My new friends, lost beneath a cumulus of greenish pot smoke and resolved never to succeed at anything, paved the way for my four-year stint at the loose and liberal Oberlin College, where I soon gave up on the idea of turning into a vengeful Texan oil man and instead eventually became a novelist.

In the end, I never made good on the Stuyvesant program of working hard, pleasing my parents and making a killing. But as for becoming an American, I think I've finally found my way. Or, put differently, America found me. The big bear coat I wore on the plane from Russia twenty years ago, the one that my teacher told me would bring me nothing but trouble, is a dream down at the hip watering holes of Williamsburg, Brooklyn. The squid-and-noodle lunches that embarrassed my compatriots in Stuyvesant High School are now the stuff of fusion menus in overpriced SoHo restaurants. Even our strange accents and the music of our homelands are now part and parcel of global culture: made in America, but not necessarily *of* America.

Today, people like myself, Russians by birth and Americans by education, don't need to choose a single, exclusive identity. Equally at home (and equally homeless) in both cultures, we are global citizens of an increasingly borderless world. We swear our allegiance to America, not because we can identify with its purple mountain majesty or its fruited plains—neither of which we have spotted as of late in Brooklyn—but because America offers what constitutes for most immigrants a normal life rooted in a sense of upward mobility and relative fairness.

America is essentially becoming a clearinghouse for global talent and creativity. This may not sound as patriotic as "the land of the free and the home of the brave," but it is a lot more accurate. The country attracts the most talented computer programmers and heart specialists, to be sure, but it's also a beacon for the most able greengrocers and the most enterprising furniture movers. Our nation's success is built squarely on its continued ability to compete favorably with other industrialized democracies for the labor pool of talented immigrants. The economic travails of a country such as Japan are at least partly the result of policies designed to homogenize the population and make naturalization almost impossible for newcomers. It is no surprise that the relatively welcoming United Kingdom has done so remarkably well in the past decade, with London becoming a multicultural city in many ways comparable to New York—while countries such as Germany, where German ethnicity is valued over talent and entrepreneurial ability in granting citizenship, have floundered economically.

Editorials in Berlin newspapers sometimes wistfully paint the city as a future New York, but Berlin is hardly diverse enough to qualify for such a comparison. At one point during a visit to Berlin in 2000, I was mistaken for an Indian by a crowd of young, poorly dressed East Berliners who complained that the influx of highly skilled computer programmers from the subcontinent was straining the educational and social welfare system for ethnic Germans. The slogan the young men chanted at me over several vodkas too many was *"Kinder statt Inder,"* meaning "Children instead of Indians."

They were wrong on two counts. First, I'm not Indian. And second, an influx of Indian computer experts has not hurt the social and educational opportunities for ethnic German children. On the contrary, the high taxes paid by these foreign professionals bolsters the social welfare system. The real issue here is racism: it would be hard to imagine those young men chanting "Children instead of Norwegians." Even more disconcerting is the fact that *"Kinder statt Inder"* was a phrase invented not by barroom hooligans but by a leading member of the Christian Democratic Union, one of Germany's two leading political parties.

"Children instead of Indians" is not a slogan we will soon hear in the halls of Congress because immigrants and America are too dependent on each other. Immigrants have helped make America the world's leading economy, while America has offered them an escape from some of the world's most stifling plutocracies and theocracies. (And it would be a shame if immigrants from failing Muslim states, from Pakistan to Iran to Sudan, were denied that escape because of the backlash from the September 11, 2001 attacks.)

What's more, immigrants have the opportunity both to assimilate into American culture and at the same time reshape it to fit their needs. The rules of the game have changed since my own attempts to become American. Assimilation no longer means giving up kasha for burgers; it means making the best kasha-burger the American palate can bear. But some things have not changed. Assimilation continues to mean learning English to the extent that is required by one's job and participation in the democratic process. Contrary to popular wisdom, most immigrants are quite eager to learn the English language—in fact, for better and worse, knowing English is also the key to advancement in their home countries.

Assimilation also means sloughing off the intolerant and antidemocratic feelings that many immigrants bring with them from intolerant and antidemocratic countries. I am often shocked by the ingrained racism I hear from Russians both in America and Russia, even among those considered to be progressive intellectuals. After hearing these Russians' easy stereotypes and cruel ethnic jokes, I consider the anti-immigrant rhetoric of conservative American pundits and politicians to be the ultimate irony. The truth is that most immigrant adults are Pat Buchanan's dream—they constitute an ultraconservative religious constituency that doubles as a cheap and highly flexible labor pool.

But assimilation has become a two-way street. Today, native-born Americans have to assimilate to a new country as well. It is a country where foreign alphabets are scrawled along subway walls; where city blocks can offer French, Chinese and Ethiopian restaurants side by side, some requiring different utensils, some none at all. Following the lead of entry-point cities such as New York and Los Angeles, America is rapidly casting itself into a global country, a nation where even Republican native-born politicians must often speak Spanish to compete for votes.

This winter, I will, once again, approach immigration at New York's JFK airport, my blue passport with its embossed golden eagle snug in my fake-fur bear coat, the one that my Russian friends say makes me look like a bookkeeper from the provinces. American passport, Immigrant Chic coat. It's how we live now, and it works.

23

WHAT IT MEANS TO BE AMERICAN IN THE 21ST CENTURY

by Tamar Jacoby

OF ALL THE THINGS that have changed in the wake of the attacks of September 11, 2001, one of the most evident is the way people think and feel about being American. Not only are many people experiencing a new pride; large numbers are also mulling more deeply than ever before just what "American" means. Still, for all the new awareness and reflection, it's hard not to feel that the issue remains surrounded by question marks. This ferment was brought home to me recently at an event at a public library. Though it was a beautiful Saturday afternoon, a good-sized audience had gathered in the stuffy hall to hear five experts talk about immigration. One of these panelists, hurrying through his notes, mentioned something in passing about the need to balance what we all have in common with the ethnicity that we inherit from our parents and grandparents—only to find during the question-and-answer period that the audience could talk of nothing else.

What exactly, people wanted to know, did he mean by what we all have in common? Just what is it that unites us—what beyond the theoretical concept of shared nationality? Someone in the room, taking the speaker literally, invoked a telling image: an old-fashioned scale—like the scales of justice—with a fulcrum and two baskets. "Okay," she said, "I'll put my ethnicity in one basket: my memories of my grandfather, the food we still eat at home, the bits of colorful language I inherited from my parents. But what goes in the other basket? What really does it mean to be American?" And though several other members of the audience cut in with words like "freedom" and "democracy," the conversation plainly left her and others perplexed. "You can talk about McDonald's or George Washington—and maybe, in some foreigners' eyes, America is about gunboat diplomacy," another person said. "But what exactly is our *national* identity?"

Though intensified in the wake of 9/11, this is hardly a new problem for Americans. For all the clarity and eloquence of the Founders' vision, it can be surprisingly difficult to get at the essence of our shared heritage. People all around the world, people who have never been to America or met an American, know it when they see it, and they generally find it so powerful that they either love it or hate it. Still, it could be argued, most American literature and much of our political discourse over two and a half centuries has been devoted to a search for this elusive meaning. The target never seems to stand still. Though its core is unchanging, it is always in flux. Every individual American makes it his or her own—a variety that can make it seem all but impossible to capture the essential spirit. And, of course, the riddle is especially puzzling for immigrants.

As every schoolchild knows, we are a unique nation: defined not by blood or ancestry, but by a set of shared ideas. Most of us can name those ideas, but they also leave many of us scratching our heads—for try as we might, it's hard to grasp how an entire nation can be characterized, much less held together, by a few abstract ideals. Freedom, democracy, "life, liberty and the pursuit of happiness": the concepts are so often invoked and so familiar that it can be difficult to enter into them—to bring them alive for oneself again or to understand how they can give rise to something as rich and dense as a national way of life. No wonder, some observers suggest, ethnicity plays such an important part in our culture: "The American in the abstract does not exist," Nathan Glazer and Daniel Patrick Moynihan wrote in 1963. A "simple 'American' identity" is "unavailable." The upheavals of the 1960s and the culture wars that followed clouded the mystery even further—and so, more and more these days, people like the woman in the library audience take refuge in their relatively colorful and comforting ethnic backgrounds instead.

The question is particularly pressing for young newcomers like Eddie Liu, the twenty-something Chinese-American whose uncertainty about how he fits in was the seed that grew into this volume. (See the Introduction for his story). Raised by foreign-born parents with little feel for the country or its culture, Eddie had nothing but the big, abstract ideas—and maybe what he saw on TV—to nourish his understanding of what it means to be American. How does the Declaration of Independence translate into a code of behavior for a young Californian? How much of what he sees on television is really part and parcel of the American way of life—and how much is optional? Most important to him, raised as he was in the era of multiculturalism and identity politics, can he reconcile this national identity with the strong sense of ethnicity he inherited from his parents? Does the American ethos leave room for other habits and loyalties—and if so, how much room? Other essays in this volume have asked whether, and how, Eddie is likely to assimilate. But the question remains: what exactly is he assimilating to? What sense of himself and the larger community is he buying into, and what is going to be expected of him?

Like the speaker in the library, most contributors to this collection would argue that Eddie can hold onto his ethnic heritage, or much of it, and become an American, too. Whether it was true throughout the nation's history—and it certainly wasn't for someone of Eddie's ethnic origin—this has traditionally been the American ideal, enshrined in the motto *e pluribus unum*. The immigrant pattern that evolved over time—and was endorsed in most eras by the mainstream public—involved maintaining a balance between the old and the new. At home, with their families and in their private lives, newcomers clung to the customs they brought with them from the old country—while at work, as citizens and in the public sphere, they adapted to American ways. Or at least that's how the story went. Still, young people like Eddie wonder, how exactly does this play out in practice today? Is the ideal finally real—and realizable? Doesn't assimilation mean ethnic death? Or, something new, has the expected balance shifted, so that now, prodded by multiculturalism, it leaves more room for ethnic difference?

The essayists in the book differ on that last, critical question. Some feel that the more things change, the stronger the current of American history and tradition flows. Others disagree: for them, everything is different now, and the old immigrant balance must be recalibrated—readjusted or indeed refashioned for a new, "post-ethnic" America. But there is also a third possibility: that while the value we as a nation put on ethnicity *is* different now, this need not in the long run alter the old immigrant bargain. As long as we remember what it is that holds us together, our national identity may be strong enough to offset and complement considerable difference.

*   *   *

Where do we even begin to look for the essence of our shared national heritage? The literature of American ethnicity has as many answers as there are voices. Everyone starts, of course, with the Founders and their ideals: the proposition that all men are created equal and the system of self-government that flows from it. But few over the years have simply left it at that, particularly not when they were postulating how it should be understood by immigrants. Industrialist Henry Ford, who spent liberally to Americanize his foreign-born workers, saw the national identity as all-encompassing—to the point that it meant, among other things, giving up garlic. President Theodore Roosevelt, who shaped a generation's views on the subject, similarly expected newcomers to forsake most if not all of their old ways: he wanted all immigrants to Anglicize their names and threatened to deport those who failed to learn English. Other thinkers have clustered at the opposite end of the spectrum, positing few if any expectations for newcomers. World War I–era cultural pluralists like philosopher

Horace Kallen felt there was no specifically American content to American nationality: for him, it was merely a frame to contain but not color or interfere with "the federation of ethnicities" he saw emerging in the nation's cities.

The range of views—and expectations—is as wide as ever today. The predominant trend echoes Kallen: a spectrum that runs from mild multiculturalism to radical transnationalism. But even those who hold out for a paramount American identity differ significantly on just what it is. For some, what binds us together is the kaleidoscopic culture created over the centuries by the many groups that have coalesced to make up the nation. Other contemporary thinkers suggest that what really matters is an approach to life: a fundamental faith in individualism, say, or the ability to reinvent yourself. Still others hold fiercely to a specific content that they believe immigrants must absorb if they are to claim to be American: content that ranges from the Gettysburg Address to baseball trivia and the words to songs from popular musicals.

Perhaps a better place to look—a way to make sense of these divergent views—is to ask how the American *people* through history have understood the essence of our national identity. Past generations cannot decide for us—for an individual like Eddie Liu or anyone else. What worked in 1910—or 1790 or 1840—may no longer be appropriate today, and surely could not be enforced even if it seemed apt to a few thinkers. Still, it can be argued, history has been building, albeit by a zigzag course, to the conception that prevails today, and a review of history may help us see more clearly just what the contemporary conception is.

✳   ✳   ✳

In fact, a sense of American identity—and of the American ethnic bargain—crystallized fairly early, in the first three or four decades of the nation's history. New as the country and its people were, the national self-image that emerged then was remarkably complete, with most of the key features that we know today already in place.

Already at the beginning, the emphasis was on ideas rather than ethnicity. Not only did the Founders emphasize the ideological dimension of what it meant to be an American, but so apparently did the first generations of settlers. The early republic was more diverse than is sometimes thought: already in 1790, when the first census was taken, 40 percent of the population was of non-English stock. Yet national origin does not seem to have been a topic of particular concern. The motto *e pluribus unum* was not initially a reference to racial or ethnic origin: it seems rather to have symbolized the political unity of the thirteen colonies. Though the Founders themselves were divided on immigration—some more optimistic than others about the absorptive capacity of the new nation—early apprehensions had less to do with new settlers' ethnic backgrounds than with the political ideas they were likely to bring with them from the Old World. (Thus pessimists such as Benjamin Franklin and Alexander Hamilton worried mainly that newcomers, often from tyrannical European states, might abuse the liberty they found in America.) And the only significant anti-immigrant legislation passed in the first century of the nation's existence, the infamous Alien and Sedition Acts of 1798, was entirely ideological in intent: meant to protect the republic from the radical political ideas popularized by the French Revolution.

Of course, whether they intended so or not, the framework that the Founders established was close to a perfect scaffolding for what would become a nation of immigrants. The proposition that all men are created equal, that inherited status should play no role in the nation's life, that the law should treat all citizens alike, that government be designed first and foremost to prevent the majority from tyrannizing minorities: it's hard to imagine a system better suited to provide freedom and opportunity for the millions who would eventually arrive on American shores. And while the ways in which the new nation implemented this vision were far from perfect, either at the start or later, the early republic seems to have fastened, in theory at least, on two of its most important tenets: the universality that undergirded the Founders' ideas and their understanding that a new kind of government would create a new kind of society and, in turn, a new kind of men and women.

The universalism found its way immediately into the new nation's immigration code. Apart from the Alien Act, which was never enforced, the federal government placed no restriction on immigration for the first hundred years after the Founding. The result was effectively open borders, and indeed many states in need of labor sent representatives abroad to recruit foreigners. Meanwhile, though the bulk of newcomers came from European countries made up of largely white racial stock, this was not the result of any American law or policy. So, too, with naturalization: though not open to blacks or Indians, it came with no other racial distinctions. To join the new republic, one needed only swear to uphold the Constitution and abjure all other political loyalties. Until the late nineteenth century, no national, linguistic, religious or ethnic backgrounds were barred.

Meanwhile, a communal ethos was emerging—and it was surprisingly minimal, even for such a young nation. Not only were the criteria for joining unusually spare. But even settled residents seemed to share little beyond the Founders' ideals—only that they and the nation were making a new start. The national creed was abstract. If it came with cultural corollaries—like the speaking of English—these were rarely discussed. In part, no doubt, this was because the new nation was only just coming into its own and developing a culture. But equally important seems to have been the expectation, by most accounts widespread and largely unquestioned, that over time the act of joining would fundamentally alter the newcomers—as indeed it was thought to be altering all who participated in the new political system.

This faith in the transformative power of the new ideals was reflected in the mythology of the new nation—the holidays, emblems, folklore and the like—which centered almost exclusively on the Founding and its clean break from the past. Even before the creation of the common school, which didn't appear until the 1820s or 1830s, it was assumed that freedom itself and republican government would spur men to rise to the challenges they posed, so that over time most citizens would learn to take advantage of and appreciate the new institutions. The French-born St. John de Crevecoeur stated the assumption most famously in one of his *Letters from an American Farmer,* published in 1782: "What then," he asked, "is the American, this new man? . . . He is [someone] who, leaving behind him all his ancient prejudices and manners, receives new ones from the new mode of life he has embraced, the new government he obeys and the new rank he holds." Early Americans seemed to have felt little need to coerce the transition: they were confident that it would happen of its own accord. And in keeping with the nation's fundamental commitment to liberty, they showed little concern about the habits that immigrants brought with them from the old country. Language, religion, whom one married, customs in the home and the ethnic enclave: from the beginning, all were considered private matters of little consequence to the rest of society.

Thus already by the early nineteenth century, the elements of an American identity were firmly in place. Not only were most Americans clear from the outset that the criteria had nothing to do with blood or ancestry. But well before the nation itself was particularly evolved—before it had a distinctive culture or even recognizable manners and mores—there seems to have been a fairly solid sense of what belonging entailed. Largely ideological rather than cultural, indifferent to national origin, leaving plenty of room for private ethnicity and yet at the same time intensely confident of the nation's power to absorb newcomers and make them Americans: a fundamental paradox was already emerging. The hallmark of the American identity was that it was minimal yet transformative.

Still, it was also clear early on that there were limits to how much ethnicity was acceptable outside the immigrant community—in the common, public square. Already at the time of the Founding, a full third of Pennsylvania's residents hailed from Germany, and they along with Germans in other states remained distinctive through the nation's early years: they maintained schools and other communal institutions, and a significant number spoke German rather than English at home. Few people questioned this or attempted to interfere with it. Nevertheless, occasional attempts by German settlers to gain more official status for their ethnicity—to have their language recognized in

Pennsylvania schools or courts—were firmly repelled. Already, the lines of the immigrant bargain were clear, and they allowed newcomers to square what still seems to many an anomalous circle—to have their ethnicity and become Americans, too.

✱   ✱   ✱

The next century of American history would prove much harder for immigrants and for the fledgling American identity that had emerged in the nation's early decades. Beginning in the 1820s, famine and political upheaval in Europe sent thousands and then millions streaming to our shores—a flow that continued until the 1920s, provoking wave after wave of nativist backlash and what historian Philip Gleason has called two major "crises of nationality," one in the 1840s and another around the turn of the century. Each of these bitterly xenophobic episodes was nearly fatal for the minimalist, ideological identity of the Founding era, and the turmoil they created lasted well into the twentieth century—arguably until World War II. Yet once this long period of testing was finally over, the old American immigration bargain emerged if anything stronger than before.

The first of the two great national identity crises seemed to be about faith. The first wave of nineteenth-century immigrants came largely from Ireland and Germany, and though they were similar in stock to most native-born citizens, they were much more heavily Catholic. As many as one-third to a half belonged to the Church of Rome, and as they poured into American ports, Catholicism emerged as the largest denomination in the country, generating decades of ferocious conflict and profoundly threatening the nation's sense of itself. This was the era of the infamous anti-immigrant Know-Nothing Party. There were riots in the streets of Philadelphia; Catholic churches were burned to the ground. In city after city, Catholics and Protestants fought bitterly over parochial schools—and gradually, as the conflicts wore on, many Americans' idea of the national identity began to harden. The native-born were troubled not just by the newcomers' beliefs but also by their poverty, their unfamiliar manners, the seemingly clannish way they went about politics. And though for the most part these concerns were cast in a religious guise, some nativists began to argue in explicitly racial terms that only Anglo-Saxons could ultimately become Americans.

The second crisis was much more blatantly about race. The second great wave of new arrivals began immediately after the Civil War, as the country expanded westward and the modern commercial economy took off in earnest. Already in the 1880s, the influx dwarfed any earlier flows, and it continued, spiking ever upward until nearly 1920. By 1890, over a third of the population was foreign-born or a child of a foreign family. And once again, the nativist backlash was fierce—so virulent and ugly at times that it threatened to overwhelm American democracy. This reaction took a variety of forms: populist and intellectual, from the merely anxious to the viciously aggressive. But by and large, this time it centered unabashedly on ethnicity, to the point that large numbers of newcomers—swarthy Southern Europeans, Jews, the Chinese—were seen by many of the native-born to be simply unassimilable. In this era, too, there was violence, particularly against the Chinese in western states. Fueled by anti-immigrant sentiment, Ku Klux Klan membership swelled dramatically to a peak of several million. And beginning in the early 1870s, the legislative noose began to tighten—first restricting who could naturalize, then limiting the immigrant flow and finally all but ending it in 1924.

Today, these two periods of reaction are often seen as typical: *the* traditional American response to immigrants and immigration. But in fact, it can be argued, they were the exceptions that prove the rule: ugly as they were and sustained—lasting, together, some fifty years or more—they did not succeed in altering what it means to be American for either newcomers or the native-born.

Even when the xenophobia was most fierce and the outcome of the identity crises still uncertain, some Americans kept faith in a more expansive vision of the national character. Writers like Ralph Waldo Emerson, Walt Whitman and Herman Melville countered the prejudice of the anti-Catholic movement with confident optimism about what the foreign influx would mean for the growing nation. None of these thinkers or their readers pretended that the new immigrants weren't different—considerably more different than those who had come before. Nor did they deny that the newcomers would have to be transformed if they were to become truly American: Emerson's prescient phrase for this was "the smelting pot." Yet all believed that the change would happen more or less automatically, part and parcel of the new settlers' life in the new country. Even more important, none of these thinkers suggested that the transformation need obliterate all that was foreign about the newcomers, and no one thought the nation that resulted would be homogenously Anglo-Saxon or Protestant. On the contrary, it was in this period that terms like "federated" nationality, "cosmopolitan" and "hybrid" came into use—all with positive connotations.

Ordinary Americans also often looked favorably on immigrants even in this bleak period. A full 25 percent of those who fought in the Civil War were foreign-born. Irish troops, which were the most conspicuous, sometimes went into battle wearing kilts and shouting Gaelic war cries. And when these units came home, often mauled beyond recognition, the native-born quickly put aside whatever concerns they had had about the foreigners' manners and religious practices, reverting once again to the early, minimalist definition of what it meant to be America. In time of war, as in the republic's early years, it was clear that the most and perhaps only important criterion was loyalty to the nation and its ideals.

This old, looser sense of national identity reemerged with a vengeance in the years after the war. Enthusiasm for immigration surged as the economy expanded. Evolving attitudes toward the freed slaves nourished the idea that all men were brothers, regardless of origin. The experience of the frontier was not only deeply Americanizing for newcomers; it also reinforced the affinity between immigrants and native-born Americans willing to uproot their lives and reinvent themselves in a new place. Meanwhile, the very success of the Catholic influx—particularly the children and grandchildren of the Irish who had come at mid-century—reassured a doubting mainstream of the nation's absorptive power. Perhaps most interesting—

most telling for what it means to be American—was the way the old immigrant bargain persisted through this period. Many immigrant enclaves remained separate and distinctive. German communities were still the largest and most conspicuous, with their own newspapers, schools and foreign-language sign-boards. Yet over time, mischievously, some German ways started to catch on in the mainstream: most noticeably the newcomers' more relaxed attitude toward weekend leisure—an approach that emphasized athletic activity, spectator sports and drinking beer.

Turn-of-the-century xenophobia obscured these trends but did not extinguish them. Israel Zangwill's famous play, *The Melting Pot,* spoke to the pro-immigrant sentiment that coexisted with tightening pressure for restriction. First produced in 1908, it tells the story of a Jewish boy and Christian girl, both of them foreign-born, who fall in love and, despite all obstacles, vow to marry and fuse their strengths to create a still more robust and productive America. Far from urging that ethnic differences be obliterated, the drama argues that each group of newcomers brings a characteristic set of strengths; it also promises that assimilation can and does happen naturally, to the benefit of both newcomer and the native-born. A huge success with a long run on Broadway, the play then toured dozens of other American cities—suggesting that many ordinary Americans thought so too.

Pressure to adopt an all-encompassing American identity began to build in the early years of the new century and escalated steadily through World War I. Still, even then, for all the heavy-handed coercion, ethnicity remained an ever-present fact of life in the vast immigrant neighborhoods of the nation's cities. The Americanization movement that emerged in the 1910s helped many immigrants learn English, and large numbers who might not otherwise have done so became citizens—but this hardly robbed newcomers of their inherited identities. Even in later years, when the movement grew bullying, for all those who Anglicized their names, millions declined to do so. Garlic did not disappear from immigrant kitchens; at most, it went briefly underground. And in retrospect it's hard to imagine a more spectacular flop than Teddy Roosevelt's infamous campaign against the ethnic hyphen. Despite his forceful insistence that only "100 percent American-ism" would do—a campaign taken up later by Woodrow Wilson and perpetuated through the war years—if anything, the hyphen became the symbol of America: an emblem of the immigrant bargain that is among the most distinctive features of our culture.

By the time the Golden Door slammed shut in 1924, the double-barreled, private-public immigrant pattern was well established. New-comers still clustered in enclaves. Virtually all the first generation and many of their children still spoke a language other than English at home. They maintained extensive networks of communal institutions, most of them different from anything to be found in the old country, but also distinct from mainstream institutions: foreign-language news-papers, ethnic theater, an endless variety of social clubs and fraternal or-ganizations, religious hospitals, mutual aid societies, big-city political machines and more. Still, when called upon to join or participate in the mainstream, the newcomers and their children did so more than read-ily: naturalizing, serving in the military and acceding with little if any protest to the notion that the larger society should remain ethnically neutral and nonsectarian, a place where individuals advanced as indi-viduals and not generally as members of a group. (The one exception was arguably politics, but even there, above a certain level, the ethnic organization gave way to a more open process.)

By the middle of the twentieth century, the outcome of the nation's two identity crises was clear—and, in a way, remarkable. For after all the turmoil of the previous 150 years, despite an all but complete de-mographic makeover and in the face of venomous nativist challenges, the basic national identity remained much like what it had been in the early nineteenth century: still minimal but transformative.

All the key elements were still in place and, if anything, stronger. With the defeat of the Anglo-Saxon movement and the repeal of Asian exclusion laws in the 1940s, the idea that being American had anything to do with blood or ancestry had been permanently discred-ited. The national identity still left plenty of room for ethnicity: the landscape was dotted with remnants of the old communal institu-tions that had sustained the great migration, and millions of Americans still clung to memories of the foreign folkways they had grown up with. Even in the 1950s, when television first appeared and began to mold the nation's psyche, it was hard to argue that it left no room for ethnic traces: what was Milton Berle, after all, or Desi Arnaz? Meanwhile, the gradual assimilation of the Ellis Island wave gave new force to the old argument that new settlers adapted best when they did it in their own way and on their own schedule, not as part of a forced march. By the middle of the twentieth century, as before, it seemed clear enough that newcomers would and could be transformed—could emerge from the crucible as loyal, 100 percent Americans—without obliterating their ethnic allegiances. Think of the typical World War II movie with its trademark scene, the melting pot foxhole: Italian, Irishman, well-to-do WASP, Pole and Jew, all in it together, and all devoted Americans, despite their distinctiveness.

If anything was different, it was the hybrid culture that had evolved through the decades. From African-American music to Jewish humor, from the German work ethic to Irish eloquence: more and more of what it meant to be American was something that had been brought here by an outsider and then, like German Sundays, had gradually seeped into the mainstream. Unlike in the nineteenth century, when the blanks had yet to be filled in, a uniquely American ethos was taking shape. But unlike the culture of almost any other nation, it was still largely optional—after all, nobody has to love jazz or follow baseball to be an American. The nativists—and more moderate Americanizers—had lost even on this score. Beyond the ideological dimension framed by the Founders, there was little specific or concrete content to the American identity. The one thing that was mandatory, now as in the past, was the fairly minimalist rules of the game—democracy, the rule of law, the language used in public and the tolerant habits tested but eventually strengthened by more than a century of tumultuous ethnic history.

✳   ✳   ✳

The last forty years have brought a new kind of challenge for the traditional immigrant bargain and for American identity: multiculturalism. Welcomed by some, deplored by others, multiculturalism and the identity politics that come with it test the age-old balance from the other side, pushing seriously for the first time in our history not in the direction of conformity but for more ethnic attachment. How much difference can the American identity accommodate? Will it hold against these new pressures? Can and should it resist them? Or should it be amended, even redefined, to take account of the new emphasis we all now put on our origins? Americans have been debating these questions since the 1960s. And while this test is not yet over—these issues have hardly faded from the op-ed pages or from heated campus disputes—in the wake of 9/11, it already seems less intense, allowing us perhaps to begin to look toward a new synthesis.

There can be little question: ethnicity plays a new role in American life and will from now on. The reasons are complicated: it's not simply a new idea that took off in the 1960s and 1970s and then was spread, as some frightened observers would have it, by a few left-wing ethnic activists. Globalization, the integration of international labor markets, a more or less permanent refugee crisis, the ease of international air travel, even the maturing of the American middle class and its ever more cosmopolitan consumption habits: we live in a much smaller world than we once did and this inevitably has consequences—for American nationality and many others. Immigrants and their children now account for a full one-fifth of the U.S. population; modern communications make it much easier for them to stay in touch with their home countries. Even if ethnic studies had never been invented, many if not most of these newcomers would surely view America with a kind of "double consciousness" not unlike the one the great black man of letters, W.E.B. Du Bois, described a century ago: "One ever feels his two-ness—an American, a Negro; two souls, two thoughts, two unreconciled strivings." Substitute "immigrant" or "Latino" or "Asian-American" for "Negro": even if multiculturalism were to disappear, few newcomers are going to outgrow this overnight, or want to, and that will inevitably mean changes for America.

Critics of identity politics make much of the ideological shift that fans and fuels this dual consciousness—and they aren't wrong to bemoan the excesses, intellectual and political, of the past decades. Ethnic activists with a stake in maintaining their constituencies play to exaggerated feelings of factional grievance. Misguided government policies grant benefits on the basis of race and ethnicity, spurring the establishment of permanent color-coded interest groups. Popular culture reminds people of what makes them different, not what we have in common. Corporate marketers see an easy way to score with ethnic customers, even if this means spreading stereotypes and promoting insularity. Etcetera, etcetera. Worst of all, it sometimes seems that the mainstream has lost the confidence to assert its values or to champion the American ideals that would ensure allegiance and unity. But troubling as all this is, it doesn't mean there can be no place for difference—even a somewhat more pronounced sense of difference—in American life. If history teaches anything, it's that robust ethnicity is as American as the frontier or the automobile. And today as in the past, it doesn't seem unreasonable to believe that the old American immigrant bargain will be able to contain and accommodate it.

Of course, there's difference and there's difference—some kinds more likely than others to coexist with national unity. The great-grandfather of multiculturalism, Horace Kallen himself, championed two different kinds of diversity over the course of his long career. His early writings, published in the 1920s as part of the reaction to the Americanization movement, stressed a vision of ethnicity that, he thought, neither could nor should be modified in any way as a result of contact with the American mainstream. Radically anti-assimilationist, deeply distrustful of the coercion that seemed to come with any kind of unity, this was also a vision planted firmly in racial essentialism—and it has proponents today, on both ends of the political spectrum: militant separatists *and* mainstream bigots who believe biology is destiny and cannot grasp the mystery that is *e pluribus unum*. Yet even Kallen eventually softened his view, never quite grasping how we as a nation might hold together, but still dropping the racialism of his early years and acknowledging the possibility that individuals can choose their identities and embrace more or less of the ethnicity they inherit.

Years later, Nathan Glazer and Daniel Patrick Moynihan made much the same point, even as they celebrated the persistence of communal difference in the 1960s and 1970s. Their classic *Beyond the Melting Pot* distinguished between two ways of embracing one's diversity: one called "ethnic," the other, more toxic in their view, "racial." (What mattered was your attitude, not your origins: both blacks and immigrants could choose either approach.) The difference was that the ethnic model allowed for choice: even if you couldn't change your color or your facial features, you could still move beyond the category you were born into—categories that, for Glazer and Moynihan, were more about political interest than biology. What's more, unlike racial identification—which seemed already in the early 1970s to come with a heavy burden of separatism—more flexible, less demanding ethnic attachments allowed even those who felt most closely tied to the group to seize opportunities in the mainstream culture.

Thirty years and much divisive debate later, we have new ways to talk about these different kinds of difference—and about just what makes some varieties seem more desirable than others. Nobody on either side of the discussion seems to see much problem with what is now called "symbolic ethnicity": the kind of fuzzy, feel-good diversity that surfaces generally in the third generation and feels more like a hobby than anything that could affect the outcome of one's life. Ethnic food, "roots tourism," ethnicity as folklore and nostalgia: this is what identity means now for most non-Hispanic whites, and no one thinks it threatens the nation's cohesion or identity. The harder questions have to do with the way ethnicity plays out among newer groups, and, fairly or not, this means they are posed mostly about people of color. Does this or that kind of group self-definition allow one to advance as an individual, or only as a part of a group? Does it require that one see oneself as a permanent victim? Does it lock you into a life of self-defeating anger and alienation? The social scientists' term for this is an "oppositional" identity, and no matter what your politics, it isn't hard to see how it might be harmful. Think of the black or Latino teen in an inner-city school who doesn't bother to apply himself because he thinks that's "acting white."

Can we as a nation encourage one kind of diversity and discourage the other? We won't get there through exhortation—by scolding ethnic activists or denouncing multiculturalism or trying to force-feed anyone an American identity. We've tried that kind of coercion in the past—in the early twentieth century and more recently—and it never works. On the contrary, it usually backfires, if anything increasing the alienation of the people on the receiving end. They feel singled out and put upon, and many react defensively, with the result that they ultimately feel more cut off and retreat further into their oppositional identities. The alternative is to create incentives for a more hopeful and flexible kind of ethnicity to take root. The perceived advantages of identity politics are not going to vanish overnight, but the only way to trump them will be to offer something better: a national identity that leaves room for ethnic loyalties and gives everyone, no matter what their origin, a sense that they have a stake in the larger community.

Does this mean that we as a nation need a new identity? It may. But before we take on the arduous, and possibly perilous, task of reinventing ourselves from scratch, perhaps we should to look back at history and at the national identity we've inherited. The 1920s, and arguably the 1950s, gave the old bargain a bad name, but in fact it leaves lots of room for diversity, without encouraging separatism. Tested by time, tempered by previous crises, perhaps this inherited answer is still useful today. It may work just as is, or—better yet—like earlier tests, the multicultural challenge may have clarified and improved it.

What does the old identity offer someone like Eddie Liu? Remember, the essence, inherited from the Founding era, is a nationality that's minimal but transformative. The basic legacy—the ineluctable common core—is a set of ideas about how the American people should govern themselves. Like all newcomers and the native-born, Eddie must accept these basic rules of the game—the simple framework that allows us all, no matter how different, to live equitably and peaceably to- gether. But today, as in the past, this largely political identity comes with few if any cultural corollaries. Eddie and his peers may like MTV—or they may discover Walt Whitman and fall in love with his America. Yet here, unlike, say, in France, neither kind of knowledge is required for membership: not literature, not music, not folkways, not even American food. The one cultural element that is part of the bargain is English. But even that obligation is surprisingly loose: immigrants and their children have been expected to use English in public—when they sought to participate in mainstream life— but untold millions have spoken a language other than English at home.

If the old bargain holds, this is the line that should matter for immigrants: the line between public and private. American identity leaves ample room for all kinds of ethnicity: for communal enclaves and all that goes on there. What it does not do—or did not do in the past— was allow those divisions to play any official role in the public life of the nation as a whole. The mainstream did not traditionally formalize, sponsor or celebrate—and certainly did not pay for—ethnic attachments. The public square—whether business or government, in a mainstream school or on the job—was expected to be common ground. And when someone like Eddie ventured into the public square, he was expected to feel and act like a 100 percent American. Contemporary thinker John Fonte suggests a test for this: imagine a Korean-American schoolgirl, a child of immigrants or an immigrant herself. When she talks about the Founders, when she recalls the Civil War, when she studies the Depression or thinks about what happened on September 11, does she think "they"—or "we"? Does she identify as an American or not? This is the transformation that the American identity requires—no more and no less than this.

The multicultural challenge has clarified but also raised questions about some of this legacy. As the identity crisis of the early twentieth century discredited the Anglo-Saxon movement and its claim that all Americans must share a common ancestry, so the ferment of the last forty years has discredited any notion that what's necessary is what social scientists call "Anglo-conformity"—identical manners. This isn't new: it's just a return to the essence of bargain. At the same time, more controversially, the multicultural era has tested the provision that the mainstream remain neutral—that it should not formalize, sponsor, celebrate or pay for ethnic divisions of any kind. Today, we do just that—in an endless variety of ways: from ethnic preferences to campus ethnic theme houses to foreign-language ballots and more. Many people oppose this, of course, and argue that we're risking dire consequences. After all, the nation is tinkering with a balance that worked, for more than two hundred years, for immigrants and the native-born. Whose interest does that serve? Does it really help newcomers to sharpen the dividing lines and emphasize what makes them different? The battle is far from over.

Still, even those of us who deplore this reinforcing of difference and struggle against it can recognize the need felt by someone like Eddie Liu to see himself reflected in the way the nation thinks and talks about itself. What the country needs is a way to honor his dual consciousness while also strengthening his connection to America—and without compromising our commitment to a neutral public square. And here, once again, the past may have something to teach us. After all, minimal as it is, the national identity has always come with an explanatory story. As journalist and historian Michael Lind has pointed out in his important book, *The Next American Nation,* no set of abstract ideas, no matter how brilliant, can mold a nation or hold it together over the long haul. The Constitution and the Declaration of Independence alone are not what bring people to fight and die for the country. That requires a kind of attachment that is built up over a lifetime, reinforced by memories and bolstered by a rich web of shared lore: not just ideas, but beloved symbols, oft-told stories, intense common experiences and the history of how the nation's ideals worked to hold us together in the past, in crisis and in victory. What the multicultural era has reminded us is that individuals need to find a way into this history—need to see their grandfathers and grandmothers' struggles or to identify with someone who played a part something like theirs—if they are to experience that sense of "we" that is the essence of belonging. This doesn't or shouldn't necessarily mean that they can identify only with someone who looks like them. But it probably does mean that the national story has to be told somewhat differently to reflect its full complexity.

One possibility, perhaps already taking place, would be a shift of emphasis in the national mythology to highlight the long, hard struggle that has been the forging of our national identity. This needn't mean a de-emphasis of the traditional central story, the Founding. Abraham Lincoln would remain a towering figure, the Civil War a decisive chapter. But perhaps the immigrant experience, broadly defined, should play a larger part. Not that all American history would become the history of people of color—a bitter chronicle of "us" and "them." On the contrary, it would emphasize what we all have in common: that what it means to be American is essentially to arrive as a newcomer—to start over and make a new life. From the Pilgrims to the slaves to the Ellis Island generation, this is the one experience that all Americans share: this and what follows—finding a way to fit in, or hang together, eventually by balancing your particularity against the common culture that accrued over time. Our history—indeed, some would say, the secret of our strength—is the history of the melting pot.

The new narrative would have to be written honestly. Yes, it would tell of prejudice—the hypocrisy as well as the idealism that has gone into realizing *e pluribus unum.* But it would also describe a slowly emerging tolerance and warn of excesses in both directions, including extreme forms of multiculturalism that could tear the nation apart. The cultural side of the story would be the easiest to tell: what, after all, is American popular culture if not a fossil record of the melting-pot experience—a story about hybrids and cross-pollination. Call the new narrative sensible, tempered multiculturalism: multiculturalism with a key caveat—that ultimately, although it talks about differences, it emphasizes how we coalesce as a nation. Of course, different groups of Americans, and not just ethnic groups, will want to tell it their own way, with their own highlights, and there will never be a single, "right" version. Still, in the long run, all the variants would

point in the same direction: toward the shared ideals that hold us together—the ideals of tolerance, democracy and meritocracy already
emphasized by our national mythology.

Is this a fundamental re-calibration of the national identity? It's a
slightly different emphasis, but hardly a wholesale change. On the
contrary, it could be argued, this would be a refinement of the traditional national identity: another clarification and improvement,
spurred by an identity crisis, that brings out the essence of the idea.
Instead of simply asserting more insistently that newcomers forget
the past and drop their difference—as some alarmist opponents of
multiculturalism suggest—let's tell the national story in a way that
everyone can find a place in it. Assimilation happens, but ethnicity
has always persisted—and if balanced against what we have in common, there's no reason it should threaten us now.

This doesn't mean that anything goes. The American identity is a
big tent, but not an infinitely big tent. A young man like Eddie Liu
still has to make choices—hard choices—about who he is and where
his loyalties lie. He has to know that being American means something: to say that it's minimal is not the same as nonexistent. It's
more than just "white-skin privilege" or a neutral framework to contain ethnic diversity. And there are limits to even the "two-way assimilation" that has made American culture the rich braid it is:
American political principles—and the values that flow from them—
are nonnegotiable. One can debate about whether Eddie and others
like him should be allowed, as they are now, to vote in more than one
country and serve in two armies—and arguably, on these points, we
should insist on more complete loyalty. Still, with or without that adjustment, the traditional immigrant bargain is clear: much as we celebrate the hypen, one side of it is more important than the other. Not
only must being American come first in a foxhole; but, Eddie and his
peers should also know, like it not, no matter how much they resist,
in the long run, it will change them. That, history teaches, is the
American way—and perhaps the meaning of being American.

ACKNOWLEDGMENTS

E VEN AN ANTHOLOGY stands on more shoulders than it's possible to count. At the top of the list of those to whom I am grateful is the Manhattan Institute, my professional home through the years that I was preparing this volume. President Lawrence Mone was supportive from start to finish, always ready with valuable counsel. David DesRosiers helped raise the money for the project; Lindsay Young watched my back and helped me get published in the meantime—and many others at the institute stood by me in an endless variety of large and small ways. No less important than MI was the Smith Richardson Foundation, which helped shape the project and supported it generously and patiently. Program officer Mark Steinmeyer deserves special thanks for a wise, forbearing manner and encouragement all along the way.

Thanks to Yale University for hosting a conference to frame the ideas in the book. Cynthia Farrar made that happen and—as she has for many years—helped me sharpen my thoughts. Among those who participated in the event and helped set the book on the right track: David Hollinger, Michael Lind, Douglas Massey, Orlando Patterson, Alejandro Portes, Douglas Rae, Rogers Smith and Stephan Thernstrom.

In the world of publishing, my first thanks go to my literary agent, Andrew Wylie, who peddled the book with characteristic brio. But others at the Wylie Agency have also been wonderfully supportive: Sarah Chalfant, Zoe Pagnamenta, Andrew Woods and others.

There would be no contract at Basic Books if John Donatich had not grasped the idea and encouraged me to pursue it. But editor William Frucht deserves thanks for the form it finally took and for shepherding the volume through the house with understanding and care. *Commentary, The American Enterprise, The New York Sun* and *Civitas* published earlier versions or pieces of chapters.

Among friends and colleagues, it's hard to know where to start: I've bent so many people's ears on this topic. Among the particularly helpful, if not always in agreement with me (how useful would that be?): Mitchell Duneier, Tom Klingenstein, Joel Kotkin, John McWhorter, Joel Millman, John Mollenkopf, Noah Pickus, Rubén Rumbaut, Fred Siegel, Peter Skerry, Abigail Thernstrom, Ron Unz, William Voegeli and Aristide Zolberg. There can be no way of adequately thanking Gregory Rodriguez and Frank Sharry, with whom I've had countless hours of conversation on these issues and both of whose friendship means more than I can say.

Most writers reserve the last thanks for family, but in this case a colleague takes precedence. There would be no book without Adam Kirsch, whose ever helpful manner and deft editing made these essays what they are and made the volume possible.

CONTRIBUTORS

Richard Alba is Distinguished Professor of Sociology and Public Policy at the University at Albany, State University of New York, and author of *Ethnic Identity: The Transformation of White America*. His teaching and research focus mainly on ethnicity and international migration. His most recent book, with Victor Nee, is *Remaking the American Mainstream: Assimilation and Contemporary Immigration*.

Michael Barone is a senior writer for *U.S. News & World Report*. He is the co-author of *The Almanac of American Politics* and author of *Our Country: The Shaping of America from Roosevelt to Reagan* and *The New Americans: How the Melting Pot Can Work Again*. He is also a contributor to Fox News Channel.

George J. Borjas is the Robert W. Scrivner Professor of Economics and Social Policy at the John F. Kennedy School of Government at Harvard University, and a research associate at the National Bureau of Economic Research. He is the author of several books, including *Friends or Strangers: The Impact of Immigrants on the U.S. Economy* and *Heaven's Door: Immigration Policy and the American Economy*. In 1998, he was elected a fellow of the Econometric Society.

Stanley Crouch is the author of three collections of essays: *Notes of a Hanging Judge, The All-American Skin Game, or the Decoy of Race* and *Always in Pursuit*. His first novel, *Don't the Moon Look Lonesome,* was published in 2000. He is a founder of Jazz at Lincoln Center and has been one of its major consultants since 1987.

Amitai Etzioni is the founder and director of the Communitarian Network and the Institute for Communitarian Policy Studies at the George Washington University. Among his twenty-two books are *My Brother's Keeper, The Monochrome Society* and *The New Golden Rule: Community and Morality in a Democratic Society*.

Herbert J. Gans is the Robert S. Lynd Professor of Sociology at Columbia University. His research and writing on ethnicity and race have appeared in general magazines, academic journals and in several of his books, including *The Urban Villagers, People, Plans and Policies, The War Against the Poor* and *Making Sense of America.* He is also an immigrant, having come to America as a refugee from the Nazis in 1940.

Nathan Glazer is professor of sociology and education *emeritus* at Harvard University and the former editor of *The Public Interest,* a quarterly of public affairs. He is the author and editor of many books and articles on ethnicity and race relations, including *American Judaism, Beyond the Melting Pot, Affirmative Discrimination, Ethnic Dilemmas, The Limits of Social Policy* and *We Are All Multiculturalists Now.*

Pete Hamill is the author of fifteen books, including the novel *Snow in August* and a memoir, *A Drinking Life.* He has been a columnist for the *New York Daily News, New York Post,* the *New York Newsday, The Village Voice, New York* magazine and *Esquire,* and has served as editor-in-chief of the *Post* and the *Daily News.*

Tamar Jacoby is a senior fellow at the Manhattan Institute and author of *Someone Else's House: America's Unfinished Struggle for Integration.* Formerly with *The New York Times* and *Newsweek,* she writes regularly on race, ethnicity and immigration for *The Weekly Standard, Commentary, The Wall Street Journal* and other publications.

Joel Kotkin is a senior fellow at the Davenport Institute for Public Policy at Pepperdine University. He is the author of *The New Geography: How the Digital Revolution Is Reshaping the American Landscape* and *Tribes: How Race, Religion and Identity Determine Success in the New Global Economy,* among other books. A former columnist for *The New York Times,* he is currently a columnist for Reis.com and a contributing editor to the *Los Angeles Times Sunday Opinion Section.*

Douglas S. Massey has taught at the University of Chicago and the University of Pennsylvania and is currently professor of sociology and public policy at Princeton University. He is the author of *American Apartheid: Segregation and the Making of the Underclass* and *Beyond Smoke and Mirrors: Mexican Immigration in an Era of Economic Integration,* among other books. He is a member of the National Academy of Science and the American Academy of Arts and Sciences and a past president of the American Sociological Association.

John McWhorter, formerly an associate professor of linguistics at the University of California at Berkeley, is a senior fellow at the Manhattan Institute. He is the author of *Losing the Race: Self-Sabotage in Black America* and an essay collection, *Authentically Black,* as well as several books on language. He is a contributing editor to *The New Republic* and writes regularly for other newspapers and magazines.

Victor Nee is Goldwin Smith Professor of Sociology at Cornell University, where he also directs the Center for the Study of Economy and Society. With Richard Swedberg, he is editing a new book, *The Economic Sociology of Capitalism.* Among his other books is *Longtime Californ': Documentary Study of an American Chinatown,* written with Brett DeBary.

Alejandro Portes is Howard Harrison and Gabrielle Snyder Beck Professor of Sociology and director of the Center for Migration and Development at Princeton University. His books include *City on the Edge: The Transformation of Miami,* co-authored with Alex Stepick, and *Immigrant America: A Portrait.* He served as president of the American Sociological Association in 1998–1999.

Gregory Rodriguez is a senior fellow at the New America Foundation and contributing editor to the *Opinion* section of the *Los Angeles Times.* He has written widely on issues of ethnicity, race, immigration and assimilation for such publications as *The New York Times, The Washington Post, The Wall Street Journal* and *The Economist.*

Peter D. Salins is Provost and Vice Chancellor for Academic Affairs of the State University of New York and a professor of political science at SUNY Stony Brook. He is also a senior fellow of the Manhattan Institute, trustee of the Lavanburg Foundation and member of the College of Fellows of the American Institute of Certified Planners. He is the author of *Assimilation, American Style,* among other books.

Gary Shteyngart was born in Leningrad, USSR, in 1972, and came to the United States seven years later. He is the author of the prize-winning novel *The Russian Debutante's Handbook,* and his work has appeared in the *New Yorker, Granta, GQ, Slate* and many other publications.

Peter Skerry is professor of political science at Boston College and nonresident senior fellow at the Brookings Institution. The author of *Mexican Americans: The Ambivalent Minority* and *Counting on the Census? Race, Group Identity, and the Evasion of Politics,* he is currently working on a book about Arabs and Muslims in America. He serves on the editorial advisory board of *Society* magazine.

Stephen Steinberg is a professor of sociology at Queens College and the Graduate Center of the City University of New York. He is author of *The Ethnic Myth: Race, Ethnicity, and Class in America* and the prize-winning *Turning Back: The Retreat from Racial Justice in American Thought and Policy.*

Stephan Thernstrom is Winthrop Professor of History at Harvard and a senior fellow at the Manhattan Institute. His books include *Poverty and Progress: Social*

Mobility in a 19th-Century City, The Other Bostonians: Poverty and Progress in the American Metropolis, 1880–1970, A History of the American People and *America in Black and White: One Nation, Indivisible,* co-authored with Abigail Thernstrom. He is also the editor of the *Harvard Encyclopedia of American Ethnic Groups.*

Roger Waldinger is professor and chair of the sociology department at UCLA. His most recent books are *Strangers at the Gates: New Immigrants in Urban America* and, with Michael Lichter, *How the Other Half Works: Immigration and the Social Organization of Labor.*

Min Zhou is professor of sociology and chair of the Asian American Studies inter-departmental degree program at the University of California, Los Angeles. She is the author of *Chinatown: The Socioeconomic Potential of an Urban Enclave,* co-author of *Growing Up American: How Vietnamese Children Adapt to Life in the United States,* co-editor of *Contemporary Asian America* and co-editor of the forthcoming *Asian American Youth: Culture, Identity, and Ethnicity.*

AUTHOR COPYRIGHTS

INDEX